WORKING MEMORY
AND LANGUAGE

Working Memory and Language

Susan E. Gathercole
Memory Research Unit,
Lancaster University, UK

and

Alan D. Baddeley
MRC Applied Psychology Unit,
Cambridge, UK

LAWRENCE ERLBAUM ASSOCIATES, PUBLISHERS
Hove (UK)   Hillsdale (USA)

Lawrence Erlbaum Associates Ltd., Publishers
27 Palmeira Mansions
Church Road
Hove
East Sussex, BN3 2FA
U.K.

British Library Cataloguing in Publication Data
Gathercole, Susan E.
    Working Memory and Language. - (Essays
    in Cognitive Psychology Series, ISSN 0959-4779)
    I. Title II. Baddeley, Alan D.
    III. Series
    153.1

ISBN 0-86377-265-X (Hbk)
ISBN 0-86377-289-7 (Pbk)

Printed and bound in the United Kingdom by BPCC Wheatons Ltd., Exeter

To our parents
Peter and Marjorie, and Donald and Nellie

Contents

Preface

We are interested in whether the processing of language in children and adults depends upon the support of short-term or working memory and, if so, in what way. In order to translate our interest in this issue into specific research projects, it has been convenient to decompose language into more tractable subdomains of skill, such as vocabulary, reading, and comprehension. To guide our evaluation of the contribution that working memory makes to the psychological processes and mechanisms involved in the learning and processing of language, we have drawn on existing theoretical models of each subdomain. Our choice of relevant theory to guide our thinking about working memory has necessarily been biased, in that we have focused exclusively on those aspects of research and theory concerning language that seem to be relevant to the issue of working memory involvement.

In this book we present our current understanding of the relationship between working memory and vocabulary, speech production, reading, and comprehension. From our own experience, a guide of this kind may be particularly useful as a consequence of the multidisciplinary nature of the literature. Each component of language that has been studied from a working memory perspective is represented by distinct research traditions and theories, and relevant research material derives from a number of quite different subject populations. In particular, theories of working memory involvement in each aspect of language have been informed by neuropsychological investigations of brain-damaged patients and by studies of children, as well as by experimental investigations of normal adult subjects. The community interested in this area is correspondingly multi-disciplinary, including members of professional groups, such as educational psychologists, speech therapists, and teachers in addition to linguists, neuropsychologists, developmental psychologists, and experimental psychologists. Our thinking on the issues raised in the book has been greatly enriched by discussions with colleagues from many of these areas.

The aim of this book is to make the research and theories linking working memory with a range of important language processes accessible to anyone with an interest in the area. No specialist knowledge is assumed. The first two chapters outline the current theory of working memory and of its development during childhood. Subsequent chapters focus on individual subdomains of language. In each of these chapters, a brief theoretical introduction to the domain of language processing provides the basis for our empirical and theoretical assessment of the nature of working memory involvement. In the case of reading development, the literature is so extensive that we have devoted the whole of Chapter 5 to a broad introduction to relevant research and theory, prior to consideration of working memory involvement in the acquisition of reading skills in Chapter 6. Where available, relevant data are drawn from experimental, neuropsychological and developmental sources, and we attempt to provide a theoretical integration of these different strands of evidence. The aim has been to provide a survey of research and theory that is illustrative rather than exhaustive, although in less well-developed areas such as vocabulary acquisition, speech production, and word recognition (Chapters 3, 4 and 7) it has been possible to cover most relevant recent work. However, in the more extensive research areas, such as reading development and language comprehension (Chapters 6 and 8), where other recent recent reviews are available, exhaustive coverage is neither possible nor desirable. These chapters only include work that is either of major influence on current research and theory, or of illustrative value. In the final chapter, more general theoretical and practical considerations arising from the study of working memory and language are considered.

The choice of subdomains of language to explore from a working memory perspective in this book has been dictated simply by the volume of research interest over the past 20 years. We consider that sufficient numbers of researchers have asked questions about whether working memory contributes to word learning, to the production of speech, to the process of learning to read and to skilled reading, and to the understanding of language, to warrant their inclusion in an analysis of working memory involvement in language. On current evidence, however, working memory does not contribute equally in the different aspects of language processing. For example, it appears to be rather less critical to speech production than language comprehension. In the interests of completeness, though, the principle subdomains of language that may be linked with working memory are included in this book. Readers will be able to use this text to judge for themselves the nature of working memory involvement across a wide range of language skills.

Both in our research and in writing this book we have benefited greatly from discussions with many colleagues and friends. Particular thanks go to Martin Conway for his interest and support at all times, to Graham Hitch for providing valuable insights into the development of working memory that have guided us in this book, and to David Howard for his detailed and constructive comments on an earlier manuscript. We would also like to thank Julia Darling for her assistance in preparing the manuscript.

A NOTE ON THE AUTHORS

At the time of publication, Susan Gathercole is at the Memory Research Unit, Lancaster University, UK and from September 1993 will be a Reader in Psychology at Bristol University, UK. Alan Baddeley is Director of the MRC Applied Psychology Unit, Cambridge, UK.

CHAPTER ONE

Introduction to Working Memory

Most adults produce and comprehend their native language rapidly, accurately and effortlessly. Speaking and listening can be combined with many of other everyday activities with little detectable cost to the language user. It is only when more objective indices of linguistic behaviour are considered that the huge reserve of expert knowledge that is necessary to support this "language skill" becomes apparent. The typical adult knows the sound structure, meaning and spelling of many tens of thousands of words, constituting a kind of mental dictionary acquired through personal experience. Knowledge about language is not, however, restricted to lexicon-like entries about individual words. The skilled language user has also mastered the grammar of the native language. The grammar is a complex system of abstract syntactic rules that allows the speaker to combine words in an infinite number of phrases and sentences. It also enables the listener to understand the messages produced by others. In addition, the production and comprehension of language is guided by knowledge about both the pragmatics of language use and the conventions governing discourse between individuals.

The unique ability of humans to develop this extensive knowledge base for their native language has been attributed to innate capacities specialised for the acquisition and processing of language (e.g. Chomsky, 1957). However, this position does not explain the psychological mechanisms by which linguistic knowledge is either acquired during childhood or used in the course of language activity. In this book, we focus on the contribution to acquisition and processing of language of one particular mechanism, *working memory*. Baddeley and Hitch (1974) used this term to describe the short-term memory system, which is involved in the temporary processing and storage of information. They suggested that working memory plays an important role in supporting a whole range of complex everyday cognitive activities including reasoning, language comprehension, long-term learning, and mental arithmetic.

Intensive research activity has been stimulated by the working memory approach. The adequacy of the working memory model as a theoretical account of short-term memory in both adults and children has been investigated and the model itself has been refined (Baddeley, 1986). In addition, researchers have been concerned with identifying those everyday cognitive activities which involve working memory. In recent years, there has been considerable interest in the contribution of working memory to language, resulting in a broad and diverse range of evidence. Some of this evidence points to a clear involvement of working memory in language, whereas other studies identify aspects of language processing in which working memory appears to play little part. It is, however, clear that working memory is important in language processing, and that the richness and complexity of its role is such that it is likely to be a fruitful research area for many years to come. The research literature on this topic is already extensive and distributed across a wide range of both general and specialised journals. We believe that a review of the area is timely and that it may help the area to advance. The aim of this book is to provide such a review. Inevitably, some aspects of language processing have been more fully investigated than others. For this reason, interpretation in some parts of the book is by necessity speculative, representing "first passes" at theory rather than polished theoretical conclusions. We hope that these speculations are useful in stimulating further research and counter-theorising.

The task of evaluating working memory involvement in language is not a straightforward one, partly because of the inconsistent usage by psychologists of the term "working memory". It is often not clear whether different researchers are talking about the same psychological mechanisms when they discuss working memory involvement in various aspects of language processing. Some researchers use the term to denote a general processing system that has a limited capacity (Daneman & Carpenter, 1980; Kintsch & van Dijk, 1978; Pascual-Leone, 1970). Others use the term to refer to an essential component of production system models of cognition, a component that is not necessarily limited in capacity (Anderson, 1983). The term "working memory" is used more specifically in this book to refer to the current version of the working memory model developed by Baddeley and Hitch (1974). This well-specified theoretical model of short-term memory is used as a framework for the analysis of the contribution of working memory to language. Although we personally have found this framework to be productive, the principal aim of the present review is not to argue for such a model, but to use it to structure an overview of the available evidence concerning this crucial interface between memory and language, an overview that we hope will be useful to readers of a wide range of theoretical persuasions.

The aspects of language processing considered in the following chapters are *vocabulary acquisition*, *speech production*, *reading development*, *skilled reading*, and *language comprehension*. For convenience, each of these language processes is considered in separate chapters although, of course, in practice these distinctions are far from clear cut. Where available, evidence concerning the nature and extent of working memory involvement in each aspect of language processing is drawn from three traditionally distinct but increasingly interrelated types of study that differ principally in their subject population. The studies we term *experimental* employ normal adult subjects, the *developmental* studies use children, and the *cognitive* neuropsychological studies involve the testing of patients with acquired brain damage.

Data from children and adults has obvious value in elucidating the nature of working memory involvement in the acquisition of language skills and in skilled language behaviour. The relevance of neuro-psychological data may, however, require more explanation. The cognitive neuropsychological approach has had increasing impact on theorising in mainstream cognitive psychology over the past decade (see Ellis & Young, 1988, for an evaluation of its contributions), and has been particularly influential in the evolution of the working memory model discussed later in this chapter. The unique value of neuro- psychological studies for theories of normal cognitive function arises from the opportunities provided by "natural experiments" in which brain damage selectively impairs a particular psychological mechanism. Studies of patients with highly specific deficits of working memory have been of exceptional value in identifying the contribution of working memory to language. It has become increasingly apparent that investigations of such patients can provide a rich source of information about the structure and functioning of short-term memory which both supplements and enhances the findings obtained from studies of normal skilled language users.

THE WORKING MEMORY MODEL

Baddeley and Hitch (1974) identified three components of working memory. The *central executive* component is the most important. Its functions include the regulation of information flow within working memory, the retrieval of information from other memory systems such as long-term memory, and the processing and storage of information. The processing resources used by the central executive to perform these various functions are, however, limited in capacity. The efficiency with which the central executive fulfils a particular function therefore depends on whether other demands are simultaneously placed on it. The greater the competition for the limited resources of the executive, the more its efficiency at fulfilling particular functions will be reduced.

The central executive is supplemented by two components which are termed "slave systems". Each slave system is specialised for the processing and temporary maintenance of material within a particular domain. The *phonological loop* maintains verbally coded information, whereas the *visuo-spatial sketchpad* is involved in the short-term processing and maintenance of material which has a strong visual or spatial component. Figure 1.1 provides a simple schematic representation of the working memory model.

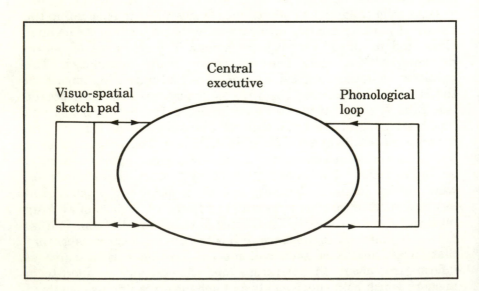

FIG. 1.1. A simplified representation of the Baddeley and Hitch (1974) working memory model.

The Central Executive

The central executive fulfils many different functions. Some of its primary functions are regulatory in nature: It coordinates activity within working memory and controls the transmission of information between other parts of the cognitive system. In addition, the executive allocates inputs to the phonological loop and sketchpad slave systems, and also retrieves information from long-term memory. These activities are fuelled by processing resources within the central executive, but which have a finite capacity. Cognitive tasks that have been suggested to involve the central executive include mental arithmetic (Hitch, 1980), recall of lengthy lists of digits (Baddeley & Hitch, 1974), logical reasoning (Baddeley & Hitch, 1974), random letter generation (Baddeley, 1966a), semantic verification (Baddeley, Lewis, Eldridge, & Thomson, 1984a) and the recollection of events from long-term memory (Hitch, 1980).

Theoretical progress on the central executive has been relatively slow, and experimental methodologies for studying the nature and extent of executive involvement in particular tasks are still under development. There have been, however, a number of important advances in understanding this component of working memory in recent years. Much of the current work on the regulatory functions of the central executive is guided by a model of the attentional control of action developed by Shallice (1982, 1988; Norman & Shallice, 1980). This model is shown in schematic form in Fig. 1.2. Action is controlled

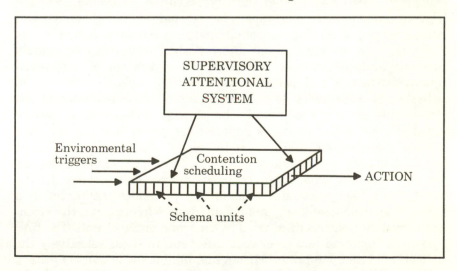

FIG. 1.2. A model of the control of action. Adapted from Shallice (1988).

in two ways. Well-learned or "automatic" activities are guided by schemas that are triggered by environmental cues. Schemas can be hierarchically organised. Skilled drivers, for example, will have a *driving schema* that activates subroutines such as *steering, gear-changing* and *braking schemas*. When driving, the driving schema will be activated and all its subroutines primed, so that the sight of red lights at the rear of the car ahead should be sufficient to provide the environmental cue to trigger the braking schema.

Potential conflicts between ongoing schema-controlled activities can be resolved routinely by the *contention scheduling* system. However, when novel activities are involved, or when the environment presents an urgent or threatening alternative stimulus, the higher-level Supervisory Attentional System (SAS) intervenes to control action. The SAS inhibits and activates schemas directly, and so can override the routine process of contention scheduling. By combining the powerful but resource-demanding SAS and the autonomous process of contention scheduling, human action is controlled by an efficient and responsive system.

Baddeley (1986) suggested that the SAS may correspond to the central executive. Useful insight into the nature of the SAS (and thus, the central executive) is provided by neuropsychological patients who, through either accident or disease, have experienced damage to the frontal lobes. It has long been known that damage to these cortical areas leads to disturbances in the conscious control of action which Baddeley (1986) has termed the "dysexecutive syndrome". Frontal lobe patients typically show a paradoxical combination of behavioural perseveration, when they repeatedly perform the same action or say the same word or phrase, and distractibility, when they repeatedly pick up and use objects within reach, regardless of the social appropriateness of such actions. Shallice (1988) explains both types of behavioural disturbance as manifestations of an impairment to the SAS resulting from the frontal lobe damage. Perseveration results when the control of action is captured at a low level by a single powerful schema that continues to inhibit all other schemas. Because the SAS is impaired, it cannot intervene in order to damp down the activation of the schema. In contrast, distractibility arises in the absence of a highly activated schema. The patient is bombarded by a range of environmental triggers for different schemas, and the attentional system becomes dominated by environmental stimuli. The SAS system is impaired and so cannot intervene to boost selectively the activation of an appropriate schema and inhibit the activity of others.

There have been some important recent empirical and methodological developments concerning the central executive. Firstly, work with frontal lobe patients indicates that the executive may play a crucial role in the planning of future actions (Shallice & Burgess, 1991). A second advance was the development of an experimental task which appears to occupy the central executive. As tasks become more routine and automated, their demands on the central executive are assumed to decrease. A task that denies the possibility of automatisation should therefore put great demands on the central executive. One such task is that of random generation where, for example, the subject is required to produce a stream of letters in as random a sequence as possible. The existing alphabetic schema will tend to produce such stereotypes as ABC and WXY, and any simple alternative strategy is unlikely to be able to simulate randomness under rapid paced conditions, as indeed proves to be the case (Baddeley, 1966a). It is assumed that in order to generate successfully an unsystematic sequence of letters, the SAS is needed to overrule the routine processes which produced stereotyped and non-random letter sequences (Baddeley, 1986). Consistent with this view, the sequences become significantly less random (and more stereotyped) when the pace of the task is increased, and when the subject is involved in other concurrent activities. In other words, when the task either becomes highly demanding of the limited SAS resources or has to share them with other activities, its efficiency in controlling the production of unsystematic letter sequences is diminished.

One of the strengths of the random letter generation task is that it can potentially provide a tool for identifying central executive involvement in other activities. The way in which this can be done is by combining random letter generation with other tasks and measuring the cost for subjects of performing both activities concurrently rather than alone. If the central executive does have limited resources, tasks which also tax the executive should either show sizeable decrements when performed concurrently with random letter generation, or should lead to the generation of less random letter sequences. Recent work by Teasdale, Proctor, and Baddeley (in prep.; see Baddeley, in press) using this methodology has yielded intriguing results which directly link the central executive with conscious awareness.

It would, however, be misleading to suggest that the central executive is as yet uniquely identified with a single mechanism or model such as the Supervisory Attentional System. Some researchers do view the executive as a unitary system that may form the basis of the general factor of intelligence (Duncan, Williams, Nimmo-Smith, & Brown, 1991; Kyllonen & Chrystal, 1990). Other work, though, suggests that it comprises a range of relatively independent subprocesses (Duncan, in press) that may include planning (Shallice & Burgess, 1991; in press), task coordination (Baddeley, Logie, Bressi, Della Salla, & Spinnler, 1986), and conscious awareness (Baddeley, in press), as well as the previously described capacity to select and control action. We are clearly only just beginning to understand this rich and complex component of cognition.

The Phonological Loop

The phonological loop is a slave system specialised for the storage of verbal material. It comprises two components, as shown in Fig. 1.3 (Baddeley, 1986). The phonological store represents material in a phonological code which decays with time. A process of articulatory rehearsal serves to refresh the decaying representations in the phonological store and so to maintain memory items. The rehearsal process is also used to recode nonphonological inputs such as printed words or pictures into their phonological form so that they can be held in the phonological store. In contrast, spoken speech information gains direct access to the phonological store without articulatory rehearsal.

The two-component architecture of the phonological loop is based on a large body of experimental evidence accumulated during the past 20 years. More recently, it has also been supported by studies of neuropsychological patients with deficits that appear to correspond to subcomponents of the loop. The principal experimental phenomena associated with the phonological store and the rehearsal process are summarised below.

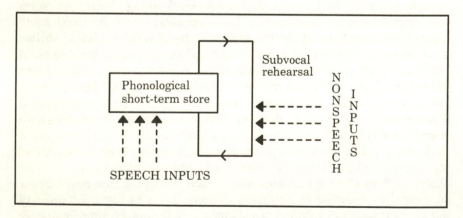

FIG. 1.3. The phonological loop model, based on Baddeley (1986).

Articulatory Suppression
The articulatory suppression technique involves the subject articulating irrelevant material, such as repeatedly saying "the, the, the". Short-term memory for lists of printed words is greatly depressed when subjects engage in articulatory suppression during presentation of the memory list (Estes, 1973; Levy, 1971; Murray, 1967; Peterson & Johnson, 1971). According to the working memory model, the disruptive effect of articulatory suppression arises because it prevents subjects from rehearsing (see Fig. 1.3). There are two consequences. Phonological recoding is disrupted and hence subvocal rehearsal is prevented, with the result that the contents of the phonological store cannot be refreshed and so will decay and be forgotten.

Word Length
Baddeley, Thomson, and Buchanan (1975) showed that immediate memory performance is directly influenced by the spoken length of memory items. Ordered serial recall of lists of one-syllable words (e.g. *sum, wit, hate*) was considerably better than recall of lists containing five-syllable items (e.g. *university, opportunity, aluminium*). This word length effect in immediate memory was found both for memory lists that were presented visually (in the form of printed words) and for those that were presented auditorily (spoken by the experimenter).

A subsequent experiment demonstrated that the word length effect was due to the articulatory duration of the memory items and not simply the number of syllables they contained. Serial recall was compared for lists of two-syllable words with either relatively short spoken durations (such as *wicket* and *bishop*) or long durations (such as *harpoon* and *Friday*). Recall was significantly better for the "short" words than the "long" ones. This result suggests that the word length effect does not reflect a memory system with a limited number of syllabic "slots" available, but instead is due to a sensitivity of the phonological loop to articulatory length of the to-be-remembered items. More specifically, it was argued that articulatory rehearsal takes place in real time, so that words that take longer to produce also take longer to rehearse. Subjects are therefore able to rehearse more short than long items in a given time, and so lose less of the short items from the phonological store as a consequence of decay.

Further convergent evidence that spoken length is a critical factor in immediate memory was provided by an experiment that directly compared reading time for memory items with the levels of memory performance for those same items. In one part of this experiment, the time taken for subjects to read aloud words varying in length from one to five syllables was calculated. In a second phase, subjects were tested on serial recall of lists of the items of each length. Reading time for memory items was highly and linearly correlated with level of memory performance ($r = 0.685$, $p < 0.005$). Figure 1.4 shows that as reading rate decreased for the longer items, so did recall level.

The linear function relating serial recall performance to the speed of articulating the memory items has shown considerable generality across memory materials, extending even to comparisons across languages. Ellis and Hennelly (1980) found that the better digit span of children speaking English than of those speaking Welsh could be explained simply in terms of the shorter spoken duration of English compared to Welsh digits. Subsequent research (e.g. Naveh-Benjamin

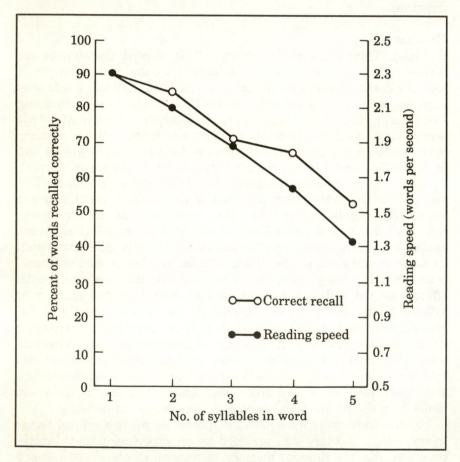

FIG. 1.4. Mean reading rate and percentage correct recall of sequences of five words as a function of length (Baddeley, Thomson, & Buchanan, 1975).

& Ayres, 1986) has shown that short and rapidly articulated digits are associated with longer digit spans across a range of languages. These findings of close correspondences between immediate memory performance and speech rate are readily explained in terms of the subvocal rehearsal component of the phonological loop. Longer items take more time to articulate both subvocally and overtly, so that rehearsal is less effective at maintaining decaying traces in the phonological store for long than short items. Thus, the memory representations in the phonological loop will be increasingly susceptible to decay as their spoken length increases.

According to this account, the word length effect should be abolished under conditions of articulatory suppression, as both suppression and length effects arise from the rehearsal process. When articulation is suppressed, subvocal rehearsal should be prevented and the advantage of short over long words in the phonological loop should disappear. This prediction has been supported. Baddeley et al. (1975) found that with visually presented memory lists, the word length effect disappeared when subjects engaged in irrelevant articulation during list presentation. With auditory presentation the word length effect has also been found to disappear with articulatory suppression, although in this case it may be necessary to continue articulatory suppression during recall as well as during list presentation (Baddeley, Lewis, & Vallar, 1984b).

Phonological Similarity
Immediate recall of a list of items is much poorer if the items are phonologically similar to one another (e.g. *B, C, T,* or *cat, rat, mat*) than if they are phonologically distinct (e.g. *R, W, H,* or *man, egg, boat*). This phonological similarity effect was first reported by Conrad and Hull (1964) with lists of letters presented visually to the subjects, which indicates that the phenomenon is not due to problems in auditory discriminability. The phenomenon has been found over many studies to be robust. In contrast, immediate memory performance shows little sensitivity to either the orthographic or semantic similarity of the memory list (Baddeley, 1966b).

The disruptive consequences of phonological similarity on immediate memory performance can be readily located within the phonological store component of the phonological loop. Salamé and Baddeley (1982) suggested that the phonological representations of memory items are liable to partial loss from decay or interference from other phonological material. The consequences of partial degradation of a memory item's phonological representation will be most disruptive when that item is similar in phonological structure to the other items in the memory sequence for the following reason. The probability of losing a phonological feature which discriminates that item from other members of the memory set will be greatest when the number of discriminating features is smallest. Thus, loss of the first phoneme of the sound of the letter C will render it indiscriminable from B and D, but nonetheless distinct from R and W.

This account of the phonological similarity effect fits well with more complex patterns of findings. In particular, the phonological similarity effect disappears under conditions of articulatory suppression *when the memory list is presented visually* (Baddeley et al., 1984b; Levy, 1971; Peterson & Johnson, 1971). With auditorily presented lists, though, the disruptive effects of phonological similarity remain intact even when rehearsal is prevented via articulatory suppression (Baddeley et al., 1984b). The reason for this selective effect should be clear from Fig. 1.3. Articulatory suppression blocks rehearsal, and so prevents visual material from ever gaining access to the phonological store. Because the phonological similarity effect is believed to be located within the phonological store, it will not occur in this condition. However, spoken material gains access to the phonological store irrespective of whether rehearsal is prevented or not. Performance will thus be sensitive to the phonological structure of the memory list even under articulatory suppression.

Irrelevant Speech
If subjects hear an irrelevant stream of speech during presentation of a verbal memory list, recall accuracy is disrupted (Colle & Welsh, 1976). This deleterious effect of concurrent speech occurs even when the memory lists are presented visually. This phenomenon is explained in terms of the automatic access of the irrelevant spoken material to the phonological store. Once there, it interferes with phonological representations of the memory items.

Findings from Salamé and Baddeley (1982) are consistent with this view. Figure 1.5 shows the principal results from Experiment 5 of their paper. In this study, the subjects' task was to remember the sequences of visually presented digit lists. During presentation of the memory list, one of three different types of irrelevant speech sounds were presented. These were either digits (e.g. *one, two*), words constructed from the same phonemes as the digits (e.g. *tun, woo*), or disyllabic words that were phonologically dissimilar from the digits. The memory disruption was found to be greatest for the first two of these conditions, when the irrelevant material was phonologically similar to the memory items. Relative to the control condition of no concurrent noise, there was also a reduced but significant residual

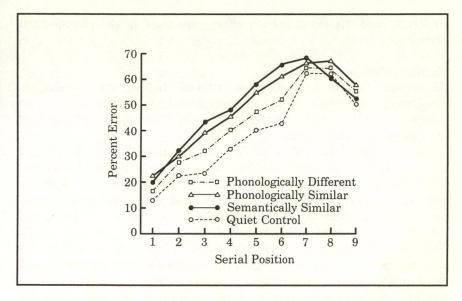

FIG. 1.5. Immediate memory for visually presented digit sequences accompanied by unattended material (Salamé & Baddeley, 1982).

disruption of recall performance by the irrelevant speech material which contained words that were phonologically unrelated to the memory items. Speech streams containing digits and nonwords that were phonologically similar to digits disrupted performance to an equivalent degree, indicating that it is the *degree of phonological similarity* between the irrelevant material and the memory items that underlies the irrelevant speech effect, rather than interference at the lexical or semantic level. The results are therefore entirely consistent with the view that the irrelevant speech effect arises from interference within the phonological storage component of the phonological loop.

Experimental Fractionation of the Phonological Loop
The findings from the experimental studies briefly outlined here are consistent with the fractionation of the phonological loop into two dissociable subcomponents. The first comprises a phonological store that is subject to decay and interference. The second involves a subvocal articulatory rehearsal process, which is used both to recode nonauditory material into a form suitable for the phonological store, and to refresh decaying representations in the phonological store. Word length and articulatory suppression effects on short-term memory are located in the rehearsal process, and the phonological

similarity and irrelevant speech effects are sited in the phonological store.

Neuropsychological Evidence

Neuropsychological evidence has proved to be very useful in developing this model of the phonological loop. In this section we review some influential investigations of the working memory skills of neuropsychological patients.

Shallice and Warrington (1970) described a patient, KF, whose memory span was limited to two digits despite relatively normal language function and preserved long-term learning. KF had a much-reduced recency effect in free recall, showed very rapid forgetting of even a single letter in the Peterson short-term forgetting task, and was better at remembering visual than auditory memory lists. Shallice and Warrington interpreted this pattern of results as reflecting a severe deficit in the operation of a short-term phonological input store. This interpretation was subsequently supported by a number of similar cases studied (see Vallar & Shallice, 1990, for review).

Vallar and Baddeley (1984a) studied one such patient who they suggested might have a highly selective deficit of the phonological loop system. PV was a young Italian woman who suffered damage to the left hemisphere as a result of a stroke. Following the immediate post-traumatic period, her problems were largely restricted to impaired short-term memory for verbal material. She had fluent speech and a normal articulation rate, normal written language, and no detectable auditory processing deficits (Vallar & Baddeley, 1984b). Her profile on a range of working memory tasks suggested a specific impairment of the phonological short-term store. With auditory presentation, PV had a very poor memory span of about two items, which was insensitive to word length but was influenced by phonological similarity with auditory but not visual presentation. She performed better with visually presented material, although her recall of such material was uninfluenced by either phonological similarity, word length or articulatory suppression.

Vallar and Baddeley (1984a) suggested that PV had a defective although still functioning phonological store, and that this was the basis for her poor auditory memory span. As the store is still believed to make some contribution to PV's memory performance with auditory presentation, the observed effect of phonological similarity in this condition is explained. In addition, Vallar and Baddeley proposed that PV failed to use the optional articulatory rehearsal process as this would simply feed information into her defective phonological store.

The consequences of this are that no word length effect occurs for auditory material, and there is no access to the phonological store with visual material. The improved memory performance of PV with visual presentation, combined with her lack of sensitivity to any of the usual phonological loop factors such as similarity and word length in this presentation condition, suggests that an alternative nonphonological aspect of the working memory system is being used to support short-term retention of visual material.

This working memory interpretation of PV's short-term memory deficits certainly provides a more adequate account of this neuropsychological case than other less well-specified views of short-term memory. It also provides strong convergent evidence, in combination with the experimental studies of normal adults, for the account provided by the two-component phonological loop model of the range of working memory phenomena. This study, and subsequent investigations of PV (her language processing skills have also been explored, and are discussed in detail in Chapters 3 and 8), provide clear illustrations of the value of studying neuropsychological cases for testing and developing models of normal human cognition.

The neuropsychological studies reviewed so far have provided important convergent evidence for the current two-component model of the phonological loop. Other investigations of patients with pathological cognitive deficits have been influential in developing our understanding the nature of the loop system, by virtue of providing, for the cognitive neuropsychologist, serendipitous natural experiments. Baddeley and Wilson (1985) investigated the short-term memory characteristics of a young adult, GB, who, as a result of closed head injury, had normal language as assessed by written communication but was completely unable to speak as a result of paralysis of speech motor mechanisms. Prior to the brain trauma, GB had normal speech production ability. If the articulatory control component of the phonological loop is genuinely articulatory in nature, in that it involves the activation (either overtly or covertly) of articulatory musculature, this patient should be unable to encode visually presented material in the phonological store, or to rehearse. In other words, he should behave like normal adult subjects under conditions of articulatory suppression. In direct contrast to these predictions, testing of GB revealed entirely normal working memory function (using a pointing procedure to measure recall). He had an unimpaired memory span, and showed the usual deleterious effects of phonological similarity and word length with visual presentation. This pattern of findings was generalised to five other patients also suffering severe acquired dysarthric impairment. Similar results have also been reported by Logie, Cubelli, Della Salla, Alberoni, and Nichelli (in press) and by Vallar and Cappa (1987).

These results rule out the involvement of peripheral articulatory and speech mechanisms in the operation of the phonological loop as these mechanisms did not function for GB. The interpretation favoured by Baddeley and Wilson (1985) was that the critical process for active rehearsal is the central speech programming mechanisms rather than overt operation of articulatory actions. All of the patients tested in this case series had acquired normal language prior to brain injury, and so had presumably developed high-level control of articulatory structures. The suggestion was that these central articulatory skills were preserved, despite the total disruption of articulatory output mechanisms.

Support for this view is provided in a recent study by Waters, Rochon, and Caplan (1992) of the short-term memory characteristics of six neuropsychological patients with apraxia of speech, which is a high-level impairment of speech motor planning in which low-level speech output processes are relatively preserved. These patients behaved exactly like normal subjects being tested under conditions of articulatory suppression, suggesting that the subvocal rehearsal process may call upon the speech production mechanisms used for high-level articulatory planning.

Recent findings reported by Bishop and Robson (1989), however, challenge this interpretation of the nature of the subvocal rehearsal process. This study explored the short-term memory characteristics of a group of cerebral-palsied individuals who were either congenitally speechless or seriously speech-impaired. Their memory profiles did not differ from those of control subjects; they showed normal sensitivity to both word length and phonological similarity. It therefore seems that the phonological loop system was functioning normally in this group, and comprised both a phonological store and a subvocal rehearsal process. As these individuals had never been able to speak, and so were most unlikely to have developed high-level articulatory planning skills, an account of subvocal rehearsal in terms of abstract speech motor programming looks implausible. Instead, Bishop and Robson (1989) suggest that the rehearsal process involves activation of an abstract phonological representation that can be constructed solely on the basis of speech perception: a sort of phonological "echo" (see Gathercole & Hitch, in press).

The issue of whether the rehearsal component of the phonological loop has an articulatory or purely phonological basis is currently being debated, and unfortunately cannot be resolved here. The differentiation of the phonological loop into both a phonological storage component and an active maintenance control process does, however, appear to be securely grounded in both experimental and neuropsychological evidence. The developmental work reviewed in Chapter 2 also fits well with this two-component conceptualisation of the phonological loop.

Much of the working memory research on language, however, is not sufficiently specific to allow us to identify which specific subcomponent of the phonological loop or working memory is involved in a particular use of language. For this reason, where necessary, we use the more neutral terms *phonological working memory* and *phonological memory* to refer to those aspects of working memory that are used to maintain verbal material, while avoiding making theoretical claims that are stronger or more specific than the available data can support.

The Sketchpad

The visuo-spatial sketchpad is a slave system specialised for the processing and storage of visual and spatial information, and of verbal material that is subsequently encoded in the form of imagery. Unsurprisingly, there is little indication that this component of working memory plays a significant role in language. In the interests of providing a complete account of the working memory model, though, current ideas about the nature of this subsystem of working memory are briefly outlined here.

Theoretical progress concerning the structure and functioning of the sketchpad has been less rapid than for its sister slave system, the phonological loop, but some important characteristics of visual working memory have now been established. The first systematic investigation of the visuo-spatial sketchpad was reported by Baddeley, Grant, Wight, and Thomson (1975). In a number of experiments, a version of the imagery technique developed by Brooks (1967) was used as a memory task that demands storage of visual information. In this task, subjects are shown an unfilled four-by-four matrix, with one cell marked as the starting square. In the spatial conditions, the experimenter reads out a series of instructions which enable to subject to mentally "fill" cells of the matrix. For example, subjects might hear the following instructions: "In the starting square put a 1. In the next square to the right put a 2. In the next square up put a 3 ..." and so on, typically up to the number 8. One of four spatial adjectives is used in each sentence to guide subjects—either up, down, left or right. Recall is tested by requiring subjects to repeat back sentences in the order presented. Subjects typically report encoding the sentences as a path through the matrix, and recalling by regenerating the sentences from their image of the path.

A nonspatial version of this task was also used, in which the spatial adjectives in the instructions were replaced by four nonspatial adjectives—good, bad, slow and quick. Thus, for example, the instructions might be "In the starting square put a 1. In the next square to the quick put a 2. In the next square good put a 3 ..." and so on. With these instructions, subjects cannot readily recode the sentences into an interpretable imaginal form that can be represented within the matrix, and so are forced to rely instead on nonvisual and predominantly verbal encoding.

It seems plausible that the spatial form of the task could be represented in the visuo-spatial sketchpad, whereas the nonspatial form could not. Baddeley et al. (1975) tested this hypothesis by requiring subjects to engage in a visuo-spatial tracking task during memorisation of the instructions in half of the trials. The results of this experiment are summarised in Fig. 1.6. Memory performance on

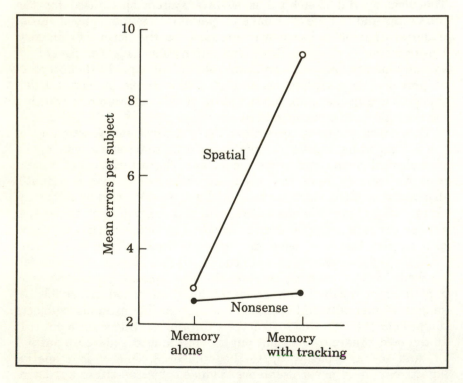

FIG. 1.6. Influence of concurrent tracking on memory span for visualisable and nonvisualisable sequences (Baddeley, Grant, Wight, & Thompson, 1975).

the spatial and nonspatial forms of the Brooks task were about equivalent in the no tracking conditions. When subjects engaged in this concurrent visuo-spatial task, however, errors in the spatial memory task increased dramatically, whereas nonspatial memory performance remained intact. This pattern of selective interference indicates that a different component of memory did indeed mediate memory for the spatial and nonspatial instructions. The disruptive influence of the tracking task on the spatial memory task is clearly consistent with the view that a memory component specialised for the processing and maintenance of visuo-spatial material contributes to spatial recall.

Subsequent research by Baddeley and Lieberman (1980) suggested that the component underpinning memory performance on the spatial task may be more spatial than visual in nature. Tracking using a pursuit rotor, which was the concurrent task used by Baddeley et al. (1975), is both visual and spatial in nature, as indeed are most everyday "visual" events. Baddeley and Lieberman (1980), however, devised two relatively pure concurrent tasks, one of which was spatial only, and one of which was predominantly visual. The spatial task involved subjects pointing to a moving sound source while blindfolded. The visual task involved judgement of the brightness of a patch of light.

Concurrent blindfolded tracking of the moving sound source selectively disrupted performance in the spatial memory task, but did not influence nonspatial memory performance. Conversely, the concurrent brightness judgement task impaired recall of the nonspatial instructions to a greater extent than the spatial instructions. These findings of selective interference indicate that the memory component underpinning performance on this particular memory task is spatial rather than visual in nature.

Imagery mnemonics have also been used to explore the visuo-spatial sketchpad. The beneficial consequences of using imagery as opposed to rote verbal learning to support the retention of verbal material were well established in the 1970s by researchers such as Paivio (1971) and Bower (1970). One attractive possibility is that the visuo-spatial sketchpad provides the medium for the generation and maintenance of information in imaginal form, and so provides the basis for the imagery benefits found in memory.

Baddeley and Lieberman (1980) reported findings that are consistent with this hypothesis. They instructed subjects to remember lists of unrelated words either by using rote repetition or by using the pegword mnemonic. This mnemonic has been used extensively by researchers interested in the use of imagery in memory, and involves teaching the subject to associate each of the numbers between one and ten with a rhyming and highly imageable word. For example, the subject is taught to associate the number one with an image of a bun, the number two with an image of a shoe, etc. Subjects are then trained to use the images as a way of remembering sequences of items by associating each memory item with an image of the word associated with that word's position in the memory list. So if the first two words in the memory list were *table* and *glass*, the subject would attempt to generate an image incorporating a table with a bun, and another image involving an interaction of a glass and a shoe. Once learned, this pegword technique has been found to provide an extremely effective means of improving memory for unrelated sequences.

The involvement of the visuo-spatial sketchpad in the imagery mnemonic was assessed by comparing the consequences of concurrent visuo-spatial tracking on memory following either pegword learning or rote learning. It had already been established that spatial recall in the Brooks task was disturbed by concurrent tracking. If imagery also involved the same visuo-spatial component of working memory, the effectiveness of the pegword mnemonic should also be reduced if subjects are simultaneously tracking.

This prediction was supported. In Experiment 3, Baddeley and Lieberman (1980) found that pursuit rotor tracking disrupted performance in the imagery condition but not in the rote learning condition. This result was generalised in a further experiment on a location mnemonic, an alternative imagery technique that involved using images of familiar locations to encode and retrieve memory items.

The findings reviewed so far suggest that a specialised visuo-spatial component of working memory is involved in both retaining visual information and in generating and maintaining images, and that the nature of this medium is primarily spatial in nature. Recent results do, however, suggest that the sketchpad has a visual as well as a spatial component. Logie (1986) devised a concurrent task in which subjects had to look at a plain coloured square which was either the same or different in colour to the one preceding it. The presence of the squares disrupted recall via the pegword mnemonic but not by rote learning. Because there is no spatial patterning in a plain coloured square, this finding indicates that a heavy spatial component is not an essential feature for the operation of the visuo-spatial sketchpad.

More serious problems for interpretation of spatial and imaginal memory performance in terms of a specialised visual working memory system arise from the results of Phillips and Christie (1977). Using lists of nonverbal stimuli consisting of three-by-three matrices in which the cells were randomly filled, they found that performance was considerably enhanced for the last item in the list. This one-item visual recency effect seemed likely to depend on the visuo-spatial sketchpad. However, the recency effect was abolished when subjects engaged in mental arithmetic after the end of the list and prior to recall. Visual working memory seems unlikely to be involved in mental arithmetic; rather, this task is typically viewed as a task requiring both phonological and central executive resources. These results therefore raise the possibility that performance in tasks such as spatial memory and imagery, which have been attributed to the sketchpad, could in fact be mediated by both the central executive and the sketchpad (see also Logie, Zucco, & Baddeley, 1990).

The proposal that working memory contains independent verbal and visuo-spatial components has, however, received strong empirical support. One recent study on imagery reported by Brandimonte, Hitch, and Bishop (1992) provides a particularly convincing demonstration that verbal and visual memory capacities are dissociable. An imagery manipulation task was used in which subjects were shown a picture of a familiar object and then asked to subtract part of the picture in order to discover a new pattern. For example, a picture of a skipping rope becomes two ice cream cones if the rope is subtracted.

In Experiment 1, recall of the pictures was tested after completion of the subtraction task. Four different learning conditions were contrasted. In the control condition, subjects were given the task without being told to remember the stimuli. In each of the three remaining conditions, instructions were given to memorise the sequence of the composite pictures, either before participating in the subtraction task, after training, or while engaging in articulatory suppression prior to training. The results are summarised in Fig. 1.7, which shows the mean number of items correctly called in the different experimental conditions.

Recall was better in the control condition than in either of the nonsuppression conditions involving memorisation, but at a corresponding level to the condition involving memorisation with articulatory suppression. Thus, when subjects were actively trying to remember the picture sequence, recall was better when they engaged in irrelevant articulation than when there was no concurrent task. This counter-intuitive finding of an *improvement* in recall in a "distractor" condition is explained by Brandimonte et al. (1992) in terms of the use of phonological recoding. It is suggested that when

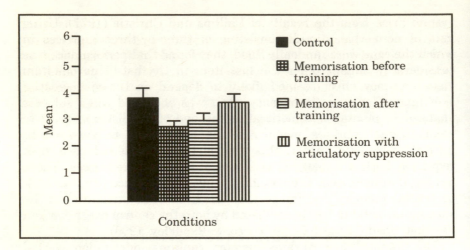

FIG. 1.7. Mean number of correct answers on the four conditions of the subtraction task (Brandimonte, Hitch, & Bishop, 1992). (Reproduced with permission.)

subjects explicitly attempt to learn the sequence of pictures, they recode the stimuli phonologically and in doing so, fail to rely on the more effective visual codes resulting from imagery transformation. Articulatory suppression prevents subjects from carrying out this phonological recoding, and so forces them to exploit their superior visual memory for the stimuli. Convergent evidence for this conclusion is provided in a later experiment, which establishes that the beneficial consequences of suppression only arise when the visual stimuli to be learned are nameable.

As in the case of the phonological loop, neuropsychological evidence has complemented that from normal subjects (Hanley, Young, & Pearson, 1991). Such evidence has been particularly influential in supporting the view that the sketchpad has separable visual and spatial subsystems, with the visual component being dependent on the functioning of the occipital lobes, whereas spatial working memory is more parietally based (Farah, 1988; Farah, Hammond, Levine, & Calvanio, 1988).

OVERVIEW

According to the working memory approach, short-term memory plays an active role in processing and storing information in the course of complex cognitive tasks such as language processing. The specific model of short-term memory that has emerged from research motivated by the working memory approach has three principal components. The central executive possesses limited-capacity processing resources, which can be used for particular processing activities, and also for controlling action and the transmission of information between other components of the memory system. The central executive is supplemented by the operation of two specialised subsystems. The phonological loop is capable of processing and maintaining phonological information, and consists both of a phonological short-term store and a subvocal control process used both for rehearsal and recoding information into phonological form. The visuo-spatial sketchpad is involved in generating images and in retaining information with visual or spatial dimensions.

CHAPTER TWO

The Development of
Working Memory

Several aspects of *language development* are considered in the course of
this book. We discuss the psychological mechanisms and processes
involved when children learn new words (Chapter 3), when they produce
speech (Chapter 4), when they learn to read (Chapters 5 and 6), and
when they attempt to comprehend language produced by others (Chapter
8). In each case, our primary interest is in identifying what role, if any,
is played by working memory in the development of the particular
domain of language ability. Before the working memory contributions to
language development can be assessed, though, it is necessary to know
the ways in which working memory *itself* develops during childhood.

Between infancy and adulthood, there is a dramatic increase in an
individual's ability to retain temporarily verbal material such as a
new word or a list of numbers. The most convenient and widely used
index of this developmental increase is provided by auditory digit
span, which is the maximum number of spoken digits that someone
can immediately remember and repeat back in the same order. An
average four-year-old child has a span of between two and three
digits. Ten years later, he or she will have a digit span of about seven
items, representing a threefold increase in memory capacity.
Short-term memory for purely visual material undergoes a similar
increase during the same developmental period.

Our interest here is in what components of the working memory
model underpin this developmental improvement in short-term

memory. If the working memory model provides an accurate account of a mature short-term memory system, as we claim it does in Chapter 1, it should be possible both to use it to identify which *components* of short-term memory change in functioning during childhood, and to characterise the *nature* of the change that results in the adult working memory system. In principle, there are many different ways in which working memory could develop during childhood. For example, components of the "adult" working memory system could be initially absent in young children and emerge at a particular point in development. Or, each of the individual components of working memory may be present throughout childhood, but their capacities may expand as the child matures. A related possibility is that the efficiency of each component increases with age.

The evidence so far favours the third possibility. All three components of working memory—the central executive, the phonological loop and the sketchpad—appear to be present in young children. For each component, the major developmental changes identified so far have been in the operating efficiency of the working memory subsystems, and in the increasingly effective use of strategies to maximise working memory functioning. Most experimental studies of working memory development have focused on the changes that take place in *phonological loop* function during school years, and this work is reviewed first. Some of the findings arising from these investigations have direct implications for the development of *central executive* function in children, and these are considered next. Finally, work on the development of *visual memory* skills during childhood is summarised.

THE PHONOLOGICAL LOOP

Two important conclusions have emerged from the application of the working memory approach to children's memory. Firstly, the phonological loop is present and functioning from the preschool years onwards. Secondly, the developmental expansion in memory span during childhood is largely due to an increase in the rate of subvocal rehearsal with age.

Evidence critical to both of these conclusions was provided in an influential study by Hulme, Thomson, Muir, and Lawrence (1984; see also Nicolson, 1981). They tested the serial recall abilities of three groups of children—aged four, seven and ten years—and a group of adults. Each subject heard lists of spoken words that contained either one syllable (e.g. "egg, pig, bus, car") or three syllables (e.g. "elephant, umbrella, banana, kangaroo"). In each case, the child's or adult's task was to immediately recall the words in the same sequence. In order to avoid ceiling effects in memory performance with the older age groups, older age groups of subjects were given longer sequences of words. At recall, subjects attempted to repeat the memory items in the order in which they had been presented.

In addition to the serial recall test, a measure of articulation rate was taken for each of the different lengths of word. Subjects were asked to repeat pairs of either one-syllable or three-syllable words 10 times each, as fast as possible. For each subject, the amount of time to repeat each word pair was measured, and these scores were used to calculate a measure of articulation rate (in mean number of words per second) for each length of word.

Memory performance increased with age in this study. However, subjects in all age groups were better at recalling short than long words. According to the logic of the working memory approach (see Chapter 1), the presence of a word-length effect indicates the use of subvocal rehearsal to maintain the memory sequence. Thus, even the youngest children appear to have been rehearsing the memory lists. Why, though, did memory performance increase with age? The answer seems to lie in the close relationship between recall and articulation rate. As the number of items recalled increased across the age groups, so too did the subjects' articulation rates. This relationship is illustrated in Fig. 2.1, which shows articulation rate plotted as a function of mean number of words recalled per list in the four age groups. Articulation rate and recall were closely linked with one another: the faster the words were spoken by subjects, the better the recall performance. This linear relationship explained both the word-length effects in each groups (long words take longer to articulate than short words) and the developmental effect (articulation rates were more rapid for the older than the younger groups). Data points from all age groups fell on the same regression slope, and there was no significant effect of group on the slope.

Rehearsal is believed to involve subvocal articulation in real time (Baddeley et al., 1975). Thus, limitations on the speed at which subjects explicitly articulate directly influence their rates of rehearsal. The common function linking articulation rate to recall scores across the different age groups therefore suggests that the developmental increase in recall performance arises because older children and adults rehearse more rapidly than young children, and hence lose fewer items due to decay from their phonological stores during the delay between successive rehearsals. The same argument is also extended to words of different articulatory durations. For each age group, it takes longer to rehearse long than short items, so recall will be better for lists containing one- than three-syllable words.

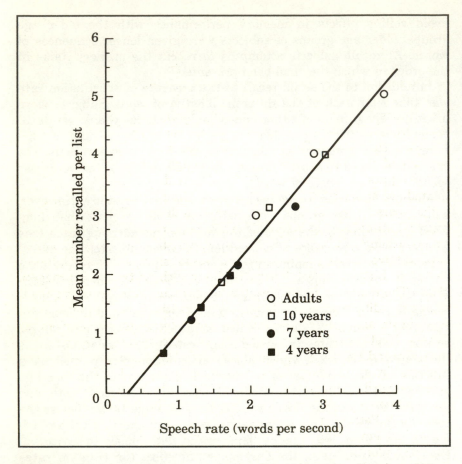

FIG. 2.1. The relationship between word length, speech rate, and memory span as a function of age (Hulme, Thomson, Muir, & Lawrence, 1984). (Reproduced with permission.)

It appears, then, that the phonological loop is present and functioning in four-year-old children, but that rehearsal is more efficient in older age groups. Results from memory tasks using slightly different presentation procedures, however, indicate that this conclusion only holds when the memory lists are spoken, as in the Hulme et al. (1984) study. When pictures are used as memory items, children below the age of about seven years show no sensitivity to word length. This dissociation in the way that young children maintain spoken and pictorial material in working memory was clearly demonstrated by Hitch and Halliday (1983). They tested the memory span of three groups of children—aged six, eight and ten years—for words containing either one, two or three syllables. The memory lists were either spoken by the experimenter at presentation, or displayed to the subjects as a sequence of pictures. In each case, at the end of the list the children were required to recall aloud the names of the memory items in the original input sequence.

The results are summarised in Table 2.1. Word-length effects were found for all groups when the memory lists were presented auditorily. With pictures, however, there was no difference in the level of recall of the words of different lengths for the six-year-olds, and a significant word-length effect on recall was only found in the ten-year-olds. This pattern of findings indicates that although young children retain heard inputs in the phonological loop, they do not use it to mediate immediate memory for nameable picture stimuli until after the age of eight years. The absence of a word-length effect on memory for pictorial stimuli for young children has been replicated several times since, although the specific age at which length effects emerge varies between five and ten years across individual studies (Hitch, Halliday, Dodd, & Littler, 1989a, Hitch, Halliday, Schaafstal, & Schraagen, 1988). The reasons for this variation across studies is not as yet clear, although differences in both the sensitivity of experimental procedures and sampling variability seem likely to be contributory factors. Most importantly, though, the existence of a common developmental trend has been replicated on a number of occasions: Whereas memory for spoken sequences is sensitive to word length from four years onwards (Hulme & Tordoff, 1989), with pictorial stimuli this phenomenon only emerges fully some time later (Halliday, Hitch, Lennon, & Pettifer, 1990).

Studies employing another technique designed from work with adults to identify the use of rehearsal—articulatory suppression (see Chapter 1)—have yielded findings that are consistent with this conclusion. The articulatory suppression technique involves subjects

TABLE 2.1

Effects of Word Length (Number of Syllables) and Method of Presentation on Number of Items Recalled by 6-, 8- and 10-year-olds (Hitch & Halliday, 1983)

		Number of Syllables in Memory Items		
Age in Years	Presentation	1-syllable	2-syllable	3-syllable
6	pictures	2.33	2.17	2.10
	spoken words	2.85	2.58	1.81
8	pictures	2.29	2.07	1.96
	spoken words	3.13	2.85	2.21
10	pictures	3.00	2.63	2.28
	spoken words	3.11	2.93	2.18

in repeating irrelevant material during the presentation of the memory list, and appears to prevent subjects from rehearsing the memory list (Baddeley et al., 1975). Halliday et al. (1990) found that five-year-olds' recall of sequences of pictures was insensitive to both word length and concurrent articulatory suppression. In contrast, a group of eleven-year-old children showed a significant word-length effect in a control condition which was eliminated with concurrent articulatory suppression. The disappearance of the word-length effect with suppression in the older age group is characteristic of normal adult subjects (Baddeley et al., 1975). The contrasting *insensitivity* of the young children's recall of picture names to both word length and articulatory suppression indicates that they do not use rehearsal as a means of remembering the names of pictures. The lack of any effect of suppression here, and in an earlier neuropsychological study (Vallar & Baddeley, 1984a), also reinforces the view that suppression affects performance via its disruption of rehearsal. It does not appear to operate as a general source of distraction as has occasionally been suggested (Parkin, 1988).

Similar developmental patterns have also been found using the phonological similarity rather than the length of the memory items as an indicator of phonological loop involvement. With pictorial presentation, Halliday et al. (1990) found significantly lower recall in 11-year-olds for lists of words that sounded similar to one another (e.g. *cap, rat, bag*) than for lists containing matched different-sounding words (e.g. *horse, train, hand*). This phenomenon is the well-established phonological similarity effect in serial recall found with adult subjects (e.g. Conrad & Hull, 1964) discussed in Chapter 1. For five-year-olds, however, Halliday et al. found no similarity effect for pictures, nor was there disruption of performance under conditions of articulatory suppression. The emergence of a phonological similarity effect with pictorial stimuli at around seven years of age is now well established (Conrad, 1972; Hitch & Halliday, 1983; Hitch, Halliday, Schaafstal, & Heffernan, 1991). Phonological similarity effects in children as young as five years of age do, however, emerge when the memory lists are presented auditorily (Hulme & Tordoff, 1989; Hitch et al., 1991). Once again, the pattern of findings suggests that the phonological loop is not used by children to maintain the names of pictures until the age of about seven years.

In summary, young children are sensitive to both the phonological similarity and spoken duration of items in immediate memory tasks. In terms of the current model of the phonological loop, this result suggests that both the phonological store and subvocal rehearsal are fully operational from the age of about four years. The increase observed in memory for spoken material as children grow older therefore appears to be explicable simply in terms of the simultaneous developmental increase in articulation rate. As speaking rate increases, so does the speed of subvocal rehearsal. As a consequence, more items can be held in the phonological loop without decay.

Use of subvocal rehearsal to recode *visual* material into a form appropriate for the phonological loop, however, appears to emerge between the ages of about six and eight years. Although young children appear to be capable of engaging in subvocal rehearsal, they do not select it as a strategy for recoding nonauditory material until the early school years. It is worth noting here that rehearsal appears to emerge at about the time at which the children start becoming skilled readers. At around this time, the child becomes proficient at silent reading; that is, in translating orthographic information into a linguistic form that is not explicitly articulated. This process has obvious features in common with the subvocal articulatory process which appears to underpin rehearsal. Perhaps, then, full use of a rehearsal strategy is a consequence of becoming proficient at reading silently. Cross-cultural studies based in countries in which reading instruction is received either early or late would be particularly informative on this issue.

The suggestion that children as young as five years do have the cognitive architecture necessary for recoding via subvocal articulation, even though they may not use it spontaneously for nonauditory material, is supported by Johnston, Johnson, and Gray (1987). In this study, groups of five-year-old children were trained to rehearse as a means of remembering the names of pictures presented serially. Although in the control group, which received no training, there was no effect of word length on recall, children taught to rehearse either overtly or covertly did show significantly better recall of lists of short rather than long words. The implication of this finding is that that although young children do not spontaneously adopt the optimal strategy of recoding via subvocal rehearsal, they can be trained to do so.

More recently, though, there has been uncertainty as to whether very young children do indeed rehearse in the same way as older children and adults. Articulatory suppression does not have the reliably disruptive effect on recall of five-year-old children for auditory lists that it has with older children and adults (Henry, 1991). This result is very puzzling, as it suggests that very young subjects are *not* actively rehearsing spoken lists, despite the well-established finding that they are highly sensitive to word length with auditory presentation (e.g., Hulme et al., 1984). One possibility is that their word-length effects do not necessarily have their origin in subvocal rehearsal, but may instead be, in part at least, a result of processes involved in extracting information from the phonological store prior to output (Campbell & Wright, 1990; Cowan, Saults, Winterowd, & Sherk, 1991; Cowan, Day, Saults, Keller, Johnson, & Flores, 1992; Gathercole & Hitch, in press). This type of account clearly requires both further experimentation and theoretical specification. At present, it seems that while the phonological loop does contribute to young children's immediate memory for spoken material, the system operates in a relatively rudimentary fashion, and may not involve sophisticated rehearsal processes of the kind used by older children and adults.

THE CENTRAL EXECUTIVE

According to the working memory model, immediate memory for verbal material is mediated by both the phonological loop and the central executive. The evidence reviewed earlier concerns the changes that take place in phonological loop function during childhood. What changes, if any, occur in the nature and organisation of the more general working memory resources provided by the central executive?

The most well-developed theoretical stance in this area is provided by Case and colleagues (Case, Kurland, & Goldberg, 1982). They distinguish between two general cognitive resources in working memory—storage space, which is the space available for storing the products of perceptual-cognitive processing, and operating space, which consists of the pool of resources available for carrying out intellectual operations. Total processing space consists of the sum of storage and processing space.

An important feature of Case et al.'s approach is that total processing space remains constant throughout development, but that older children need less processing space to perform intellectual operations as a result of the increased efficiency of encoding and retrieval operations. A prediction of the constant total space hypothesis is that as operational efficiency increases its processing demands will be reduced, leaving more processing space available for storage. Experimental evidence for this predicted negative relationship between efficiency and storage space is provided in a series of four studies using groups of children aged between three and six years (Case et al., 1982). In Experiment 1, operational efficiency was measured by the time taken for subjects to repeat back single words; this was assumed to involve both perceptual analysis and motor speech planning activity. Storage capacity was measured by a memory span procedure. As predicted, an approximately linear monotonic relationship was found between processing speed and memory span: As processing speed increased, so did memory span.

Further experiments reported by Case et al. (1982) compared performance on a combined measure of processing storage space (counting span, in which the children had to count the number of dots on a series of cards, and then recall the series of numbers) and on a processing measure (speed of counting). Similar results were obtained: Counting span and counting speed were highly correlated with one another.

Case et al. (1982) claim that their findings show that increased efficiency of processing operations in general working memory underpins the developmental increase in short-term span. Their idea is that memory storage space increases as the child develops, due to a decline in the amount of processing resources required. In terms of the working memory model, this would approximate most closely to an explanation in terms of the central executive. As we have already discussed, however, the developmental increase in speed of subvocal rehearsal in the phonological loop also provides a very good account of the improvement in memory span during childhood. How should these two conflicting interpretations be resolved?

It could be argued that Case et al.'s (1982) approach is just a more general version of the working memory account. In both cases, the critical change with age is that the efficiency of control processes increases—these processes are termed intellectual operations by Case and colleagues, and subvocal rehearsal by working memory researchers. Both approaches also claim that the increased efficiency has direct beneficial consequences for memory storage (either by freeing up storage space, or by reducing decay of phonological representations). Perhaps, then, the two approaches are describing the same process of cognitive development, using language and concepts which vary only in specificity.

The results of a series of experiments by Hitch, Halliday, and Littler (1989b) indicate that developmental change in the phonological loop and central executive can be dissociated experimentally. Memory span for lists of visually presented words was tested in groups of eight- and eleven-year-old children. The memory lists contained words of either one, two or three syllables, and in half of the trials subjects engaged in articulatory suppression during presentation.

Hitch et al. also took two measures of spoken output rate for the different sets of words. These were the speed of reading aloud a list of words (oral reading rate), and the speed of continuously repeating two words (articulation rate). Articulation rate was calculated as usual in terms of numbers of word produced per second. In addition, two measures of "item identification time" were taken. Subjects' speed of reading aloud single words presented visually was measured, as was their rate of repeating single words that had been presented auditorily. These visual and auditory item identification measures were chosen to provide estimates of operational efficiency that match closely those used by Case and collaborators.

The aim of the study was to determine which measures best predicted memory span—the output rates implicated by the working memory model, or the identification rates emphasised by the Case et al. (1982) approach. The results were intriguing. Both articulation rate and oral reading rate provided very good predictors of memory span in the control conditions ($r = 0.97$, $p < 0.001$, both cases). Memory performance under conditions of articulatory suppression, however, was not significantly related to articulation rate, although there remained a significant, although somewhat reduced, link between span and oral reading rate ($r = 0.84$, $p < 0.05$). Different results were obtained with the identification time data. Both visual and auditory identification time were only related to span in the articulatory suppression conditions ($r = -0.96$, $p < 0.001$, for visual identification time, and $r = -0.98$, $p < 0.05$, for auditory identification time). Under the control conditions of no concurrent suppression, the identification times were not significantly associated with memory performance.

These results demonstrate dissociable influences of output rate and identification time on the effects of word length and age on immediate memory. Both articulation rate measures provide very good predictors of memory performance when subjects are not engaging in articulatory suppression. This finding confirms previous findings in the working memory tradition, and supports the phonological loop hypothesis that the effects of word length and age on memory span reflect the subvocal rehearsal process.

On the other hand, memory performance under articulatory suppression was not associated significantly with the articulation rate measure, and was most strongly linked with the item identification measures. This finding suggests that increasing operational efficiency does indeed enhance available storage space, but that this developmental change reflects central executive rather than phonological loop function.

Hitch et al.'s (1989b) results are important, as they clarify the nature of the developmental changes in verbal working memory skills with age. The speed of articulatory rehearsal is a powerful determinant of immediate verbal memory which underpins both the word-length effects on memory and some of the developmental increase in memory. Central executive function improves in efficiency with age, resulting in the availability of additional processing resources for storage and retrieval of memory items. In combination, the changes in the operations of these two components of the working memory model readily account for the sizeable increase in verbal memory performance which occurs between childhood and adulthood.

In our recent work with a group of language-disordered children, we too have found clear evidence that phonological working memory and central executive function can be separated developmentally (Gathercole & Baddeley, 1990a; see Chapter 3 for more details of this study). The disordered group was significantly impaired on all measures of phonological working memory skill, even when compared with younger children of matched verbal abilities. Yet on two non-memory measures obtained with verbal stimuli—articulation rate and articulation latency—the language disordered children performed at a normal level. These results reinforce the notion that phonological processing skills and general processing efficiency are indeed developmentally dissociable.

THE SKETCHPAD

So far, we know that before the age of about seven years, young children do not use the phonological loop to store the names of picture lists. Nonetheless, four- and five-year-old children can typically remember a sequence of two or three pictures. How do they do it, if they are not encoding verbally? The answer may be that they are using the visuo-spatial sketchpad. Hitch, Halliday, Schaafstal, and Schraagen (1988) explored this hypothesis directly. Groups of five- and ten-year-old children were tested on their oral recall of the names of sequences of pictures. Three sets of pictures were used. In one set they were visually similar to one another. Objects depicted pictorially in this set all had one-syllable labels, namely *nail, bat, key, spade, comb, saw, fork* and *pen*. Another set consisted of pictures of objects with three-syllable names, such as *umbrella, kangaroo* and *banana*. The control set were visually dissimilar from one another, and all had short names such as *pig, cake* and *leaf*. Examples of these materials are given in Fig. 2.2

The following predictions were made. If five-year-olds do use visual memory in remembering picture sequences, they should be uninfluenced by the articulatory length of the memory items, thus replicating previous findings for children of a similar age (e.g. Hitch & Halliday, 1983). Remembering a sequence of items that are visually similar to one another may well be difficult if the items are being

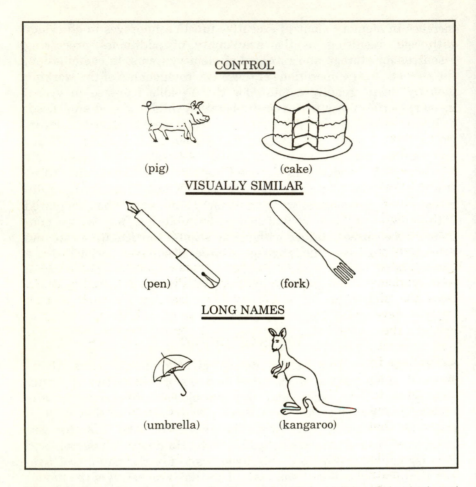

FIG. 2.2. Examples of memory stimuli used by Hitch, Halliday, Schaafstal, and Schraagen (1988). (Reproduced with permission.)

represented visually, because loss of visual features of the representation in memory due to either decay or interference could render items indiscriminable from one another. In contrast, if the eleven-year-olds were using the phonological loop to remember the pictures, as suggested by the research reviewed earlier in this chapter, they should be sensitive to the spoken length of the memory items, but not to their visual characteristics.

These predictions were largely borne out by the results. The older children were indeed uninfluenced by the visual similarity of the picture lists, but showed poorer retention of lists containing pictures with three-syllable rather than one-syllable names. The younger children were poorer at recalling the visually similar than dissimilar sequences. However, the five-year-olds were also disrupted by increasing word length, although to a significantly lesser extent than the older group. This pattern of findings is clearly consistent with a developmental shift from dependence on visual working memory for the retention of picture sequences towards the use of the phonological loop to retain picture names. For the older children, there appears to be a tendency instead to use the phonological loop to maintain any stimuli that can be verbally recoded, irrespective of their input form.

The work reviewed so far reveals a greater tendency for young rather than older children to remember pictorial information in visual form. There are, however, visual memory items which cannot be recoded verbally, and which even adults would presumably have to remember in terms of their visual characteristics. Examples of such tasks were described in the section on the visuo-spatial sketchpad in adults and would include, for example, grids composed of cells which were randomly either filled on unfilled (e.g. Phillips & Christie, 1977). Does the ability to use visual working memory for such stimuli improve developmentally, as the functioning of both the phonological loop and the central executive appear to do, or do visual memory skills remain constant as the child grows older?

Findings from Wilson, Scott, and Power (1987) suggest that visual memory span undergoes a developmental increase equivalent in magnitude to the expansion of verbal memory span between the preschool years and late childhood. They devised a visual span technique that was closely analogous to the verbal memory span task. Subjects of a range of ages were shown matrices in which half of the cells were filled, and half unfilled. Two seconds later, they were shown a second matrix which was identical except that one previously filled cell was unfilled. The subject's task was to identify the missing cell. The first matrix tested consisted of only two cells, with matrix size increasing by two after each correct response, until the matrix size was reached at which two successive incorrect responses were made. Span was calculated as the last length at which the subject made a correct response.

The results are summarised in Fig. 2.3. The solid line depicts mean visual pattern span in the condition in which recognition was delayed by two seconds. Visual memory span increased with age, showing a developmental improvement comparable with that already established for verbal memory span. Thus, although younger children may tend to rely on visual rather verbal recoding of memory items, this result shows that the capacity to retain material in nonverbal as well as verbal form does improve with age.

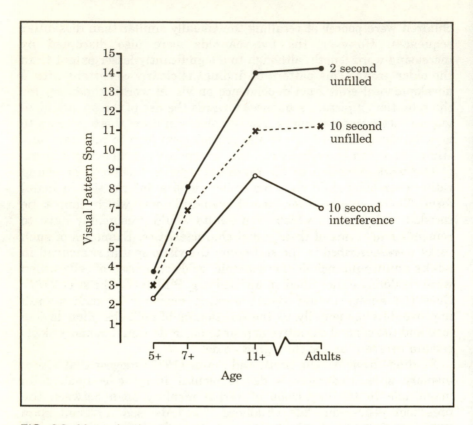

FIG. 2.3. Mean visual pattern spans as a function of age and the nature of the retention interval between presentation and test (Wilson, Scott, & Power, 1987). (Reproduced with permission.)

While the study by Wilson et al. (1987) shows a clear developmental trend, it does not necessarily reflect an increase in the capacity of the sketchpad. Tasks involving the retention of complex visual patterns may place relatively heavy demands on the central executive (see Chapter 1), and it is possible that it is the capacity of the executive rather than the sketchpad that is responsible for the developmental expansion in visual memory span. This interpretation is supported by results from two other conditions in the Wilson et al. study. In both conditions presentation was followed by a 10-second pretest delay which was either unfilled, or occupied by a written arithmetic task. The results are shown in Fig. 2.3. All age groups showed poorer performance following the filled than the unfilled delay, with the disruption being much greater for older subjects. Since mental arithmetic probably disrupts the central executive rather than the sketchpad (Hitch, 1980), the developmental improvement in visual memory span seems to be attributable in part at least to an increased central executive contribution rather than to a simple increase in sketchpad capacity. Separating the development during childhood in the sketchpad from parallel increases in executive and phonological loop performance offers an intriguing experimental challenge.

OVERVIEW

The working memory model has proved to be a very useful tool in guiding analysis of the developmental changes in short-term memory function during childhood. All three principal components of working memory appear to be present at the youngest age at which short-term memory is typically tested, four years. At this age, children appear to retain auditory speech information within the phonological loop, although nonauditory material such as pictures of objects seem to be remembered in terms of their visual rather than sound-based characteristics. A rudimentary form of rehearsal, possibly akin to an immediate echo of the phonological form, appears to be used. Full strategic rehearsal for all linguistically codable material emerges some years later, at around seven years of age.

Children's phonological loop skills appear to be separable from their more general processing abilities, which probably provide an index of central executive function. Recent work on memory for nonlinguistic visuo-spatial material also points to a significant increase in visual memory capacities during the school years. However, whether these capacities reflect the improved functioning of the specialised sketchpad component or improvement in central executive efficiency is as yet unclear.

CHAPTER THREE

Vocabulary Acquisition

The ability to learn new words is central to becoming a skilled language user. The typical pattern of vocabulary development is now well-established. Children usually produce their first word at some time around their first birthday. The first 10 words or so are acquired relatively slowly, at the rate of between 1 and 3 words per month. Rate of acquisition of new words then accelerates rapidly, leading to a period of "vocabulary explosion" (Bloom, 1973). Between about 19 months and 2 years, children typically learn about 25 words per month (Nelson, 1973). This rate of acquisition increases during infancy, so that by the age of 5 years, mean vocabulary is in excess of 2000 words. Peak rates of vocabulary growth occur during the school years; recent estimates are that between the ages of about 7 and 16, children typically learn on average 3000 words every year (Nagy & Herman, 1987). Vocabulary development does not stop at later adolescence. Adults learn new words too, although the rate of natural vocabulary acquisition during adulthood is much slower, and is likely to be dependent on social and occupational factors. Foreign languages can be learned at any time, of course; successful acquisition of a second language involves massive vocabulary growth in which the number of phonological forms familiar to an individual can be almost doubled.

The important role played by vocabulary knowledge in the development of other language abilities is borne out by studies from a number of different developmental traditions. Detailed investigations of the lexical development of individual children have illustrated the importance of single-word knowledge in the first few years of life for the subsequent emergence of complex syntactic and semantic structures (see Barrett, 1989, for review). Similar conclusions emerge from correlational studies of measures of intellectual development in older children. Vocabulary size is strongly associated with a range of abilities including general intelligence, reading ability, reading comprehension, and school success (e.g., Anderson & Freebody, 1981; Thorndyke, 1973). Accordingly, vocabulary knowledge has been widely employed by experimental, developmental, and educational psychologists as a useful indicator of verbal intelligence, using standardised tests such as the Wechsler Scales for children (Wechsler, 1974) and the British Picture Vocabulary Scales (Dunn & Dunn, 1982).

The central role played by vocabulary knowledge in language processing, and in intellectual development more generally, makes the psychological study of the processes involved in learning new words an issue of both exceptional theoretical interest and practical relevance (Sternberg, 1987). Psychological research on the acquisition of vocabulary is largely represented by two traditions, both of which focus on the influence of exogenous factors on word learning. Firstly, developmental psychologists have devised methods for simulating word learning in very young children, and have demonstrated the remarkable facility of young children in acquiring new names and concepts even in experimental situations where exposure to the novel words and their concepts are strictly controlled. Secondly, many researchers have addressed the educational issue of how best to facilitate vocabulary acquisition in school children, and there is now a large body of pedagogical research concerning optimal methods of word learning. Findings arising from these traditions, both of which study environmental influences on vocabulary learning, are briefly reviewed in the following section.

ENVIRONMENTAL FACTORS

One important area of research on vocabulary development is concerned with how much young children learn about new words when their exposure to the novel items is controlled experimentally. The work of Carey and colleagues has been particularly influential in this area, providing both an experimental methodology and an interesting theoretical perspective. The "fast mapping" paradigm closely simulates natural vocabulary acquisition, and has the important feature of being suitable for use with very young children. A good example of the paradigm is provided in a study reported by Carey and Bartlett (1978). In this study, three- and four-year-old children encountered a new word in the form of a command from the experimenter. The children were seated in front of an array containing two plates of different colours, and told "Bring me the chromium plate. Not the red one, the chromium one." In this way, the new label was defined by the experimenter by reference to familiar concepts present in the environment. The child was later asked either the colour of the plate, or to identify an object signalled by the experimenter by the new label. After just one exposure to the new word, and when tested a week later, half of the children displayed some knowledge of the new word.

Carey (1978) used this evidence of rapid word learning to suggest that children are able to acquire new names and their referents by an early stage of vocabulary acquisition which is termed "fast mapping". She proposed that following initial exposures to a word and its context, information about the word's phonemic, visual, semantic, and syntactic characteristics may be stored together in memory in a temporary form. This interim representation is necessarily simple in nature, given the limited information possessed by the child about a word from initial exposures, and will be updated and refined by subsequent relevant experience. By this account, rapid vocabulary acquisition reflects the child's preparedness to store the word's phono-logical representation with preliminary hypotheses about its referents' physical and syntactic–semantic properties. The conceptual repres-entation is "roughed out" in memory, rather than structured elaborately.

This paradigm has been applied and extended by other researchers, too. Dickinson (1984) introduced groups of six- and eleven-year-old children to a single exposure of a new word either in the context of a conversation, a story, or an explicit definition. The children later had to judge which of a pair of items consisting of the novel word and a nonword was a real word. There were no differences in performance across the three contexts in which the child was exposed to the new items. However, the younger children were 21% successful at identifying the novel word after only one encounter with it. For the older children, the success rate was 30%. In both cases, performance was significantly more accurate than would be expected by chance. Similarly, the children were found to be above chance at identifying whether the new word was initially encountered as a noun or verb. This evidence that children can retain some information about a new word's phonological and syntactic form even after a single exposure fits well with Carey's notion that young children operate a strategy of fast mapping to facilitate rapid and flexible vocabulary growth (similar conclusions can be drawn from work reported by Dollaghan, 1985; and Taylor & Gelman, 1988).

The results from "fast mapping" tasks therefore establish experimentally that children very readily pick up information concerning new words, and can appropriately use partial knowledge about words at a later point in time (see also Rice, 1990). The sources of children's natural exposures to new vocabulary items have also been investigated. Unsurprisingly, the earliest words to emerge in infants tend to be words most frequently used by their caretakers (Harris, Barrett, Jones, & Brookes, 1988). Older children learn new words from television programmes (Rice & Woodsmall, 1988), stories (Elley, 1989) and books (Nagy & Anderson, 1984; Cunningham & Stanovich, 1991), as well as from formal vocabulary instruction given in school (White, Power, & White, 1989).

A number of methods have been found to be useful for promoting vocabulary learning in the classroom. In general, combinations of different instruction methods are recommended by researchers as being most effective in promoting vocabulary growth and comprehension. Instances of such techniques include formal instruction on morphological knowledge (White et al., 1989), the teaching of individual word meanings via definitions (Elley, 1989; Herman & Dole, 1988), providing the new word in context and practice in deriving word meaning from context (Jenkins, Matlock, & Slocum, 1989; Stahl, Jacobson, Davis, & Davis, 1989).

PHONOLOGICAL WORKING MEMORY

The work described in the previous section demonstrates the ease with which young children learn new words, and identifies those environmental factors which are likely to promote vocabulary learning in educational contexts. It fails, however, to cast any light on why there are such wide individual differences in vocabulary knowledge. One possibility is that all individuals share the same capacity for learning new words, and that all individual differences in vocabulary knowledge are consequences of unidentified exogenous factors such as the parents' vocabulary and exposure to vocabulary-enhancing television programmes, books, and stories. This seems unlikely. A more plausible possibility is that children differ in the component cognitive skills involved in learning new words. Here we consider recent research, which indicates that one such source of individual variation that directly influences the ease of word learning is the phonological component of working memory.

Convergent evidence that phonological working memory contributes directly to the long-term learning of the unfamiliar phonological structure of new words is provided by neuropsychological, developmental, and experimental studies. This work is reviewed in the following sections. In anticipation, phonological working memory appears to contribute directly to the learning of new words. In particular, the ease of learning new words seems to be limited by the adequacy of an individual's phonological memory skills.

Neuropsychological Studies

The first direct evidence that the phonological loop component of working memory is directly involved in learning new words was provided by the neuropsychological study of a patient with a severe and highly specific impairment of phonological working memory. The short-term memory deficits displayed by PV, a young woman who suffered a stroke, were described in Chapter 1. PV's phonological memory abilities were studied in detail by Vallar and Baddeley (1984a), who interpreted her performance as reflecting two deficits of the phonological loop system. It was suggested that PV's primary impairment was a damaged phonological store, which led to very poor retention of auditorily presented material. In addition, PV appeared not to use subvocal rehearsal either to maintain decaying representations in the phonological loop, or to recode visually presented material into phonological form, presumably because subvocalisation would simply feed information into her grossly impaired phonological short-term store.

Of principal interest here is a later study performed by Baddeley, Papagno, and Vallar (1988), in which PV's abilities to learn new phonological information were explored. Two important character-istics of PV were established in this study. Firstly, she showed a very poor immediate memory span for nonwords, failing to repeat any nonwords containing more than two syllables. This finding is consistent with the explanation of her poor auditory memory performance in terms of a defective phonological store. Secondly, PV's learning of unfamiliar phonological material was correspondingly severely impaired. In Experiment 3, she was presented with eight high-frequency words in her native Italian language, each of which were paired with nonwords derived from Russian. For example, one pair to be learned was "Rosa–Svieti". On each learning trial all eight word–nonword pairs were spoken by the experimenter, and PV's learning was then tested by giving her the Italian stimulus word, and asking her to say the paired nonword. A maximum of 10 learning trials were given to PV, and also to 14 control subjects.

Performance in this experiment is illustrated in Fig. 3.1. Whereas by the final trial 12 of the 14 control subjects had achieved perfect recall of the Russian paired associates, PV failed to learn any of the nonwords. She also showed a total lack of learning in a further version of this experiment in which presentation rate of word–nonword pairs was greatly slowed down. In contrast, she learned some visually presented word–nonword pairs (although not as many as control subjects), and learned pairs of familiar words at a normal rate.

The correspondence between this patient's long-term phonological learning deficits and her phonological working memory impairment is notable. She was unable to learn pairs of spoken word–novel word pairs when the links between the stimuli could not readily be mediated by either semantic or orthographic information. Thus, PV's phonological loop deficits were most apparent when the task involved genuine long-term phonological learning. Without adequate temporary phonological storage, it appeared that the process of constructing a more stable long-term memory trace had to fail.

This interpretation is consistent too with a recent report by Vallar and Papagno (in press) of a single case study of a girl suffering from

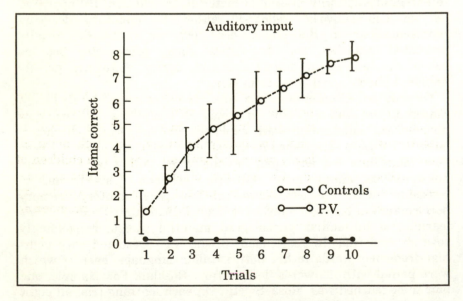

FIG. 3.1. Performance of PV and matched control subjects on word–nonword paired associate learning with auditory presentation (Baddeley, Papagno, & Vallar, 1988).

Down's syndrome who showed the opposite dissociation. Despite her relatively low general intelligence, she showed very good performance on phonological short-term memory tasks. As predicted, her pattern of word–word and word–nonword learning was the converse of that shown by PV. Her acquisition of unfamiliar Russian vocabulary items was normal, while her capacity for associating pairs of familiar words, which typically depends on semantic coding, was impaired. This pattern of results was reflected in her real-life achievements, where, in addition to her native Italian, she could speak both English and French reasonably fluently.

Developmental Studies

The notion that short-term phonological memory is involved in the acquisition of phonological forms of new words has been explored in a number of recent studies of children. The relationship between phonological working memory and long-term phonological learning ability in the neuropsychological patient PV raised the interesting possibility that phonological memory skills in children may influence their ease of learning new words. If this is the case, phonological memory skills and vocabulary knowledge should be closely associated with one another. This hypothesis has now been tested in a series of studies of both unselected samples of children, and children with pathological deficits of language processing. In both lines of enquiry, close links between phonological memory skills and vocabulary development have been found.

Normal Children

We designed a longitudinal project to test the hypothesis that phonological working memory fulfils an important developmental role in vocabulary acquisition during childhood. Specifically, we wanted to discover whether or not vocabulary knowledge and phonological memory skills were closely associated with one another in children of early school age, and also whether children's early phonological memory skills could be used to predict their later vocabulary development. Detailed reports based on this project are provided in Gathercole and Baddeley (1989a,b) and Gathercole, Willis, Emslie, and Baddeley (1992).

A number of four-year-old children were tested initially within two months of starting primary school in England. They were retested at the same time of year at ages five, six and eight years. A total of 80 children were tested at each of these waves. The tests given at each wave included measures of nonverbal intelligence, receptive vocabulary, reading, and phonological short-term memory. The principal measure of phonological memory was a test which involved the immediate repetition of nonwords. In the test given to the children in the first three waves of the study, when they were aged four, five and six years, the nonwords ranged in length from one to four syllables, and contained either single consonants only, or clustered consonants. A more difficult set of nonwords was given in the final wave of the study, at age eight, in which the number of syllables in the stimuli ranged from two to five syllables. The number of correct repetition attempts made by each child was scored as a function of the length and consonant complexity of the nonwords. At each wave, one further test of phonological memory was administered; this was either a different nonword repetition test (at ages four and five years), or auditory digit span (at ages six and eight years).

There are two reasons why we favour the nonword repetition test as a measure of phonological short-term memory in children rather than the more conventional measures such as digit span, which are based on serial recall of already familiar items. Firstly, performance on immediate memory tasks can reflect the contribution of long-term memory knowledge as well as phonological short-term memory processes. Recent work indicates that the superior immediate memory performance found with familiar rather than unfamiliar words arises from the additional availability of phonological specifications in long-term memory for familiar stimuli (Hulme, Maughan, & Brown, 1991). We therefore expect to gain a more sensitive measure of phonological memory skill by using memory items for which there are no long-term lexical representations, because subjects will be less able to use lexical knowledge to supplement phonological short-term memory. In fact, it is difficult to rule out long-term memory contribution to immediate memory performance even with nonwords. In a detailed item analysis of the nonword repetition test, we found that children's repetition accuracy was highly associated with the rated wordlikeness of the nonword (Gathercole, Willis, Emslie, & Baddeley, 1991b). For this reason, we suggest that where close phonological analogies to nonwords are available in long-term memory, subjects may use them to support working memory representations of nonwords. Nonetheless, long-term phonological knowledge, and, of course, semantic knowledge too, will make a greater contribution to immediate memory performance when the tasks involves remembering familiar rather than unfamiliar stimuli. For this reason, memory tests using unfamiliar phonological sequences seem likely to be more sensitive to children's phonological memory skills than lexically based tasks such as digit span.

We do not wish to deny here the undoubted value of tasks such as digit and word span as measures of phonological memory skill. They have proved to be invaluable tools for exploring the phonological loop in recent years, and are likely to continue to be useful techniques. And, of course, both nonword repetition and digit span measures are significantly correlated with one another in young children (Gathercole & Adams, in press; Gathercole, Willis, & Baddeley, 1991a). The point here is that in studies of young children, simpler measures such as nonword repetition may well be more sensitive to phonological memory constraints.

A second advantage of the immediate nonword repetition test over serial recall procedures such as span is its simplicity. Repeating unfamiliar sound sequences is a natural common activity for young children, as part of the process of language acquisition, and the accuracy of repetition seems likely to be less sensitive to the children's use of higher-level strategic processes, such as active maintenance or cumulative rehearsal, than in tasks requiring the ordered recall of independent lexical elements. In particular, given the evidence reviewed in Chapter 2 that full strategic rehearsal may not emerge typically until about seven years of age, the use of nonword repetition to test phonological memory function in children during the early school years seems to us to be highly appropriate.

Our main interest in the longitudinal study, then, concerned the relationship between vocabulary and nonword repetition ability between the ages of four and eight years. For the first three years of the study, the correlations between scores on the nonword repetition tests and the receptive vocabulary tests were highly significant: at age four, $r = 0.559$; at age five, $r = 0.524$; and at age six, $r = 0.562$. At age eight, the correlation between repetition and vocabulary was much smaller, although still statistically significant, $r = 0.284$. Furthermore, the relationships between nonword repetition and vocabulary scores at each of the waves remained significant even after other possible confounding factors, such as age and nonverbal intelligence, were controlled.

The close relationship between nonword repetition ability and vocabulary scores between the ages of four and six years, and to a lesser extent at eight years too, is fully consistent with the hypothesis that phonological memory contributes to the long-term phonological learning of new words. Correlations do not, however, establish the direction of causality. In particular, the significant correlations are equally consistent with a different hypothesis advanced by Snowling, Chiat, and Hulme (1991). They suggested that children may use knowledge about the structure of real words to support the repetition of nonwords. According to this account, children with more extensive vocabularies are likely to have long-term phonological specifications, which more closely approximate any particular nonword, and this may help them to retain nonwords. Note that this hypothesis assumes the opposite causal relationship between vocabulary and nonword repetition to the one we advanced earlier: Whereas we proposed that phonological memory contributes to vocabulary acquisition, Snowling et al. suggest that existing vocabulary knowledge contributes to nonword repetition ability. Clearly, the finding that vocabulary knowledge and nonword repetition ability are indeed closely linked is equally consistent with both of these competing views.

In order to discriminate between these competing hypotheses, it is necessary to identify the causal structure of the vocabulary–repetition relationship found in this longitudinal study. To do this, we used cross-lagged correlations (Crano & Mellon, 1978). This technique involves comparing the correlations obtained between two variables across two times in the hypothesised causal and noncausal directions. For example, the hypothesis that phonological memory skills at age four contribute to vocabulary knowledge at age five is tested by comparing the correlation between repetition scores at age four and vocabulary scores at age five with the converse correlation between vocabulary scores at age four and the repetition measure at age five. By the logic of cross-lagged correlations, the correlation should be greater in the causal than the noncausal direction. Thus, the first correlation (between repetition at age four and vocabulary at age five) should be greater than the second one (between vocabulary at age four and repetition at age five).

Figure 3.2 summarises the results of applying this technique to each of the four waves of the longitudinal study. We computed the partial correlations between the repetition and vocabulary scores, controlling for differences due to chronological age as well as scores at the earlier points in time on the nonverbal intelligence and outcome variable tests. By controlling for this range of factors, we were using very conservative estimates of the relationships between the two variables across time.

The results indicate that the causal underpinnings of the link between phonological memory and vocabulary knowledge changed during the course of the longitudinal study. Over the first interval—between ages four and five—early nonword repetition scores were significantly more closely associated with later vocabulary knowledge than early vocabulary was with later repetition scores. This pattern of findings supports our hypothesis that phonological memory plays a causal role in word learning, at least in the period

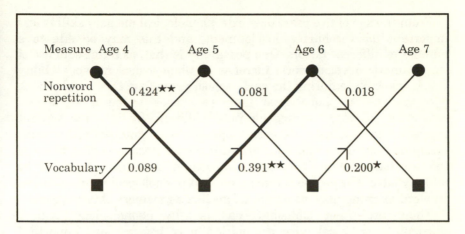

FIG. 3.2. Cross-lagged partial correlations between nonword repetition and vocabulary scores from Gathercole, Willis, and Baddeley, 1992 (see text for details). Lines shown in bold denote partial correlations that are significantly greater than the corresponding cross-lagged partial correlation.

between four and five years of age. Beyond this period, though, the causal structure appeared to change. Between the ages of five and six years, there was a highly significant partial correlation between vocabulary and later nonword repetition, but a nonsignificant converse association between repetition at five years and vocabulary at six years. These results indicate that by five years of age, vocabulary knowledge had become the pacemaker in the relationship between vocabulary and nonword repetition. Similarly, between the ages of six and eight years there was a significant forward association between vocabulary and later repetition ability, but not between early repetition ability and later vocabulary scores. Essentially the same pattern of causality emerged in the corresponding cross-lagged comparisons of partial correlations made between vocabulary and the other phonological memory measures taken during the course of the study, providing a within-study replication of the results.

Between the ages of four and five years, then, phonological memory skills do appear to critically influence vocabulary learning. To explain this causal link, we have suggested that children with good phonological memory abilities produce phonological memory traces that are highly discriminable and persistent, and that as a consequence there is a greater probability for these children that any particular phonological trace will (a) become durable, and (b) link semantically with its referent. In these ways, phonological memory skills exert a direct influence on the ease of acquiring a new vocabulary item.

From the age of five years onwards, phonological memory skill is less important for vocabulary development, and this may be due to a number of different factors. One possibility is that, as a consequence of the dramatic developmental increase in phonological memory ability which takes place during the early school years (e.g. Case et al., 1982; Nicolson, 1981), phonological memory ceases to be a significant constraint on word learning for most children. In fact, this account seems rather unlikely, as even eight-year-old children make some errors on immediate repetition of multisyllabic nonwords, and many of the vocabulary items that are acquired at about this age will be multisyllabic. The degree of constraint that phonological memory places on word learning may, nonetheless, decline as memory skill improves.

There are other plausible reasons why phonological memory constraints on vocabulary acquisition may become less important between the ages of four and eight years. One possibility is that as the children's vocabularies expand during this important developmental period, the use of analogies with existing vocabulary items to learn the phonological forms of new words increases so that the short-term phonological memory load involved in acquiring a new word diminishes (Gathercole et al., 1991b). Also, other constraints in vocabulary development, such as acquiring the meaning of a new concept, may become increasingly important. Words acquired during middle and later childhood are typically more abstract in nature, with less direct correspondence to physical objects or sensations provided by the environment, than the words acquired during the preschool years. In these later years of vocabulary development, individual differences in semantic and conceptual skills may therefore impose critical limits on the ease of learning new words, with the relative importance of phonological memory abilities declining accordingly.

Finally, it seems likely that extent of reading activity has an increasing influence on vocabulary growth during the early school years; this factor alone may be sufficiently important to overshadow the contributions of phonological short-term memory to the acquisition of new words. A number of commentators have speculated that children's exposure to print, and the extent and variety of their reading activity, explains some of the surprising vocabulary gains shown by children during the school years (e.g. Hayes, 1988; Nagy & Anderson, 1984). A recent correlational study by Cunningham and Stanovich (1991) provides direct support for this view, showing that individual differences in children's vocabulary knowledge are predictable on the basis of their familiarity with book titles. Our study also provided some evidence of this relationship. There was a strong significant association between reading ability at age six and vocabulary knowledge two years later ($r = 0.681$, $p < 0.001$), and this relationship remained significant even after variance due to age, nonverbal intelligence, and earlier vocabulary scores are taken into account ($r = 0.441$, $p < 0.001$). Together with the main analyses of the developmental relationship between vocabulary and phonological memory for this longitudinal study, this link with reading ability appears to demonstrate that there may be an important shift from phonological memory to reading as the major pacemakers in vocabulary knowledge during the primary school years.

Although the findings from the longitudinal study indicate that between the ages of four and five years there is a close link between phonological memory skills and vocabulary acquisition, there are inevitable limitations with correlational studies of this kind. The possibility must remain that correlations between two measures may simply reflect the indirect influence on both of other unidentified factors, such as the linguistic and social environment of the child. For instance, both phonological memory skills and vocabulary knowledge may be promoted by the rich and varied linguistic experiences of some children, and this could be the basis for the observed developmental association between the two abilities.

We tried to rule out differential environmental experience as the basis of the developmental correlation between phonological memory and vocabulary. To do this, the long-term learning of children with high and low phonological memory skills was compared in a task which simulated natural vocabulary acquisition. Any differences in word-learning speed obtained between the children of high and low memory skills in this situation could not be attributed to some children having heard a new word more times than others. A task was devised in which children attempted to learn the names of some brightly coloured plastic animals (Gathercole & Baddeley, 1990b). One set of toys was given familiar names such as "Peter" and "Michael", and the other toy set was assigned phonologically unfamiliar names such as "Piemas" and "Sommel". The children received the sets on different days, and in each case were given up to a maximum of 15 learning trials to learn the set of names to a criterion of correct responses on two consecutive trials. Two groups of five-year-old children were tested in this study. One group, selected from the longitudinal study, had low nonword repetition scores; the mean score for this group was more than one standard deviation below the sample mean for that age. The other group of children had high repetition scores (the mean of which was more than one standard deviation above the sample mean), but had nonverbal intelligence scores which matched the low repetition group.

The critical measure obtained from this experiment was the mean number of trials taken by each child to learn a new label. The predicted results were as follows. If phonological memory skill is involved in the long-term phonological learning of new words, the low repetition group should have greater difficulty in learning the phonologically unfamiliar names than the high repetition group. For the familiar names, stored knowledge associated with the labels could be used to support learning, so group differences were expected to be reduced, or maybe even absent, in this condition.

The results were consistent with these predictions. Figure 3.3 shows the mean number of name and non-name labels (maximum = 4) learned by each group over each of the 15 possible trials. On every trial for both sets of materials, the low repetition children had learned fewer names than the high repetition group. In addition, the learning advantage to the high repetition children was greatest for the names. The high repetition group took an average of 1.24 trials to learn a familiar name, whereas the low repetition children took 2.06 trials. This difference was not statistically different. For the non-names, the high group learned a new name in 2.96 trials on average, whereas the low group took 5.25 trials to do the same. This difference was found to be statistically reliable ($p < 0.05$). The low repetition group also remembered fewer new labels in delayed memory tests administered unexpectedly 24 hours after the original learning episode.

So, the children with poor phonological memory skills took longer to acquire new phonologically unfamiliar labels than the children with superior memory abilities. The high memory group showed more rapid learning, and also better delayed retention of the labels. The two groups were matched on nonverbal intelligence, thus the results could not simply be due to the children with high phonological memory being generally brighter. Moreover, the study used a standard learning paradigm in which the exposure of each child to the material to be learned was strictly controlled. The results therefore provide powerful support for the hypothesis that phonological memory contributes directly to the long-term learning of new words, by showing that even when exposure to new words is equated across all subjects, the speed of learning new names is still directly related to phonological memory skill.

A recent study of second-language learning in children also implicates phonological memory skill as a critical contributor to vocabulary development. Service (1992) tested the nonword repetition abilities of a group of nine-year-old Finnish children about to start learning English as part of a new educational scheme. The success of

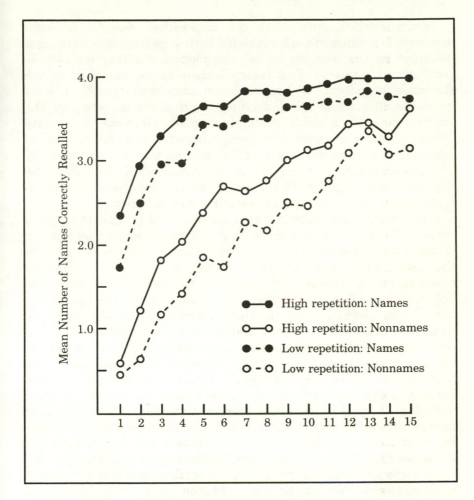

FIG. 3.3. Mean correct recall of children in the high and low repetition groups on names and nonnames as a function of trial (Gathercole & Baddeley, 1990b).

these children in learning English was monitored over a number of years. Repetition scores were found to be highly and significantly correlated with the children's grades in English two and a half years later ($r = 0.66$, $p < 0.001$), although they were not associated with arithmetic grades taken at the same time. This specificity of the relationship between repetition and English grades suggests that nonword repetition and foreign-language learning share a common component, and that this does not simply reflect differences in general intellectual ability.

Service (1992) argues that the association between nonword repetition and children's achievements in foreign language learning is mediated by the contribution of phonological working memory to vocabulary acquisition. This interpretation seems plausible, as the children's knowledge of English vocabulary was tested at least indirectly in each of the language proficiency tests used by the teachers to grade a child's ability in English. Moreover, vocabulary directly constrains both the comprehension and production of language. It is, of course, also possible that nonword repetition ability will predict the rate of acquisition of syntax, which may well also depend on the capacity to maintain the surface characteristics of spoken material. However, this issue is yet to be explored.

Another important aspect of this study is that it illustrates a link between phonological memory skills and second-language learning in children aged between nine and twelve years of age. In contrast, in the longitudinal study reported earlier we had found that the contribution of phonological memory to vocabulary acquisition appeared to decline to a nonsignificant level beyond the age of five years or so (Gathercole et al., 1992). Service's (1992) findings of a similar contribution in children considerably older than five years of age suggests that the reduced importance of phonological memory in word learning beyond this age does not reflect a maturational factor, such as the achievement of some critical level of memory skills. Instead, the findings indicate that phonological memory may still be important in word learning at a later point in time. Its contribution may be particularly critical during the early stages of learning words in a new language, when long-term memory support is minimal, as there are likely to be relatively few similar sounding words that can be used to support the temporary phonological representations held in working memory (Gathercole et al., 1991b).

Children with Language Impairments
The work reviewed in the previous section indicates that in unselected samples of school-age children, there is a close link between their phonological memory skills and the ease with which they learn new words. It is therefore particularly interesting that a common characteristic of children with developmental language impairments, and of children with more specific disorders of reading, is poor vocabulary development (e.g. Stark & Tallal, 1981; Vellutino & Scanlon, 1987). Perhaps the slow rates of word learning in children with these kinds of impaired language development are due to deficient phonological working memory skills.

Children with deficits in a range of language abilities, but with normal nonverbal intelligence and no apparent perceptual, social or emotional problems, are typically described as having a developmental disorder of language. A large body of research has documented the multiple verbal and cognitive deficits of such language disordered children (e.g. Aram & Nation, 1975; Benton, 1978; Leonard, 1982). They typically have poor language comprehension and almost always subsequently have problems when they attempt to learn to read. Two further deficits associated with developmental language disorders were of particular interest to us. Firstly, poor vocabulary knowledge is a hallmark of disordered language development (e.g. Stark & Tallal, 1981). Secondly, a number of studies have provided evidence of verbal short-term memory deficits in language disordered children (e.g. Graham, 1980; Kirchner & Klatzky, 1985; Locke & Scott, 1979; Wiig & Semel, 1976). For children with developmental language difficulties, then, poor vocabulary development and short-term memory problems appear to go hand-in-hand.

The earlier research on the vocabulary and memory deficits of language disordered children had, however, failed to illuminate the nature of possible links between the two impairments. Firstly, the specific nature of the apparent working memory deficit of language disordered children had not been identified from the perspective of a detailed model of short-term memory. Secondly, none of the earlier studies had been concerned with identifying whether there were causal links between the memory and vocabulary deficits of language disordered children. We attempted to provide preliminary evidence relating to these issues in a study of the short-term memory abilities of a group of language disordered children (Gathercole & Baddeley, 1990a). Children attending a Language Unit at a local authority school for remedial instruction in language skills were selected for the study on the basis of having vocabulary, comprehension, and reading scores on standardised tests below their chronological age, but having nonverbal intelligence scores within the normal range. On average, their performance on the verbal tests was between 18 and 24 months below the expected level for their ages.

Techniques developed in the context of the working memory model were used to provide detailed systematic assessment of the phonological memory characteristics of the language disordered children. The aim of these experiments was to identify which components of working memory were deficient in the language disordered group. In each experiment, the memory performance of the language disordered children (mean age 8 years 6 months) was compared with the performance of normal children of comparable nonverbal age, and also with younger normal children whose vocabulary and reading abilities matched those of the language disordered children (mean age 6 years 6 months). By including language-matched controls (the younger group), we were able to distinguish between two alternative hypotheses. The first hypothesis is that the poor phonological memory skills of the disordered group play a causal role in their more general language problems, such as poor vocabulary growth. In this case, the language disordered children should have even poorer phonological memory skills than the younger normal control children of matched language development. The alternative hypothesis is that the memory problems of the disordered group are a consequence of their poor language development. If so, their memory skills should be equivalent to those of the younger controls.

Tests of the nonword repetition abilities of the three groups provided direct support for the first hypothesis, namely that phonological memory deficits may be instrumental in the language development problems experienced by the language disordered group. In the course of this investigation, the children were given three separate tests of nonword repetition and in each case, the disordered groups were significantly impaired relative to both sets of control children. For the purposes of illustration, we report here our findings using the most systematic test of nonword repetition ability, one that we developed originally for use in our longitudinal study (Gathercole & Baddeley, 1989a). Equal numbers of nonwords in this test contained one, two, three, and four syllables. Consider first the overall levels of performance of the three groups of children. Whereas both the nonverbal age and language controls correctly repeated on average about 84% of the nonwords, the mean performance accuracy for the language disordered group was much poorer, at 52%. Moreover, all of the language disordered children obtained lower scores in this test (reflecting poorer repetition performance) than any of the matched nonverbal age and language controls.

Figure 3.4 shows the mean repetition performance of the experimental group and the three control groups as a function of the nonword length. The language disordered group did not perform significantly worse than the control groups on either the one- or two-syllable items as all groups were virtually perfect at this length. Note, though, that the disordered children were impaired at repeating one-syllable nonwords in the other two tests used in our study. With the three- and four-syllable nonwords, however, the language disordered children performed at significantly lower levels than both control groups ($p < 0.001$, in both cases). The extent of the separation

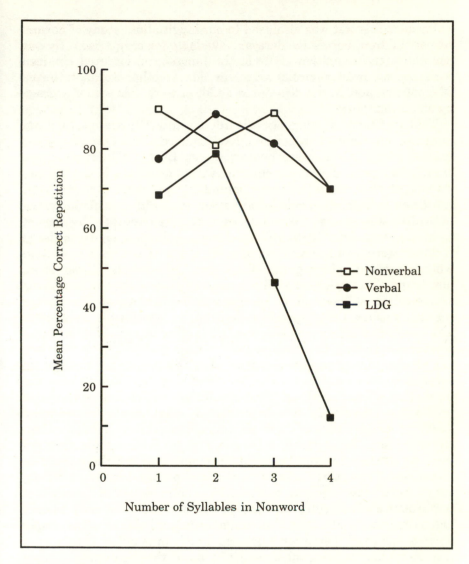

FIG. 3.4. Mean accuracy of nonword repetition of the nonverbal controls, the verbal controls, and the language disordered group (LDG) (Gathercole & Baddeley, 1990b).

in performance between the language disordered children and the control groups was such that the total number of four-syllable nonwords correctly repeated by each child perfectly discriminated all of the disordered children from both groups of controls. In other words, all of the control children were better at repeating the longest nonwords than all of the language disordered children.

Because this test was also used in our longitudinal study of normal school children, normative data are available for comparison. By our estimates, the repetition skills of the language disordered children were appropriate for normal four-year-olds. In other words, in terms of repetition ability, the disordered children were delayed on average by about four years.

This finding that language disordered children are particularly impaired on nonword repetition has been replicated in two other studies. Using our nonword repetition test, Bird (1989) found that a group of language disordered children with a mean age of seven years was lagging two and a half years behind in repetition skills. Nonword repetition deficits in an older group of children with specific language difficulties (mean age, 10 years) were reported recently by Taylor, Lean, and Schwartz (1989). In this study too, the language disordered children were significantly impaired in a test of nonword repetition when compared with a group of age-matched controls. Taylor et al. also found that repetition ability was more closely related to reading and spelling skills than to mathematical attainment. This latter result indicates that repetition deficits are specifically related to achievement in language tasks, and not to other aspects of intellectual function.

The findings from these three studies therefore converge in establishing that children with disordered language development are dramatically impaired in their abilities to repeat unfamiliar phonological forms. In fact in our study (Gathercole & Baddeley, 1990a), the magnitude of the repetition deficit was even greater than the deficits of the children in language tests. Whereas the children were on average lagging by about 20 months behind their peers in measures of receptive vocabulary, oral comprehension, and reading, they were four years behind in their nonword repetition performance. This rules out the possibility that the poor phono-logical memory skills of the language disordered children are simply a consequence of their poor language ability in general. If this were the case, the phonological memory skills of the disordered sample and of the language controls would be indistinguishable; clearly, they were not.

The interpretation of the nonword repetition deficit of the language disordered groups that we favour, and which Taylor et al. (1989) also advocate, is that it reflects impaired functioning of phonological working memory in these children. Our reasons for favouring the nonword repetition paradigm as a particularly sensitive measure of phonological memory skills in young children were discussed in the previous section, where we argued that it provides a relatively pure measure of phonological working memory which is minimally influenced by either long-term memory involvement or by strategic processes. Convergent evidence for this interpretation of repetition as a phonological memory task is also provided the poor serial recall performance of the language disordered group in our study (Gathercole & Baddeley, 1990a). There are, however, possible nonmemory deficits which could nonetheless underlie the poor nonword repetition performance of the language disordered children. Accurate repetition of an unfamiliar nonword requires adequate perception and segmentation of the input, and the planning and execution of an appropriate series of articulatory gestures, as well as maintenance of the target string in phonological working memory. Could, then, the repetition deficits of the disordered children reflect impairments of either perceptual or motor output process, rather than poor phonological memory skills?

We tested both of these nonmemory accounts of the repetition impairments of language disordered children (Gathercole & Baddeley, 1990a). Some researchers have indeed found that certain language disordered children are deficient in perceptual analysis, but the tasks have usually involved the detection of rapid transitions in synthetic auditory stimuli (e.g. Tallal & Piercy, 1975; Tallal, Stark, & Mellitts, 1985; Elliott, Hammer, & Scholl, 1989). Using undegraded speech stimuli of the kind employed in our memory experiments, however, we found no evidence that our language disordered group were deficient in their perception of speech. Perceptual analysis of the language disordered group and both the nonverbal and language control children was tested using a minimal pairs discrimination paradigm, in which pairs of nonwords or words spoken clearly were replayed to the children on a cassette recorder. The pairs were either identical to one another, or differed by one articulatory contrast. The task was to judge whether the two stimuli were identical or not. There were no significant group differences on this test. These results indicate that the poor immediate memory performance of the language disordered group was not due to inadequate perception of the stimuli to be remembered.

We also tested the possibility that the language disordered children were impaired in their motor output processing, and that this was the basis for their poor repetition of nonwords. Two measures of output speed were taken. The first measure was latency of articulation. The children were instructed to say a target word immediately that they saw a light bulb flash. A voice key was used to detect voice onset, and stopped to timer. The language disordered children were as fast as both sets of controls in their speech onset times.

The second measure was rate of articulation. The language disordered group produced on average fewer words per second than the nonverbal controls, but had equivalent articulation rates to the language controls. For the one-syllable words, for example, rate of articulation was 2.18 words per second for the disordered group, 2.13 words per second for the language controls, and 2.89 words per second for the nonverbal controls. The rate of articulation of the language disordered children compared with their language controls indicates that they may be developmentally delayed in terms of their articulatory skills, with rates of speaking more appropriate for their general level of language ability than their age.

In neither of these experiments, then, did the language disordered children reveal a deficit of speech motor output processing which could explain the magnitude of their deficits in the phonological memory experiments. In showing that the language disordered children were no slower than their language controls at either preparing their motor output, or at executing the articulatory gestures, these findings appear to rule out the possibility that their poor memory performance is simply due to decay of items from memory as a consequence of delayed output. The results also indicate that the memory deficits cannot be explained in terms of slow rehearsal rate, as rate of subvocal rehearsal and overt articulation rate are thought to be highly correlated with one another (e.g. Hulme et al., 1984). Both of the two articulatory measures did, however, focus on speed of articulatory output, so for the time being it must remain a possibility that the language disordered children have particular problems with articulatory accuracy.

In summary, it appears that children with disordered language development have severe deficits of phonological working memory, which cannot be readily explained in terms of their general levels of language ability, or their speech perceptual skills, or their articulatory output abilities. About the specific nature of their phonological memory deficits, however, we can as yet say little. The group of language disordered children that we studied were not especially slower in articulating speech, which means that their poor phonological memory performance is not simply due to slow subvocal rehearsal. The locus of their memory impairment therefore seems more likely to lie in the storage component of the phonological loop than in the efficiency of the subvocal maintenance process. Perhaps the process by which verbal material is encoded phonologically is noisy or inaccurate in these children, so that the resulting phonological representations in the store are not sufficiently discriminable. Alternatively, the capacity of the phonological store may be reduced in these children, so that either fewer phonological units can be stored, or the same number are stored less elaborately. A further possibility is that the phonological traces may decay very rapidly for these children.

Irrespective of the precise nature of the poor phonological memory function of the language disordered children, its co-occurrence with poor vocabulary development in this population fits well with the hypothesis that phonological working memory contributes to the long-term learning of the phonological forms of new words. The poor rates of natural vocabulary development in children with developmental disorders of language is certainly in keeping with the magnitude of the apparent memory deficit in language disordered children. The notion that the poor vocabulary development of language disordered children reflects basic cognitive limitations rather than exposure to an impoverished linguistic environment is supported by findings reported by Haynes (1982). She tested a group of language disordered children (mean age nine years) and younger language matched controls (mean age seven years) in an experiment which simulated natural vocabulary acquisition. The children were read stories containing 12 legal nonwords, each occurring twice in the script. The stories concerned the inhabitant of a strange planet showing a series of imaginary objects to a visiting spaceman, in order to make the use of nonwords seems feasible. As a nonword was spoken, the child was shown the object which was the nonword's referent in the story. The children performed a filler task after the end of the story, and then were tested on their recognition of the nonwords. At recognition, the child heard four versions of each nonword—the correct target form, and three phonologically incorrect forms. These forms differed from the target either in initial phoneme, medial and/or final consonants, or in all three phonemes (the "random" condition). An ingenious spatial task was designed so that children could identify the target nonword without having to produce it themselves. In this task, they had to post a letter through one of four postboxes which corresponded to the target nonword.

On average, the language disordered group correctly identified 30% of the target nonwords, a performance level which is barely above chance (25%). In contrast, the younger language-matched controls achieved a mean level of 45% of accuracy, and a group of age-matched control children scored 55% correct. Of the errors, the language disordered children incorrectly identified the three different error forms of the nonword with about equal frequency, with the random errors (selection on nonwords differing in three phonemes from the target) occurring in 34% of the error trials. In contrast, the proportion of random errors for the two control groups was considerably less than 20% in both cases.

These findings have a number of important implications. Firstly, the deficits of the language disordered children relative to younger language-matched children in an experimentally controlled vocabulary acquisition task establish that their poor natural vocabulary growth is not simply the result of linguistic deprivation, but instead of deficiencies in basic cognitive skills. And as the disordered children were matched on vocabulary scores with the language controls, it cannot be argued that the vocabulary differences were crucial. Even with the same vocabulary level, language disordered children have special problems in learning new words.

Secondly, the greater frequency of choosing phonological forms that were maximally different from the target nonword in the language disordered group than the control groups suggests that the disordered children were also less successful in storing partial phonological representations of the nonwords than the controls. Together with the reports of severe phonological memory deficits in language disordered children, these results support the view that phonological memory deficits underpin the poor vocabulary development of language disordered children. Samples of such children clearly do have phonological memory deficits, and also have problems in learning the phonological forms of new words even in experimentally controlled circumstances. Furthermore, the phonological learning difficulties of the language disordered children cannot be attributed to their current level of vocabulary knowledge. Clearly, it would be premature to claim that a direct causal link has been demonstrated here. Results from the few correlational studies designed to test the hypothesis that temporary phonological memory plays a direct role in the long-term learning of new words do, however, provide strong preliminary support.

A final comment concerns our linkage of the vocabulary deficits of language disordered children with their phonological memory impairments. It should be emphasised that the language disability of such children is by no means restricted to poor vocabulary growth, and extends invariably to the development of other language abilities, such as reading, syntax, and language comprehension (see Cromer, 1991). How then are these associated deficits explained? There are at least three possibilities. Firstly, there may be independent impairments underlying the various linguistic problems encountered by language disordered children. For example, their syntactic and comprehension deficits may have different roots to their poor vocabulary growth, possibly arising from problems at the level of abstract morphology (Gopnik & Crago, 1991), difficulties in hierarchical planning (Cromer, 1983) or impairments in temporal sequencing (Tallal & Piercy, 1975). A second possibility is that phonological working memory contributes independently to the development of vocabulary, reading, and comprehension. This position seems plausible and is certainly consistent with evidence reviewed later in the book on phonological memory contributions to the development of reading (Chapter 6) and comprehension (Chapter 8). A third view is that vocabulary knowledge is pivotal to any aspect of language use, whether it is speech production, syntactic processing or language understanding. Individual words represent the building blocks of language, and without understanding of these units the higher-level aspects of language processing cannot proceed. Difficulties in learning new words may therefore indirectly retard all aspects of language development or other aspects of language, above and beyond any direct influences that phonological memory deficits exert on vocabulary development.

Poor Readers
Children who experience specific difficulties in learning to read during the early school years but do not have the extreme and generalised language impairments of the children described in the previous section also tend to have poor vocabulary knowledge. In tests of both receptive and productive vocabulary, poor readers perform at a consistently lower level than children of the same age of normal reading ability (see Vellutino & Scanlon, 1987, for discussion of this point). Poor readers also perform badly on verbal short-term memory measures, and their memory deficits have been suggested to be located within the phonological component of working memory (e.g. Jorm, 1983). The memory characteristics of poor readers are discussed in detail in Chapter 6. The important point for this chapter is that once again, as with the language disordered children, phonological memory deficits and poor natural vocabulary co-occur. Could the memory impairments underpin the difficulty of children with reading problems typically shown in readily learning new words?

There is as yet little evidence which bears directly on this hypothesis. The long-term phonological learning deficits of poor readers have, however, been confirmed under experimental conditions that control exposure to the new words. Aguiar and Brady (1991) devised an experimental game in which nine- and ten-year-old children were asked to help a robot learn new words that would be needed for a journey to a distant planet. In the course of this game, the children were taught six new words, each of which was paired with multiple semantic attributes. For example, "taysum" was defined as a smart, helpful, talking fish, and "rimple" as irregularly shaped white berries which can be used for robot fuel. A picture accompanied the naming and definition of each new item, and the child was required to repeat the name after the experimenter.

A number of measures of learning and memory were taken. First, the number of trials taken for the children to learn the new words was calculated. Secondly, the children were asked to supply the definitions of the new words when given the name by the experimenter. Thus, whereas the first measure provides an index of phonological learning, the second measure denotes learning of semantic attributes. Finally, recall and recognition of the new names were tested at the end of the experimental session, and recognition was also retested three weeks later.

Measures of reading ability and intelligence were taken, and used as predictors of the various learning measures. Phonological learning of the new names, indexed by both the trials to learning and total errors made during the learning trials, was significantly associated with reading ability, which explained about 10% of variance in both kinds of learning score. Reading ability was not, however, significantly associated with the definition learning score: 29% of the variance in this semantic measure was predicted by general intelligence.

The results from this study indicate that reading ability is specifically associated with the long-term phonological (but not semantic) learning involved in learning new words. A similar result was also obtained by Kamhi, Catts, and Mauer (1990), who found that poor readers were much slower at learning new words in a task which combined the fast mapping paradigm developed by Carey (1978) with an intentional learning procedure of the kind employed by Aguiar and Brady (1991). An attractive hypothesis from our perspective is that the difficulties encountered by children of low reading ability in learning new words are due to their poor phonological working memory skills. However, Aguiar and Brady (1991) took a measure of auditory digit span in their study, and found that it was not a good predictor of word learning. This result suggests that the phonological memory abilities of the poor readers did not, in fact, play a role in their long-term learning problems. As we have already argued in this chapter, however, digit span may not provide the most sensitive measure of children's phonological memory skills, and Aguiar and Brady themselves suggest that it would be useful to repeat the study, including a measure of nonword repetition performance from the children. If the phonological memory deficits of children of low reading ability are the basis for their poor vocabulary growth, we would certainly expect a positive relationship between scores on this measure and measures of long-term phonological learning, as indeed we obtained in an earlier study (Gathercole & Baddeley, 1990b).

Summary
The hypothesis that phonological working memory plays a role in long-term phonological learning of words has been explored in a variety of developmental studies. Close links have been established between children's phonological memory abilities and both their native language vocabulary knowledge and their second-language learning. It also appears that the poor vocabulary growth associated with both developmental language disorders and specific reading impairments may be attributable to deficits of phonological working memory in these children.

Although the results from relevant developmental studies have been broadly consistent with the phonological memory hypothesis, there are many complexities to the relationship between phonological memory and vocabulary development that have yet to be resolved. First, it appears that the memory contribution to natural word learning in the first language is most important at around five years of age. Although we have discussed some ideas concerning why this should be, more work is needed to identify the change which apparently takes place in the nature of natural vocabulary learning after the age of about five years. Secondly, there are clear indications that long-term knowledge concerning words already in individuals' vocabularies is used in immediate memory tasks, suggesting that an earlier causal link is replaced by a more complex interaction between vocabulary knowledge and phonological memory. Factors influencing the balance of the reciprocal relationship between memory and vocabulary have still to be fully explored. Thirdly, the work with children has largely relied on correlational techniques to address the issue of phonological memory involvement in word learning. More direct evidence is also needed, using experimental procedures that manipulate phonological memory factors. For the moment, understanding of the nature of the apparently complex links between phonological memory and vocabulary acquisition in children is itself in its infancy.

Experimental Studies

If phonological working memory is involved in the long-term phonological learning of new words by children, it might be expected to contribute to the acquisition of new words during adulthood, too.

Whereas young normal adults will have substantially developed their abilities to produce speech, to understand the syntactic structure of communications, and to read, their vocabulary knowledge may well continue to develop for many more decades. New words can be learned at any time of life. So, is phonological memory involved in adults' word learning, too?

Findings reported by Papagno, Valentine, and Baddeley (1991) suggest that this is indeed the case. A series of experiments was conducted with normal adult subjects which investigated vocabulary learning under varying concurrent task conditions. If the phonological loop component of working memory in adults mediates the long-term learning of phonological information, they might be expected to have difficulty in learning new words when they are simultaneously engaged in articulatory suppression. According to the working memory model, suppression prevents visual material from being recoded into the phonological form appropriate for representation of the phonological store, and therefore rules out phonological loop mediation of visual information. For auditory material, articulatory suppression should disturb retention by preventing rehearsal, although as auditory material is thought to gain direct access to the phonological store, the consequences of suppression should not be as disruptive of auditory memory as of visual memory. However, visual presentation may provide a supplementary visual or orthographic memory trace, making it difficult to predict whether suppression of articulation will have the greatest effect with visual or auditory material.

Parallel series of experiments were run by Papagno et al. (1991) on Italian and English adult subjects. Experiments 1 and 2 involved Italian subjects learning two lists of eight pairs of items. In one list, each pair contained two familiar Italian words; in the other list, the pairs contained a familiar Italian word and an unfamiliar Russian one. Subjects learned either with no concurrent task, or engaged in articulatory suppression during learning. A maximum of five learning trials were given to each subject for each list of pairs.

The results were largely consistent with the predictions of the phonological memory hypothesis. For illustration, the main findings of Experiment 2 are shown in Fig. 3.5. The stimulus pairs were presented auditorily in this experiment. Articulatory suppression caused a greater impairment in the recall of foreign words than of the familiar Italian ones. This result provides direct support for the view that the phonological loop is indeed involved in adults' learning of foreign words, but that it plays a lesser role in the learning of phonologically familiar material for which subjects have stored knowledge concerning meaning.

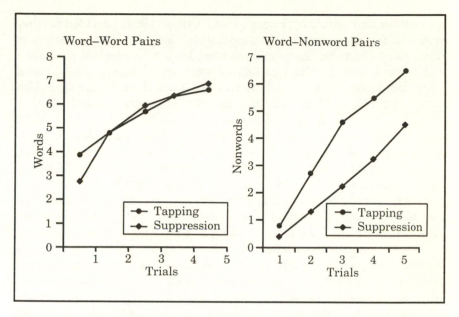

FIG. 3.5. Number of pairs correctly recalled on each learning trial, as a function of type of pair and of concurrent activity (Papagno, Valentine, & Baddeley, 1991).

Findings from the parallel English experiments in Papagno et al. (1991) initially appeared to fail to replicate this result. Using pairs of English words only, versus pairs containing both English and Russian words (e.g. *thread–netka*), no selective disruption of foreign word learning was found under articulatory suppression. When the subjects were questioned, however, it appeared that the reason why learning of the Russian stimuli was not selectively disrupted by suppression in this group was that they were using semantic coding of the stimuli to produce meaningful associations (e.g. *throat–gargle–garlo*). In this way, subjects could avoid using the phonological loop.

This explanation of the null findings of this experiment was tested in a further experiment in which new nonword stimuli were constructed from unfamiliar pairs of consonant–vowel–consonant triplets, such as *paglir*, which were more difficult for English subjects to represent in terms of existing verbal-semantic associations. The expected result was obtained. Articulatory suppression penalised learning of the word–nonword pairs to a significantly greater extent than learning of the word pairs. A similar result occurred when subjects were required to learn Finnish vocabulary items, selected to be low in association value.

A subsequent study by Papagno and Vallar (1992) provided further evidence for the role of the phonological loop in foreign language vocabulary learning. They manipulated both phonological similarity and word length in the learning of word–word and word–nonword pairs. Both variables are believed to influence directly the operation of the phonological loop. The findings were straightforward. Neither variable influenced the learning of word–word pairs. This, presumably, was mediated by semantic coding (Baddeley & Dale, 1966). Speed of learning the word–novel word pairs was, however, impaired when the novel words were either of a high degree of phonological similarity or were relatively long. Together with previous findings, these results clearly converge on the view that the phonological loop component of working memory makes an important contribution to the long-term learning of novel phonological material.

We acknowledged earlier in the chapter that the various correlational studies showing an association between phonological memory performance and vocabulary scores are open to the possibility of an interpretation in terms of some third variable, such as level of phonological awareness, or knowledge of English word structure (Snowling et al., 1991). The experimental studies of vocabulary learning in adults described previously, however, do not seem readily explicable in these terms. As the phonological storage hypothesis can readily account for both these findings and the results of the correlational studies, it provides at present the most parsimonious account of the relevant research literature.

WHAT ROLE DOES PHONOLOGICAL MEMORY PLAY IN LEARNING NEW WORDS?

The weight of evidence in favour of the notion that the long-term learning of the phonological forms of new words is directly influenced by phonological memory factors is considerable. So far, though, we have said relatively little about the mechanisms underpinning this causal association, except that the ease of long-term learning of phonological material is likely to be influenced by the adequacy and availability of temporary phonological specifications of the item to be learned. But how?

It seems probable that the process of learning a new word involves the transfer of phonological information from its temporary representation in the phonological loop into some more permanent knowledge structure in the lexical-semantic memory system. Irrespective of the nature of the precise mechanisms which control this transfer of information into a stable representation, it seems likely that the more distinctive and durable the temporary memory trace is in the phonological loop, the more readily a stable long-term memory representation can be constructed. At extremes, this interpretation is self-evident. If people cannot temporarily represent the sound structure of a phonologically unfamiliar item, as in Papagno et al.'s (1991) experiment where subjects were engaging in irrelevant articulation during learning, we would not expect the phonologically structure to be easily represented in long-term memory either. Quite simply, it seems unlikely that the phonological characteristics of the new word could be successfully encoded in long-term memory in the absence of an adequate temporary representation. And similarly, if children with disordered language development such as those we studied (Gathercole & Baddeley, 1990a) cannot immediately repeat a three-syllable nonword, it is not clear how we could expect them to reproduce that same item 10 minutes, 10 hours, or 10 days later.

A less extreme case is provided by our study of children of high and low repetition skills learning new names of toys in a learning experiment (Gathercole & Baddeley, 1990b). The children in this experiment were required to repeat each name at the beginning of every learning trial, and trial did not proceed until the names had been repeated correctly. Nonetheless, the children with lower repetition scores learned the phonologically unfamiliar names more slowly than the high repetition group. Presumably, the same general situation arose in Service's (1992) study of Finnish children learning English at school—they could correctly repeat the English word, but could not remember it some time later. This situation suggests that impaired long-term learning does not simply occur when the material to be learned exceeds the span. Instead, it seems that the ease of learning is influenced by the adequacy of the representation in the temporary phonological memory system. The better the quality of this memory trace, the greater the probability that a stable long-term memory representation will result.

Ways in which the phonological loop may vary in adequacy between individuals, and in particular between children, have already been considered earlier. Individuals with low phonological memory skills may encode phonological material in a noisy and unreliable form, or a form in which the serial order of the phonemes is not strongly represented, or their phonological representations may decay very rapidly. Alternatively, poor phonological memory skills may be a result of inefficiency of the subvocal rehearsal process. Any of these deficits would result in relatively poorly specified phonological representations which either have low discriminability, or fail to preserve their discriminability for long. Provided that the cognitive processes involved in constructing the long-term phonological representation from this temporary store do not take place as soon as a new item in encountered, and we know from the gradual learning curves that they do not, we would indeed expect poor long-term learning from people with poor phonological working memory.

THE CENTRAL EXECUTIVE

Investigations into working memory involvement in vocabulary learning have emerged only in the past five years or so, and have so far focused more or less exclusively on the contribution of the phonological loop component of working memory. As a consequence, we know a lot more about how the novel phonological form of a new word is learned, but still relatively little about working memory involvement in the processes by which the *meaning* of a new word is acquired. Successful vocabulary acquisition, of course, involves both kinds of learning: It is not very useful for a language user either to retain the phonological structure of a word while failing to learn its meaning, or to remember the word's meaning but not be able to recover its phonological form.

A notable exception to the bias towards the phonological component of word learning is provided in a paper reported by Daneman and Green (1986), which in fact predates the current wave of interest in links between phonological working memory and language understanding. Daneman and Green were interested in whether the process of inferring the meaning of a new word from a rich linguistic context called upon the more general purpose processing and storage resources of the central executive. They presented subjects with prose passages to read, each of which contained a low-frequency word with which subjects were unlikely to be familiar. Examples of the words and their meanings include *groak—To watch people silently while they are eating, hoping that they will ask you to join them*, and *ruelle—A space between the bed and the wall*. After reading the text, subjects were asked to define the novel word, and their definitions were rated for accuracy.

Daneman and Green also obtained a measure of working memory capacity known as reading span from each subject. The reading span task was developed originally by Daneman and Carpenter in 1980, and is discussed in Chapter 8. The details of the measure need not concern us at present: The important point here is that the reading span measure appears to tap subjects' abilities to both process and store linguistic information, and can be interpreted as providing an index of central executive linguistic function. Daneman and Green (1986) found high positive correlations between the accuracy of subjects' vocabulary definitions and both their reading spans ($r = 0.69$) and their scores on a standardised vocabulary test ($r = 0.58$).

The link between the vocabulary definition scores and the standardised test indicates that subjects' abilities to infer the meanings of the novel words from the passages of text effectively simulates real world vocabulary learning. Even more importantly, subjects' abilities to infer the meaning of the novel items was closely related to the measure of their working memory capacities. On this basis, Daneman and Green plausibly argue that an individual's ability to understand new words is based on the contextual cues available, and that the capacity to exploit these cues effectively will depend on the available of working memory resources. Specifically, it is suggested that subjects with low working memory capacities will be less likely to have sufficient resources available to maintain representations of text that has already been read as well as to process the incoming material. These individuals therefore have less opportunity to draw upon memory representations of the word's context in order to derive accurately a word's meaning.

This pioneering study demonstrates first that natural vocabulary acquisition does involve processing of meaning, and secondly that such nonphonological aspects of word learning are interesting specifically from a working memory viewpoint. Extending work in this tradition seems likely to yield important conceptual benefits, by enhancing and balancing our current understanding of working memory involvement in long-term learning in the real world.

OVERVIEW

The work reviewed in this chapter has largely been concerned with the involvement of the phonological loop component of working memory in the acquisition of new words. Results from developmental studies of young children that simulate natural vocabulary acquisition point to the process of learning the phonological form of a new word as being one of the most vulnerable aspects of vocabulary acquisition. The main body of research discussed in this chapter directly supports this view, and indicates more specifically that phonological memory factors may place significant constraints on long-term phonological learning. The most direct evidence in support of this view converges from four separate lines of enquiry.

Firstly, the vocabulary knowledge of children during the early school years is closely linked to their phonological memory ability, and children of low memory ability have been found to be relatively slow at learning new names in an experimental task. Phonological memory ability is also an effective predictor of children's success in learning a foreign language. Secondly, studies of children with disordered language development—who are characterised by having unusually poor natural vocabulary growth—have revealed severe deficits of phonological working memory. Thirdly, a neuropsychological patient with an apparently defective phonological store was completely unable to learn to associate familiar words with unfamiliar spoken foreign words. And finally, studies of adults learning unfamiliar foreign words have shown that ease of long-term learning is directly influenced by factors known to influence the phonological loop, such as articulatory suppression, phonological similarity, and word length.

This chapter has focused on the involvement of the phonological loop in vocabulary acquisition. Clearly, though, other cognitive skills must also come into play in word learning. The natural acquisition of new words does not simply consist of the child learning the phonological form of the word. Its semantic form must also be acquired, as well as (for some words) the physical characteristics of its referents. The contributions of working memory components other than the phonological loop to the development of the complex knowledge structures representing each word are as yet largely unexplored, but may too turn out to be critical.

CHAPTER FOUR

Speech Production

Producing connected speech requires little conscious effort. In planning speech output, the speaker is rarely aware of selecting either the grammatical structure of the intended utterance (such as choosing between active or passive form, or where to insert subordinate clauses into the sentence) or the words to be spoken. And, tongue-twisters excepted, the physical actions involved in producing connected speech seem largely automatic and involve little conscious intervention.

Despite the introspective simplicity of speech production, experimental studies have established that many complex cognitive operations occur between a speaker formulating the conceptual content of an intended message and executing the appropriate articulatory gestures which lead to its production. As an illustration, a simplified version of the influential framework for speech production constructed by Garrett (1975, 1980) in order to account for data from skilled speakers is shown in Fig. 4.1. According to this framework, there are five separate levels of representation involved in translating the conceptual content of the message to the precise articulatory instructions used to produce the desired speech signal. Once the conceptual content of the utterance has been constructed (the message level representation), the speaker then has to produce a functional level representation, in which the major lexical items are selected, and their functional roles specified (in terms of, for example, the

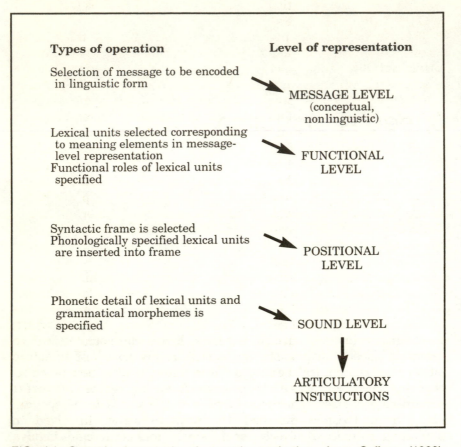

Types of operation   **Level of representation**

Selection of message to be encoded
in linguistic form
                                           MESSAGE LEVEL
                                           (conceptual,
                                           nonlinguistic)

Lexical units selected corresponding
to meaning elements in message-
level representation   FUNCTIONAL
Functional roles of lexical units   LEVEL
specified

Syntactic frame is selected
Phonologically specified lexical units
are inserted into frame   POSITIONAL
                                           LEVEL

Phonetic detail of lexical units and
grammatical morphemes is
specified   SOUND LEVEL

                                           ARTICULATORY
                                           INSTRUCTIONS

FIG. 4.1. Garrett's framework of speech production, from Saffran (1982). (Reproduced with permission.)

predicate/argument structure required by the selected verb). Following this, a specific syntactic frame is selected, and the phonological specifications of all lexical units are inserted into the sentence frame, to produce the positional level representation. In two further stages, phonetic rules are applied to the phonological specification, and then corresponding articulatory commands retrieved, to produce a set of detailed articulatory instructions which will control the production of the utterance.

Other areas of psycholinguistic research have identified many other cognitive processes involved in speech production. At output alone, for example, there appears to be a hierarchy of representation of speech units in which multisyllabic stress groups are successively decomposed into syllables, phonemes, allophones and phonetic features, prior to realisation into articulatory instructions (see Meyer & Gordon, 1984, for review).

There are at least two possible classes of functions that the working memory system may fulfil in the clearly complex sequence of cognitive operations involved in speech production. Firstly, working memory may provide *buffer storage* for speech output. Each of the levels of representation in Garrett's model will require storage while the computations necessary for translation into the next representational level are taking place. And indeed, influential theorists in the area of speech production identify the necessity of (unspecified) buffer storage in the speech production process (e.g. Bock, 1982). Correspondingly, influential theorists in the area of memory have suggested that the normal function of short-term memory is to provide a response buffer which permits the efficient programming of speech (Morton, 1970). Perhaps, then, working memory provides temporary storage either for the intermediate levels of representation, or for the final articulatory specification, prior to output.

In principle, the phonological loop component of working memory seems ideally suited to serve this speech output buffer function. Firstly, it is specialised for the representation of material in the articulatory/phonological domain. Secondly, it is a slave system which can be utilised without demanding limited capacity central executive resources. Use of the phonological loop to plan speech should therefore not impinge upon central executive functioning, unless the amount of planned speech exceeds the two seconds or so temporal capacity associated with the phonological loop.

It is the latter buffer role of working memory in language production that has received most theoretical and empirical attention by psychologists. In the first section of this chapter, we will review the most influential work that has addressed this issue of whether working memory provides temporary storage for planned speech. Experimental work in this area is restricted largely to studies of normal adults, but there have also been some neuropsychological studies whose results, as we shall see, have proved critical in settling theoretical debates.

A second possibility is that working memory contributes to the *cognitive processing* involved in speech production. In Garrett's model, a number of information processing operations are required in order to progress from one level of representation to the next level. For example, to proceed from a message level representation to a functional level representation, the speaker must retrieve abstract representations of content words from the lexicon, create the appropriate syntactic structures, and then combine the two in the functional structure of the sentence. To achieve a positional level representation, the phonological specifications of the main lexical items must then be retrieved, a planning frame for the sentence constructed, the words inserted into the planning frame, and the appropriate affixes and functions words accessed and inserted.

In each of these two illustrative cases of progression from one level of representation to the next, more specific, level in the process of sentence production, the cognitive processes involved require the retrieval of material from the lexicon, the construction of syntactic frames, and the integration of the products of both of these different processes. It seems quite plausible that the central executive component of the working memory may be involved in some or all of these processes. The central executive is typically characterised as possessing scheduling and integrative capacities, as well as flexible processing resources, and thus in principle seems ideally suited as a potential contributor to these aspects of the speech production process.

The second section in this chapter will focus on work relevant to the involvement of the central executive in the production of speech. Although the area is little researched, there are a few intriguing signs that the central executive may play a number of critical roles in the high-level cognitive processes involved for skilled speakers in planning speech output.

The third section of the chapter is much more speculative in nature, and considers the possible roles played by working memory in the the production of speech in children. There has as yet been little research directed at this issue, but there is nonetheless some evidence that the development of working memory skills may be an important factor underpinning the change in speech output abilities with age. The main concern of this section is to identify fruitful areas for future research on links between working memory and speech production during the early years of language development.

PHONOLOGICAL WORKING MEMORY

In this section, three areas of research relevant to the issue of whether the phonological loop component of working memory acts as a speech output buffer are reviewed. The first set of studies explores whether the motor output buffer for speech and the phonological loop are one and the same mechanism in skilled speakers. The second area of research is concerned with the similarities in errors arising in spontaneous speech and in short-term memory tasks. Finally, cognitive neuropsychological study of patients with acquired deficits of speech production and of working memory are covered in the third section.

Speeded Speech Production

The possible involvement of verbal short-term memory mechanisms in the preparation of speech output was first explored systematically by Klapp and associates. The following tasks and results arising from this laboratory are typical (Klapp, 1974). Subjects were tested in a simple reaction time paradigm in which they were told in advance the identity of a target word that they were to say as quickly as possible after a signal was given. The speed with which subjects started to produce the target word after the signal was measured. The number of syllables of the target word was found to have no effect on articulation latency. In a corresponding choice reaction time experiment using letters rather than words, however, in which subjects did not know what the target word was to be until it was presented visually as the signal to speak, word length did influence speech latency. Subjects took longer on average to start saying a "W"—containing three syllables—than to start saying a "T"—containing one syllable only. So, when the signal marking the beginning of the reaction time interval also informed the subject which response they were to make, the speed of initiating articulatory output increased with the articulatory duration of the target utterance.

Klapp (1976) claimed that these findings establish that there is a necessary stage of speech motor programming prior to output in which information is retrieved from long-term memory and stored in a temporary motor-programme buffer. Furthermore, it was suggested that the duration of this programming activity is influenced by the number of articulatory segments being retrieved, so that it takes less time to programme a short articulatory response than a long one. In the case of simple reaction time, it was argued, subjects can complete this motor programming prior to the signal to speak, so that their speed of responding is not sensitive to articulatory duration. In the choice reaction time case, however, subjects were unable to prepare their response in advance so that speed of speech output included the length-sensitive motor programming progress.

Most relevant to the present concerns, Klapp (1976) suggested that the mechanism involved in speech motor planning is the short-term memory component corresponding to the phonological loop, and that this component is in fact a by-product of response control, rather than a general purpose memory system. There are, however, two serious problems for the hypothesis that the phonological loop serves as a motor output buffer in speeded speech production. Firstly, the influence of number of syllables on speed of responding in choice reaction time tasks is not restricted to spoken output tasks. Klapp (1974) also found latency to make a speeded manual same/different judgement to visually presented stimuli was sensitive to syllabic length. In this case, the effect clearly cannot be attributed to articulatory motor programming, as none was required. Instead, the result suggests that the length effect may arise in the process of recognition of a lexical item, and is perhaps due to the post-lexical phonological information becoming available. This result clearly calls into question the relevance of the effect of word length on voice latency to the motor output buffer theory.

A second problematic result for the "short-term memory as a speech output buffer" view was provided by Klapp, Greim, and Marshburn (1981). They set out to test directly whether or not the articulatory loop and the speech output buffer were the same. In Experiment 1, subjects participated in one of three different experimental conditions. The first two conditions provided replications of previous experiments. In a choice reaction time condition, subjects had to say a target item as quickly as possible after it was displayed on a screen. In a corresponding simple reaction time condition, subjects were told in advance what the target item was, and spoke the item as soon as a "Go" signal appeared on the screen. In a third, critical, condition, subjects were tested under the same simple reaction time conditions as above, but silently and repeatedly articulated "La" during the period between being shown the identity of the target, and receiving the "Go" signal. In each experimental condition, the to-be-pronounced stimuli were either digits or letters, and varied in length between one syllable (e.g. *4*, and *A*), and three syllables (*W*).

The predictions from the phonological loop hypothesis are straight-forward. If the loop provides buffer storage for speech motor programming, filling the loop with irrelevant articulatory material in the silent articulation condition should prevent this advance response programming from taking place. Therefore, in the simple reaction time plus articulation condition, the results should be identical to the choice reaction time task, in which no advance programming is possible. In other words, voice latencies should be sensitive to the number of syllables in both tasks. Absence of an effect of number of syllables should only be observed in the simple reaction time condition where subjects were not silently articulating.

Table 4.1 summarises the results obtained with letter stimuli. Choice reaction time was found to be longer with items containing

TABLE 4.1
Mean Reaction Times (ms) to Respond to Letters as a Function of their Length
and of Concurrent Activity

	One Syllable			Three Syllables
	T	A	Mean of T and A	W
Choice	356	360	358	395
Simple	274	256	265	253
Simple + articulation	318	293	305	307

Adapted from Klapp, Greim, and Marshburn (1981).

more syllables, as in previous studies. However, simple reaction time with irrelevant articulation behaved like simple reaction time alone; there was no effect of number of syllables. This result suggests that irrelevant silent articulation does not suppress the formation of buffer storage for speech output. Given that in a further experiment in this series, the same concurrent articulation task did disrupt immediate serial recall performance, it appears that the phonological loop and the mechanism underpinning the length effect in speech output planning are dissociable.

One further speech production phenomenon did, however, appear to provide another possible locus of short-term memory buffer storage in the process of speech production. This phenomenon is the list length effect on speech latency. Sternberg, Monsell, Knoll, and Wright (1978) found that in a simple reaction time task, in which subjects know in advance exactly what they are to say in response to a "Go" signal, the latency of the utterance is influenced by the number of response elements in the utterance. For example, in one experiment subjects were required to say one digit (*one*), two digits (*one, two*), and so on, up to five digits (*one, two, three, four, five*), in response to the signal. Figure 4.2 shows the mean latencies in each of the utterance length conditions. Speed of responding was a linear function of the number of words in the utterance, with latency increasing approximately 13ms with each word. The linear function accounted for 98.7% of the variance in latencies across trials.

Latency did not, however, turn out to be a simple function of the number of syllables of the utterance (in this respect, the results replicated Klapp's previous findings). In a further experiment, subjects produced either one-syllable words (e.g. *cow*) or matched two-syllable words (e.g. *coward*). Although latency was influenced to a small extent (about 3ms) by an increase in length from one to two syllables, the effects of number of syllables per word and words per

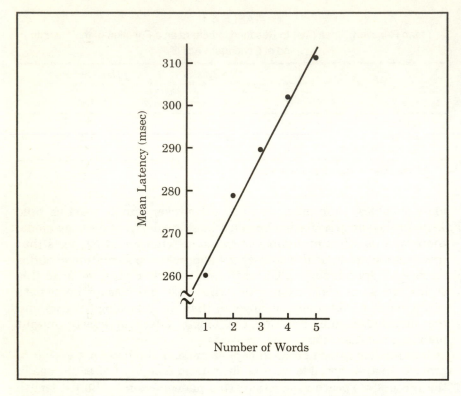

FIG. 4.2. Mean latency of responses as a function of number of words to be produced (Sternberg, Monsell, Knoll, & Wright, 1978). (Reproduced with permission.)

list were found to be independent of one another. This additivity in the speech output function suggests that the critical feature for the list-length effect on latency is the number of response elements to be programmed, where the elements are higher-order units such as words or syllable-stress units, rather than smaller length-sensitive units such as syllables or phonemes.

A further experiment within this series showed that the list-length effect on latency was also uninfluenced by whether or not subjects were given an additional memory load. These studies indicate that the phonological loop is unlikely to be the mechanism underpinning this speech output preparation effect. The insensitivity of the speech latency function to number of syllables stands in stark contrast to the sensitivity of the phonological loop to the articulatory duration of memory items (Baddeley et al., 1975). Furthermore, a concurrent verbal memory load is known to reduce or eliminate the contribution of the phonological loop (Baddeley et al., 1975). The voice latency effect, however, remained constant with a secondary memory load. Finally, it should be noted that the size of the effects of length on performance, 13ms per word, is at least an order of magnitude less than the word-length effects associated with the phonological loop.

Sternberg et al. (1978) suggest that the effect of list length on latency reflects the construction of a representation (referred to as a motor programme) of the entire intended utterance prior to response. They proposed that the programme consists of linked subprogrammes which consist of units probably corresponding either to a word or a stress group, and that the programme is retained in a motor programme buffer which is distinct from short-term memory mechanisms (and hence, the phonological loop). The programme was believed to be constructed prior to the signal to speak, but a sequential search through subprogramme addresses took place prior to its execution. Because this search is initiated after the signal to speak, the time taken to retrieve the programme is directly related to the number of subprogrammes. In principle, the account is rather similar to Klapp's (1976) account of short-term memory as a response buffer. However, although a speech output buffer does seem to be necessary for speeded speech production, it now seems unlikely that it is the phonological loop that plays the role of buffer (see Monsell, 1984, for discussion).

Speech Errors

Another source of evidence that has been interpreted as reflecting the buffer contribution of short-term memory in speech production is provided by naturally occurring and experimentally stimulated speech errors. The most notable slips of the tongue of natural origin are the result of misordering the phonemes within utterances which occur in Spoonerisms such as "keep a tape"—"teep a kape" (Fromkin, 1973). The fact that such errors occur, with phonemes that should occur later in an utterance being exchanged for early phonemes, indicates that the entire utterance was stored prior to output. The storage is presumably within a phonemic domain, as the primary unit of exchange is the phoneme. Once again, the phonological loop component of working memory looks just right for the job. A phonologically based system that does not require central processing resources should be ideal for planning speech output; the main flexible processing component (the central executive) and other slave system(s) would be left free while the loop component aids the efficient planning and production of speech.

Ellis (1979) reviewed the characteristics of naturally occurring speech errors, and argued that they reflect the imperfections of the phonological loop component of working memory. Firstly, the maximum separation of phonemes in Spoonerisms and slips of the tongue is about eight syllables (Nooteboom & Cohen, 1975). This limit corresponds closely to the estimated two seconds or so capacity of the phonological loop estimated on the basis of studies of the word-length effect in memory (e.g. Baddeley et al., 1975; Hulme et al., 1984). So, both naturally occurring speech errors and verbal short-term memory involve about the same number of phonemes.

Secondly, exchange of phonemes across words is more likely to occur when the consonants share several distinctive articulatory features (e.g. Mackay, 1970). This feature similarity effect has a close parallel in the acoustic confusions made in short-term memory tasks. In particular, Conrad and Hull (1964) demonstrated that the errors made in serial recall of visually presented letters were likely to be acoustically similar (and hence similar in terms of articulatory features) to the target letter. So in both natural speech production and short-term memory tasks, errors are strongly influenced by the articulatory/acoustic features of the target items. A number of further classes of error in short-term memory demonstrated by Ellis (1980) directly parallel errors in natural speech production—for example, the predominance of consonant over vowel transitions, and the feature similarity effect.

Despite the apparent empirical successes of this particular area, it has been restricted by its dependence on a correlational approach. To show that a common output buffer mechanism contributes to both speech production and short-term memory performance, it is necessary to advance beyond demonstrations of common influences on performance on both kinds of cognitive task. Correlational evidence is necessary but not sufficient to support arguments about functional equivalence. Direct evidence is needed, in the form of demonstrations that the two kinds of task—speech production and short-term memory—interact. Attempts to show this in the sister area of speeded speech production have failed, as discussed above. Klapp et al. (1981) found that the word-length effect in choice reaction time—viewed as a speech output buffer phenomenon—was *not* disrupted by articulatory suppression. Furthermore, the list-length effect explored by Sternberg et al. (1978)—also taken to reflect speech motor programming—remained intact when subjects maintained a verbal memory load during speech production. To survive as a convincing theoretical perspective in the face of the lack of supporting evidence from other closely related areas of research, the speech error approach requires substantial development. One priority is to provide an explanation of why short-term memory is involved in natural speech production but apparently not in the kind of speeded speech production measured in the experimental paradigms of researchers such as Klapp and Sternberg. More practically, paradigms need to be developed in which possible interactions between short-term memory and the natural production of speech can be tested. At the moment, though, the evidence for short-term memory involvement in natural speech production remains weak.

Neuropsychological Evidence

Findings from patients with brain damage resulting in specific disturbances of language production and of memory function have had considerable impact on theories linking working memory with speech output. Evidence from two distinct types of acquired cognitive disorder are relevant to the issue of whether working memory acts as a speech output buffer. The first group consists of patients with disordered speech production abilities. The principal question is: Do such patients have impaired working memory skills? And if they do, is it possible that their speech production problems are a direct result of their working memory deficits? A second and even more important neuropsychological group for this issue consists of patients with pure acquired deficits of short-term memory. The question here concerns whether their production of speech is normal. If it is, theories attributing a critical role to working memory mechanisms in normal speech production are seriously undermined.

In this section, we review some illustrative studies of both classes of patient—those with speech production deficits, and those with short-term memory deficits. In general, these studies were designed to bear on issues other than the involvement of working memory in speech production. The principal concern here, though, is to evaluate that hypothesis.

Acquired Deficits of Speech Production

The main neuropsychological condition arising from impairments in speech production is Broca's aphasia. First documented in the late nineteenth century by the neurologist Broca, and associated with damage to the anterior language area of the left hemisphere, this syndrome is typically characterised as an expressive disorder of language. The patients' language comprehension abilities are not perfect, and are discussed in detail in Chapter 8, but are spared relative to the impairment of speech output.

The speech output associated with Broca's aphasia has several main features. Firstly, the patients' speech is non-fluent—it is halting and laboured. Secondly, the impoverished output consists mainly of content words such as nouns and a limited repertoire of verbs. Output is largely "agrammatic"—it lacks the grammatical words such as "the" and "is", as well as the grammatical bound morphemes denoting inflectional endings, which mark normal connected speech. Finally, the repetition of spoken language is also severely impaired.

A number of alternative theories have been advanced concerning the basis of the speech production impairments associated with Broca's aphasia (see Saffran, 1982, for review). In terms of Garrett's speech production framework introduced earlier in this chapter, the central deficits have been variously located at the functional level, the positional level, and the articulatory level. In fact, given the mild comprehension problems accompanying Broca's aphasia, an explanation of the speech production problems located purely at the level of articulatory output mechanisms, such as the account put forward by Lenneberg (1973), seems implausible. The major issue to have occupied neurolinguists interested in this aphasic syndrome in recent years concerns whether the central deficit is in the syntactic mechanism (e.g. Berndt & Caramazza, 1980; Caramazza, Berndt, Basili, & Koller, 1981b), or in the mapping of syntactic structures onto semantic interpretations (Linebarger, Schwartz, & Saffran, 1983).

Of central interest is whether Broca's aphasics have disordered phonological memory skills. The answer is that they do indeed. Although the immediate visual memory abilities of Broca's aphasics appear to be unimpaired (e.g. de Renzi & Nichelli, 1975; Kelter, Cohen, Engel, List, & Strohner, 1977), their immediate phonological memory skills have been shown in a number of studies to be deficient. Cermak and Tarlow (1978), for example, used a continuous recognition memory paradigm to study the short-term memory abilities associated with several different neuropsychological syndromes. In this task, a series of memory items were presented, and subjects had to raise their hand if an item had previously been presented in the series. The to-be-remembered stimuli were words (either spoken, or presented in printed form), pictures, or random shapes.

The Broca's aphasic patients were significantly worse than either Korsakoff's syndrome amnesic patients or control subjects at recognising recurring spoken or printed words, but did not differ in memory for the shapes, which presumably could not be verbalisabled. Similar results were also obtained in an independent study of aphasic patients reported by Riege, Metter, and Hanson (1980). The patients' poor performance in the verbal memory test was interpreted by the authors of both studies as reflecting failure to use the phonological mediation and subvocal rehearsal functions typically attributed to the phonological loop (see also Cermak & Moreines, 1976).

Further convergent evidence for this interpretation was provided by Ostergaard and Meudell (1984). In a probed recognition memory task, a group of Broca's aphasics were found to have a selective deficit in recognition of items in the earlier (primacy) portion of the memory list when compared with a group of normal control subjects. This portion of the serial position curve is typically assumed to be sensitive to rehearsal processes, and thus the result is consistent with the notion that a subvocal rehearsal deficit typically accompanies this acquired speech output disorder.

Could the whole range of speech output deficits characteristic of Broca's aphasia be plausibly attributed to an impairment of the phonological component of working memory? It could certainly be argued that one consequence of a speech output buffer of reduced capacity might be that the individual strategically selects to preserve the major lexical items rather than the supplementary grammatical features, such as inflectional endings and function words. The result of this simplifying strategy would presumably be telegrammatic speech output. This argument is very similar to the account of the speech production problems of Broca's aphasics put forward by Lenneberg (1973); the only difference is that whereas Lenneberg's contention was that the output constraint was located in articulatory output mechanisms, the suggestion being considered here is that the restriction is in a putative speech output memory buffer.

A problem for the speech output buffer hypothesis is that the severe agrammatism in speech production associated with Broca's aphasia is usually mirrored in comprehension deficits. The speech output buffer theory therefore fails to provide a parsimonious account of the associated production and comprehension deficits of this aphasic syndrome. In contrast, theories locating the impairment in a syntactic mechanism which contributes to both the production of speech and syntactic analysis of heard speech do not have this problem (e.g. Caramazza et al., 1981b). However, phonological working memory may quite plausibly contribute to the comprehension as well as the production of speech—this possibility is considered in some detail in Chapter 8. We therefore complete this section by noting that although other more specific theories of Broca's aphasia exist, it remains at least possible that the undoubted deficits of the phonological loop component of working memory associated with this syndrome may play a role in the speech output difficulties of the patients.

Patients with Acquired Short-term Memory Deficits
The speech production characteristics of individuals with brain
damage resulting in deficits of the phonological component of working
memory provide a much more cogent test of the hypothesis that
working memory serves as a speech output buffer. The study of speech
production in patients with short-term memory impairments also
provides a classic demonstration of the theoretical power that
cognitive neuropsychological study can yield. If patients with severe
deficits of phonological working memory are found to have no
corresponding deficits in spontaneous speech production, the notion
that the phonological loop may be used as a buffer in which planned
speech is stored prior to articulation must be ruled out. This is exactly
what has been found. A number of cases have been reported of
patients with apparently normal speech output accompanying highly
specific disturbances of phonological working memory.

The most influential and systematic study of the speech output of
a short-term memory patient was provided by Shallice and
Butterworth (1977). They investigated JB, a patient who suffered
various cognitive deficits as a result of brain injury. Although when
first assessed three weeks after surgery JB made some paraphasic
errors and phonological approximations in her spontaneous speech,
the speech production difficulties soon disappeared. Other persisting
deficits were characteristic of a syndrome complex known as
conduction aphasia, and were attributed by Shallice and Warrington
(1970) to a central phonological short-term memory deficit (see
Shallice & Warrington, 1977, for review). JB's repetition of sequences
of spoken words was very impaired; although her oral comprehension
was satisfactory for simple grammatical structures, for more complex
sentences comprehension deficits were found. Immediate memory
performance was very poor, particular for auditorily presented
sequences—span was 3.4 for digits, 2.5 for letters, and 2.5 for words.
These estimates should be contrasted with the span range of 5–9
items expected of a normal adult. The errors that JB made in
short-term memory tasks did, however, appear normal, with some
acoustic errors of the type observed by Conrad and Hull (1964) in
normal adults occurring. Interpretation of JB's memory performance
from the perspective of the working memory model would probably
attribute her deficits to a deficient phonological short-term store.

Shallice and Butterworth (1977) carried out a detailed analysis of
JB's spontaneous speech. They asked her and ten control patients to
talk for approximately five minutes about their most recent holiday.
The speech was recorded, and the proportions of phonation and
silence calculated for each subject. Also, speech errors were classified

and counted. The characteristics of JB's speech and that of the controls is summarised in Table 4.2.

JB's pause duration (35.1% of the total speech time) was well within the range shown by the control subjects (mean = 37.4%, SD = 4.4). For five of the speech error classifications, JB's errors were not significantly more frequent than the controls—literal and verbal paraphasias, omissions, syntactic errors, and high-level amendments. The only indication that JB's speech output might not be normal was that she made rather more function word errors than controls (3.1 per 1000 words, and 0.6 per 1000 words, respectively).

JB's spontaneous speech output was more or less normal. Certainly, she did not appear to speak less than the controls with normal short-term memory function, and her utterances were as syntactically well-formed. The problem with function words is so specific as to make a short-term memory explanation implausible; there is no apparent reason why function words should demand output buffering when no other types of word do. It therefore appears that normal phonological loop function is not necessary for speech planning.

Similar findings of normal speech production accompanied by reduced phonological memory capacity have been reported for other adult patients with acquired memory impairments (see Vallar & Shallice, 1990, for a review). For example, the patient PV had an auditory memory span of two items, but showed no speech production problems after the immediate post-traumatic period (Vallar & Baddeley, 1984a).

Summary
The weight of neuropsychological evidence favours the view that normal phonological working memory skills are not necessary for the planning and production of spontaneous speech. The neuro-psychological evidence thus casts serious doubt on the speculative phonological memory account of the speech production deficits of Broca's aphasia discussed in the previous section. The magnitude of the immediate verbal memory deficits of PV and JB are at least as

TABLE 4.2
Rates of Speech Errors per 1000 Words for the STM Patient JB and Controls
(from Shallice & Butterworth, 1977)

	Literal Paraphrasia	Verbal Paraphrasia	Omission	Function Word Error	Syntactic Error	High-level Amendment
Controls	1.6	0.7	0.6	0.6	1.3	4.9
JB	0	1.5	0.7	3.1	1.5	2.3

great as those of the typical Broca's patient, and yet these patients show no evidence of laborious dysgrammatic speech output. On this basis, it appears that a deficit located in specific language processing mechanisms seems to represent a more plausible account of the speech production problems associated with Broca's aphasia than the speech output buffer explanation (c.f. Caramazza et al., 1981b; Linebarger et al., 1983).

In demonstrating a dissociation of phonological working memory skills and spontaneous speech production, the findings from these neuropsychological studies converge with the findings considered earlier in the area of speeded speech production with normal adults. There too, attempts to find interactions between short-term memory and speech production failed, with factors such as as articulatory suppression and concurrent memory load being found to be quite independent of phenomena attributed to speech motor programming (Klapp et al., 1981; Sternberg et al., 1978). The only positive support for the concept of the phonological component of working memory as a speech output buffer is provided by the essentially correlational evidence concerning the similarities of the errors arising in speech production and in short-term memory tasks as described by Ellis (1979).

The balance of evidence therefore suggests that the phonological store is not responsible for holding speech output as a buffer. This position is supported by the weight of neuropsychological and experimental evidence. However, the processes responsible for *controlling* articulation and rehearsal may well be the same as those responsible for controlling speech output. Hence, speech production problems will impair the operation of the subvocal rehearsal component of the phonological loop system. This account readily explains the correspondence between natural errors of speech and the errors that arise in immediate memory tasks: Both derive from speech output mechanisms, directly in the case of speech production, and indirectly, via articulatory rehearsal, in the case of immediate memory performance.

The view that speech output processes are necessary for subvocal rehearsal also provides a ready explanation for recent neuro-psychological evidence. Dyspraxic individuals, whose speech production difficulties are due to disturbances of high-level speech motor planning, have impaired phonological memory span (Waters et al., 1992). On the other hand anarthric patients, who have deficits in control of the speech motor musculature, show normal functioning of the phonological loop system (Baddeley & Wilson, 1985; Bishop & Robson, 1989). This pattern of association between phonological loop function and deficits of speech motor planning, paired with its apparent independence of the peripheral output mechanisms, is discussed in detail in Chapter 1. The findings suggest that subvocal maintenance in the phonological loop involves the processes used in the high-level planning, but not the execution, of speech output.

THE CENTRAL EXECUTIVE

Two possible contributions of working memory to speech production were considered at the beginning of this chapter. The first suggestion, which was that the phonological loop may act as a buffer for speech output, received little support from either experimental or neuro-psychological studies. The second possible contribution is to the computations involved in the spontaneous production of speech. It is clear from Garrett's framework outlined in the early part of this chapter that many complex cognitive processes are involved in producing meaningful utterances that are both syntactically legal and phonologically correct. Possible roles that the central executive may play include providing the computational power necessary to produce the different levels of representation involved in speech production, and coordinating the interaction between specialised language processing modules and the more general cognitive systems responsible for semantic and lexical processing.

The issue of whether or not the central executive is involved in speech production has not been widely investigated. The results of two studies, however, do suggest that the central executive fulfils a specific function in the planning of speech output.

In the first of these, Daneman and Green (1986) develop a measure they call "speaking span". This involves presenting the subject with a list of words, each of which must be used to generate a sentence. For example, a subject given *cabbage* and *judge* might generate the sentences *Cabbage is my favourite vegetable* and *The judge condemned the innocent man to death*. As the number of words increases, subjects reach a point at which performance breaks down and words are forgotten. Daneman and Green showed that this correlated highly ($r = 0.60$) with the capacity to produce synonyms for a word in context, a capacity that correlated significantly but less highly ($r = 0.44$) than the previously described working memory span of Daneman and Carpenter (1980). They conclude that the two span measures reflect overlapping components of a complex working memory system.

Power (1985) investigated the involvement of working memory in a task which involved subjects generating a plausible sentence to include two words provided by the experimenter (e.g. *farmer–field*, *editor–basket*). Thus, subjects have to construct a semantically plausible and syntactically legal utterance based on two stored lexical entries which specify content words to be included in the sentence. Power's hypothesis was quite simple. If the central executive component of working memory is involved in any or all of these cognitive operations, sentence production should be disrupted if subjects are concurrently engaged in a secondary memory task whose load is sufficiently great to compete for limited central executive resources with the sentence planning task.

Accordingly, subjects performed the sentence production task under conditions of either no digit load, a load of three random digits, or a load of six random digits. Immediately after producing an appropriate sentence, subjects were required to repeat the digit sequence. Previous work had shown that a six-item load cannot be handled by the phonological loop alone, and so places significant demands on the central executive (Baddeley & Hitch, 1974). Therefore, if the central executive is involved in the planning of speech, the heavy digit preload condition should disrupt sentence production ability. On first glance, the results of Experiment 1 looked disappointing for this hypothesis. Subjects were significantly faster at producing sentences under the six-digit load condition (mean latency 1.87 seconds) than in the control no-load condition (mean latency 2.32 seconds). Furthermore, the sentences produced did not differ in qualitative features, such as numbers of clauses, durations, speech rate, and judged complexity. They did, however, differ in the expected direction in terms of the predictability of the concepts within the sentence. In order to quantify the extent to which a particular sentence was stereotyped, each sentence was sorted into categories based on conceptual content, so that all sentences which were synonymous or overlapping in meaning were allocated to the same category. An index of "information value" for the sentences in that category was then calculated; the greater the resulting index, the greater the informational value (i.e. the departure from stereotype) of the sentence category. The mean information value scores were 2.05 for the no-load condition, 2.02 for the 3-digit condition, and 1.74 for the 6-digit condition. This trend to produce sentences with more stereotyped conceptual content as memory load increased was statistically significant, and was replicated in a further experiment.

So, the semantic structure of the sentences produced by subjects was more predictable and stereotyped when subjects were engaged in a concurrent task thought to demand central executive support. The increased typicality of the sentences was not, however, found in the three-digit memory load condition, which suggests (as do the results of studies reviewed in the earlier sections of this chapter) that the phonological loop is not critically involved in spontaneous speech production. Interestingly, the results did not provide evidence that the central executive was involved in the process of construction of grammatical frames for sentences, as there was no influence of digit preload on grammatical complexity. This result, together with the finding of influence of preload on the typicality of semantic context, suggests that central executive involvement in sentence production may be restricted to the earlier levels of Garrett's framework, and in particular to the cognitive processing resulting in the conceptual and functional levels of representation.

This work provides preliminary evidence concerning the nature of central executive involvement in speech production, but further detailed study of possible central executive functions using the dual-task methodology are clearly required before any strong conclusions can be drawn. One of the reasons for the apparent reluctance of psycholinguists to study this issue may reflect the prevailing view that speech production is served exclusively by a highly specialised cognitive module (e.g. Fodor, 1983). The notion that a general purpose processing system, such as the central executive, contributes to speech production does not sit comfortably with this modular perspective. Work by Power (1985) does, however, indicate that construction of semantic content in speech production may be partly controlled by the central executive. The main point we wish to make here is that the central executive is in principle equipped to contribute to many of the cognitive processes identified in the production of spontaneous speech. Before the potential nature of central executive contribution to speech production is known, however, techniques for investigating working memory involvement in the planning of speech output need to be devised.

THE DEVELOPMENT OF SPEECH PRODUCTION

Whether working memory contributes to speech production in children is, quite simply, as yet unknown. There are no studies with which we are familiar that have focused directly on the possible involvement of either the phonological loop or the central executive in planning speech output during either infancy or later childhood. Most work on children's speech production is firmly rooted in the naturalistic tradition, providing either detailed case histories of individual children (e.g. Wijnen, 1990; Veneziano, Sinclair, &

Berthoud, 1990), or grammatical analyses of utterances elicited from children in open-ended play situations (e.g. Brown, 1973; Scarborough, Wyckoff, & Davidson, 1986). In this section, we speculate about what contributions working memory might make to the development of children's speech production abilities, and point to possible routes which future research projects on this issue might usefully take. First, though, the way in which speech production ability develops during the first few years of childhood is briefly outlined, in order to provide a context for our consideration of possible working memory involvement.

Words and word-like utterances start being produced at around twelve months of age for the average child (see Barrett, 1989, and Nelson, 1973, for more detailed descriptions). For the following few months, output is typically restricted to single words (mainly salient nouns such as "teddy" and "shoes", and non-nominal words such as "gone", and "more"), and to formulaic multiword phrases like "here-you-are" that seem to be used by the child as single words. New words are acquired relatively slowly at first, at an average estimated rate of between one and three words per month up to about 18 months. There then follows a period of very rapid vocabulary growth, and the child typically starts to combine words into two-word utterances at about 20 months.

Between this age and about five years, most normal children master basic grammatical structures. The developmental sequence of grammatical abilities was examined by Wells (1985) in a longitudinal study of British children, while Crystal and colleagues have developed a standardised schedule for the assessment of speech production abilities in young children (e.g. Crystal, Fletcher, & Garman, 1976; Crystal, 1982). Two of the most widely investigated indexes of the changes in the grammatical complexity of children's speech output as they develop through the preschool years are the increase in mean length of utterance (MLU) and the related increase in mean length of response (MLR). This is due primarily to increased use of grammatical morphemes, the inclusions of determiners such as "the", adjectives and verbal auxiliaries such as "should", and to the coordination of phrases and clauses into single sentences by use of words such as "that", "and", and "with".

Mean length of utterance in morphemes has proved to be a useful indicator of children's grammatical development. Brown (1973), in particular, claimed that MLU provides a better predictor of syntactic maturity in young children than their chronological age, and used different levels of MLU to mark different stages of grammatical skill. Not surprisingly, though, MLU is highly correlated with age. Miller and Chapman (1981) combined data taken from six independent studies to produce an estimate of the MLR function between the ages of one and six years. This function is shown in Fig. 4.3. There was found to be a strong linear relationship between age and mean length of utterance between the ages of 18 months and 5 years, with age accounting for a significant 78% of the variance in MLU scores. This close association between children's age and the number of words they produce within utterances supports the use of MLU as an index of grammatical maturity. However, it has been pointed out that an exclusive focus on output length may obscure critical qualitative

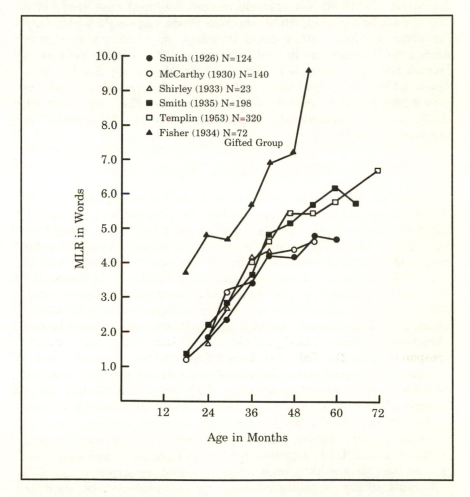

FIG. 4.3. Children's mean length of response (MLR) in words at one to six years of age, from six studies (Miller & Chapman, 1981). (Reproduced with permission.)

features of a child's grammatical skills (Crystal et al., 1976); it also appears that MLU becomes less closely associated with grammatical development as linguistic proficiency increases (e.g. Klee & Fitzgerald, 1985).

Children with disordered development of language depart in a number of important ways from this thumbnail sketch of normal speech production abilities (see Cromer, 1987, and Bishop & Rosenbloom, 1987, for reviews). They start to produce speech later than the average child, and their speech output fails to develop in complexity at the usual rate by almost any index of measurement. Crystal et al. (1976), for example, report a typical case study of a three-and-a-half-year-old child who was producing single words only. For older children with specific language impairments who have started to produce multiword utterances, the output reflects a dependence on very simple grammatical structures (e.g. Scarborough, Rescorla, Fowler, & Sudhalter, 1991). Such children also appear to have difficulties in mastering control of phonological output (Leonard, 1982), and in articulatory sequencing (Wolfus, Moscovitch, & Kinsbourne, 1980).

Phonological Working Memory

Earlier in the chapter, we reviewed evidence for the hypothesis that the phonological loop acts as a buffer for planned speech output. There was little support for this position, and our conclusion was that the converse relationship was true: The processes responsible for speech output underpin the subvocal rehearsal activity used to maintain material in the phonological loop. If this is the case, we would expect linguistic proficiency and subvocal rehearsal to be closely related during childhood, and more specifically that speech production ability should be the pacemaker in the developmental relationship.

There is some support for this view. Subvocal rehearsal of visually presented material appears to emerge at around the age of seven years in most children (e.g. Conrad, 1972; Hitch & Halliday, 1983). Studies of the development of speech production abilities have established that by this age, most children are efficient at producing the majority of phonemes, and many consonant clusters too (Berry & Eisenson, 1956). Thus, articulatory efficiency certainly does appear to precede the use of subvocal rehearsal as a memory strategy.

A rudimentary phonological loop system that can be used to maintain verbal material temporarily must, however, be available to children before this age. Children as young as four and five years are sensitive to the phonological similarity of auditory memory items (Henry, 1991; Hulme, 1987), showing that they can represent memory items in a speech-based code, presumably in the phonological store. Presumably, though, the child is not born with a fully operational phonological store; effective use of the phonological store will depend minimally on the child first having acquired a speech-based code. However, given the evidence for categorical perception of speech sounds by the age of one month in infants (Aslin, Pisoni, & Jusczyk, 1983) it seems likely that some use of the phonological store may be available during early infancy.

The presence of a phonological store may therefore precede the emergence of the child's spoken language in the form of identifiable words at around the age of one year. Is it possible, then, that the phonological store functions partly to support the early stages of speech motor planning? Although a highly specialised speech motor buffer appears to be present in adults (e.g. Bock, 1982; Klapp et al., 1981; Sternberg et al., 1978), it may only emerge in the course of acquiring language production skills. During the early phases of language development, before the component skills of speech production become automatised, the more general purpose resource of the phonological store may be used to plan speech output.

This hypothesis that the phonological store mediates speech motor planning in very early childhood raises the intriguing possibility that the steady increase in utterance lengths between the ages of about one and four years (e.g. Miller & Chapman, 1981) may be due to the concomitant increase in phonological working memory skills that we presume also takes place during this period. Perhaps, then, the considerable degree of individual variation in utterance length even within children of a similar age (e.g. Klee & Fitzgerald, 1985) reflects differences in the capacity of the phonological store in infants and young children.

This hypothesis is clearly very speculative, and indeed is undoubtedly simplistic. In fact, it seems to us rather unlikely that the capacity of the phonological store provides a simple constraint on speech motor planning and so limits the length of spontaneous utterances. More plausibly, though, phonological memory and speech production may develop reciprocally with one another. With increased phonological and articulatory proficiency, the functional capacity of the phonological store may also increase due to improved efficiency of phonological coding processes. A consequence of this increased capacity may then be to promote efficient buffering of planned speech output. Anne Adams of Lancaster University is currently exploring the nature of the developmental relationship between phonological memory skills and speech production in a longitudinal study of preschool children. The data obtained so far indicate that there are indeed significant links between phonological memory skill and the complexity of spontaneous speech output in three-year-old children.

The Central Executive

Earlier in the chapter we reviewed evidence that the central executive contributes to the construction of the semantic content of sentences in adults (Power, 1985). Although there has been no corresponding study of central executive involvement in young children's speech production, it is possible that central executive involvement is even more extensive during the development of language production abilities. The basis for this speculation is that the information processing operations involved in many aspects of speech production in adults seem to be automatic. Our lack of introspection about how we go about producing grammatical structures and generating the appropriate articulatory gestures to produce target words attests to this automaticity, as does our apparent abilities to continue producing connected speech while engaged in other cognitive activities with little cost. In contrast, during the period in which children are acquiring language skills, the effortful and error-prone nature of their speech output does not suggest the execution of highly automatic language processes. Rather, speech output during infancy and preschool years seems to be better characterised by controlled processing activity that, according to Schneider and Shiffrin (1977), typically reflects early stages of skill acquisition, and requires the allocation of limited capacity attentional resources.

A straightforward prediction that follows from this hypothesis that the central executive is heavily involved in speech production in young children is that speech output should diminish in either quality, quantity, or both when children are engaged in other activities that draw upon central executive resources. There has been no direct test of this hypothesis, although data from a study of children's speech output in different environmental contexts by Wagner (1985) fits well with this view. Wagner recorded the entire speech outputs in one day of 12 children aged between 17 months and 15 years. The situations which elicited most speech in children aged less than six years typically involved low levels of concurrent physical activity, such as eating, bedtime, and observing. For the older children, this relationship was not apparent: Conversation was produced during both physically demanding tasks, such as skipping, and intellectually demanding tasks, such as doing homework. The findings of this study suggests that high speech output is indeed associated with low physical activity situations in children up to early school age, but that speech and motor output are independent in older children. This pattern fits rather well with the contention that the central executive plays a major role in both processing and scheduling the cognitive operations mediating speech production in very young children who are still acquiring basic language skills. Beyond the age of age five, however, children have typically mastered basic grammatical skills (Wells, 1985). We may therefore indeed expect the nature of other concurrent activities to have relatively little impact on the ease of speech production after this point in time.

There are obviously many other factors potentially confounding this apparent inverse association between spontaneous speech output in young children and physical activity. For example, many low-activity situations are routine activities in which parent–child interaction is encouraged, such as mealtimes, bathtime and bedtime. The possible nature of the predicted link between speech production and physical activity does, however, seem worth pursuing further in the form of more controlled observational studies in which physical and social predictors of speech output can be gauged independently.

Finally, consistent with the notion that a limited capacity processing system such as the central executive contributes to speech production, tradeoffs have also been found across different levels of the linguistic message. For example, Nelson and Bauer (1991) provided detailed linguistic and phonetic analyses of spontaneous samples of a small group of two-year-old children. For the majority of the children, tradeoffs were found between the complexity of word combinations and the phonetic complexity of individual words. Nelson and Bauer argue that this interaction between complexity of different levels of the language production process fits well with the view that the production of language is handled by a limited capacity system capable of differentially allocating resources to different levels of linguistic processing. Perhaps the limited capacity system in question is the central executive.

OVERVIEW

Psycholinguistic research on the cognitive processes involved in language production is largely motivated by specialised issues and theories quite unrelated to those guiding research on working memory. As a consequence, there is relatively little direct evidence concerning the relationship between working memory and language production. In this chapter we have relied extensively on a combination of correlational evidence and speculation; it may therefore be unsurprising that there are no strong conclusions that we wish to draw at this point. Nonetheless, the issue of what contribution components of the working memory system may make to the production of language in children and adults seems to us to be one of considerable interest.

The phonological loop does not appear to be used as a speech output buffer in adults, as has been suggested by some theorists. Neuropsychological evidence does, however, suggest that the use of subvocal rehearsal to maintain material in the phonological loop calls upon processes involved in the high-level planning of speech motor output. With respect to the central executive, there is some indication that it may contribute to the construction of semantic content of utterances. This contribution seems both plausible and important, but as yet unfortunately little researched.

Although on *a priori* grounds there is probably more reason to believe that general purpose resources, such as those provided by the working memory system, may be most useful in the effortful stages of acquiring language ability, there is even less direct evidence concerning the interrelationships between working memory and language production processes in young children. Here we have speculated on the possible links between the phonological store component of working memory and the efficiency of speech production processes. Observational evidence that is suggestive of central executive involvement in speech production during the early stages of language acquisition is also discussed. More directed research on the links between working memory and speech production in the first few years of life is needed, however, before progress can be made from speculation to well-formed theory.

CHAPTER FIVE

An Introduction to Reading Development

The study of how children become skilled readers, and of why some children experience unexpected difficulties in learning to read and spell, has occupied psychologists and educationalists since the end of the last century. The resulting body of knowledge on how reading skills develop during childhood is extensive. Much of the research on reading development points to the importance of phonological processing, and in the next chapter we review this evidence, and consider whether the phonological component of the working memory system mediates the link between phonological processing and success in learning to read. The present chapter is intended as an introduction to the area of reading development for readers unfamiliar with the extensive body of theory and data on children's reading. In the course of this chapter, a theoretical framework for reading development is introduced, which provides the platform for the analysis of phonological processing involvement in learning to read in Chapter 6.

Of course, becoming a skilled reader does not only involve phonological processing. Learning to read also involves the mastery of low-level skills, such as visual discrimination, as well as high-level abilities, such as language comprehension, and an understanding of pragmatics (see Oakhill & Garnham, 1988, for a recent comprehensive review). It would also be misleading to suggest that there exists a consensus view on how to characterise the development of literacy skills, and on why some children fail to learn to read as readily as others. In fact, there is little agreement on the way in which reading development is most effectively studied. Whereas some researchers focus on the characteristics of reading in children of varying levels of reading ability, others are more concerned with identifying the nonreading cognitive skills which contribute to reading development. Another point of difference between researchers concerns whether all poor readers have common cognitive problems to a greater or lesser degree of severity, or whether their reading difficulties arise from one or more of a range of heterogeneous cognitive deficits.

The purpose of this chapter is to provide a general introduction to research on reading development, guided by two specific goals. The first goal is to familiarise the reader with the principal theories and methodologies that motivate current research and thinking on reading development. The second goal is to acknowledge the complexity of the processes involved in literacy acquisition, and to point where necessary to the nonphonological aspects of learning to read. The detailed nature of the links between purely phonological abilities and literacy is the main focus of Chapter 6.

In the next section of this chapter, two influential traditions in the study of reading development are discussed. In later sections, we outline the methodologies associated with each of these traditions, and summarise the major debates concerning the characterisation of poor reading development and dyslexia.

CHARACTERISING THE ACQUISITION OF LITERACY

For the newcomer to the study of reading development, the many alternative approaches to literacy acquisition can seem baffling. Even reviews of the area typically fail to embrace the full range of empirical and theoretical traditions. One influential tradition to have emerged in the past decade as a major theoretical force is the *component cognitive skills* approach to reading research (Carr & Levy, 1990). This approach is based on the study of individual differences—focusing principally on the nonspecialised cognitive skills necessary for normal reading development. It has been applied both to children with reading ability within the normal range for their age, and to unusually poor readers and spellers (sometimes termed *dyslexics* and *dysgraphics*, respectively). Other research groups focus more specifically on developmental dyslexia, and on the reading, rather than nonreading, characteristics of children who encounter serious difficulties in learning to read and write. Ellis (1985) provides a useful review of a representative range of important texts representing this tradition. In the following sections we describe two representative theoretical models which illustrate these contrasting but influential approaches to reading development.

A "Developmental" Model of Reading

A developmental model of reading and spelling development is one which describes, in terms of psychological mechanisms or processes, the way in which literacy skills change and progress as the child learns to read and write. A simple description of the reading characteristics typical of a six-year-old child and of a young adult therefore does not represent a developmental model, for two reasons. Firstly, it fails to identify how the rudimentary skills of the six-year-old reader first came into play. Secondly, this description fails to characterise the nature of the changes that take place in the psychological mechanisms used for reading during this period. Both of these features—the identification of the nonspecialised cognitive skills used in the development of reading ability, and the characterisation of change during the period of literacy acquisition—are central to a developmental model.

Frith's Three Strategies for Reading

The theory of reading acquisition advanced by Frith (1985) satisfies both of these criteria, and is currently one of the most influential developmental models of reading (see also Marsh, Friedman, Welch, & Desberg, 1981; Ehri, 1985). This theory describes the changes in reading abilities that occur as the child is learning to read an alphabetic orthography such as English. The changes are characterised in terms of the development of three main strategies: the logographic, alphabetic, and orthographic strategies. The normal progression of reading abilities reflects both the development of each strategy, and the eventual replacement of one strategy by the next, more complex, strategy. Although Frith characterises the typical child as progressing through the strategies in a fixed sequence, it is suggested that at particular points in time the child may be using two different strategies, principally when a new one is in the early stages of its development.

Children's earliest attempts at reading are suggested to arise from the use of the logographic strategy. This strategy involves the child learning to associate a familiar word with the salient graphic cues present in its printed form. These cues may include visual features such as the length of the word, the first letter, or its overall shape. At first, the visual memory specifications of the words learned via this strategy are rather approximate and unreliable. Some reading errors typical of this early stage of reading are reported by Seymour and Elder (1986) in a detailed study of children's reading attempts during the first year of formal reading instruction. A typical error was made by a child who read *policeman* as *children*; the child explained that it had to be *children* because it was a long word.

As children learn more about the visual forms of letters and hence improve their discrimination skills, though, they are able to construct fairly accurate representations for a relatively small number of words. An important feature of this strategy is that the ease of learning new words is not affected by the regularity of the letter–sound correspondences represented within the words; irregular words are learned as readily as irregular ones. The use of a logographic strategy for reading typically occupies the first year or so of a child learning to read, and is often described as the child establishing a basic "sight vocabulary".

According to Frith (1985), there are a number of basic skills which the child has to have mastered before a logographic strategy can be successfully developed. One prerequisite is that the child can understand metalinguistic terms such as *word* and *sentence*; without awareness of these basic symbolic components of written language, most children make little progress in learning to read (Ferreiro, 1978). The development of a logographic strategy will also depend on the visual discrimination and visual memory skills of the young child. This view fits well with recent findings that measures of children's visual discrimination abilities as they start to learn to read provide good predictors of their success in the first year of reading (Ellis & Large, 1988).

The child then attempts to exploit the correspondences between letters and their associated sounds as a way of guiding reading of words that are not within their sight vocabulary. Unfamiliar letter sequences are spelled out by applying simple letter–sound correspondence rules, not always successfully during the early stages. There are a number of labels for this new approach to reading, such as "cracking the alphabetic code" (e.g. Liberman, 1989), and the "alphabetic" strategy (Frith, 1985). The major advantage of this strategy over the earlier logographic approach to word learning is that the child may now be able to read successfully new regular words that are not in its sight vocabulary. Many researchers have noted that the development of this strategy equips children with an important self-teaching mechanism which enables them to successfully "read" unfamiliar words which in turn will gradually increase their sight vocabulary (Share, Jorm, MacLean, & Matthews, 1984).

The utility of the strategy has obvious limitations with an alphabetic orthography such as English where the relationship between letters and sounds is inconsistent. The printed form of many common words in our language is irregular. Mispronunciation of irregular words is therefore a central feature of this strategy for reading; the child makes what are known as "regularisation" errors, such as pronouncing *was* as though it rhymes with "has".

There is a good deal of evidence that the child's skills at processing and manipulating phonological information contributes to the ease of developing the alphabetic strategy, and this is the subject of Chapter 6. For the present purposes, it is sufficient to note that almost every measure that psychologists have taken of children's facility with the spoken form of language has been found in one study or another to be positively related to young children's reading ability.

Frith's (1985) third stage, the "orthographic" strategy for reading and spelling, follows the alphabetic strategy. It involves parsing words into multiletter orthographic segments, which map onto stored internal representations of morphemes (units of meaning, which may correspond to words), and does not require phonological mediation. The progression from dependence on alphabetic to orthographic strategies is characterised by an increasing sensitivity to the neighbouring context of a letter or letter string, and a decreasing reliance on sounding out segments. Thus, a child will learn during this period that vowels are lengthened by a final *e* in a word. When using an orthographic strategy the child's reading speed should not be directly influenced by the number of letters in the word, but instead by the number of orthographic segments.

Although this theory of reading development stops at the orthographic strategy, Frith (1985) considers it possible that skilled adult reading may be characterised by a further and final phase in reading development. In this phase, reading activity becomes independent of language processing mechanisms and is handled instead by a cognitive module specialised for reading (Fodor, 1983). Aside from this issue, skilled reading does approximate the orthographic strategy to a high degree. Normal reading in adults usually involves direct access to stored word knowledge on the basis of letter configurations (the "direct" route to word recognition), and does not depend on phonological recoding for familiar words (see Chapter 7).

The Relationship between Reading and Spelling

Frith suggests that the strategies used to guide reading and spelling may proceed out of step with one another. Figure 5.1 depicts Frith's elaborated six-stage model, in which reading and writing progress

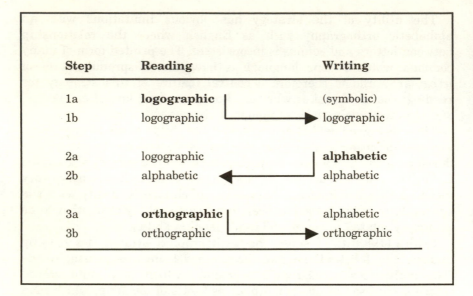

Step	Reading		Writing
1a	**logographic**		(symbolic)
1b	logographic		logographic
2a	logographic		**alphabetic**
2b	alphabetic		alphabetic
3a	**orthographic**		alphabetic
3b	orthographic		orthographic

FIG. 5.1. Frith's (1985) model of the acquisition of reading and writing skills. (Reproduced with permission.)

through the same sequence of three strategies, but do so out of phase with one another. The arrows show which activity acts as the pacemaker for the development of a new strategy at the different points in literacy acquisition.

At the earliest phase of reading, as the child begins to use a rudimentary logographic strategy to develop a small sight vocabulary, the child cannot spell because word recognition is not based on a complete specification of the visual features, but only on the salient ones. Whereas recognition of these distinctive graphic features will enable the child to successfully "read" the small set of familiar words, the specification will not be sufficient to support successful spelling, as this requires an intact representation of the letter sequence. As the logographic strategy develops, however, and the visual memory for the words becomes more precisely specified, the child will be able to attempt to spell.

It is spelling, according to Frith (1985), that acts as the pacemaker for the shift to an alphabetic strategy. The proposal is that it is relatively easy to start using letter–sound correspondence in spelling, as the number of letters is fairly small. Simple spelling–sound correspondences are, however, initially rather less useful in reading. Correct pronunciation for many printed letter strings depends on the larger orthographic context. So *eo* in people is pronounced as *ee*, not *ee-oh*. Pronunciation of other words cannot be confidently derived from mapping rules. For instance, the way to pronounce correctly the word *bow* depends not on the letter string, but on the semantic context. In due course, children do extend the alphabetic strategy to reading. In the very earliest stages, though, an alphabetic strategy may only be used to guide spelling.

At the point of transition from an alphabetic to an orthographic strategy, however, it is proposed that reading once again takes over the role of pacemaker. As with the earlier development of the logographic strategy, the specifications of orthographic or morphemic segments is assumed to be initially weak, and thus insufficient to direct spelling. With better specification, however, both reading and spelling activities will eventually be guided by knowledge of these higher-level letter units.

We have outlined Frith's theory of reading acquisition in some detail, because in addition to satisfying the requirements of a development model of reading, it captures many of the complexities of literacy acquisition that are problematic for more rigid stage theories. In particular, reports that young children can spell words they cannot read (e.g. Bryant & Bradley, 1980) fit well with the notion that towards the end of the first phase of reading development, children may be using an alphabetic strategy to spell, but depend still on the more basic logographic strategy to read.

Information Processing Models of Reading

An alternative approach to the study of reading acquisition has involved using models of skilled adult reading to guide theoretical interpretation of children's reading behaviour. In particular, cognitive neuropsychologists have attempted to apply the *logogen* model of word recognition to the study of dyslexic children, and to a lesser degree to the study of normal children learning to read. A version of this model formulated by Morton and Patterson (1980) is shown in Fig. 5.2.

This version of the model was developed largely in order to account for various "acquired dyslexias". These are syndrome complexes of highly specific impairments of reading that have been found to result from localised damage to the patients' left hemisphere. Detailed study of such patients has led to the identification of four important components of this model of reading. The *visual input logogens* are devices specialised for the recognition of printed words; there is one logogen for each word in an individual's vocabulary. The *output logogens* are devices for generating the phonological forms of words;

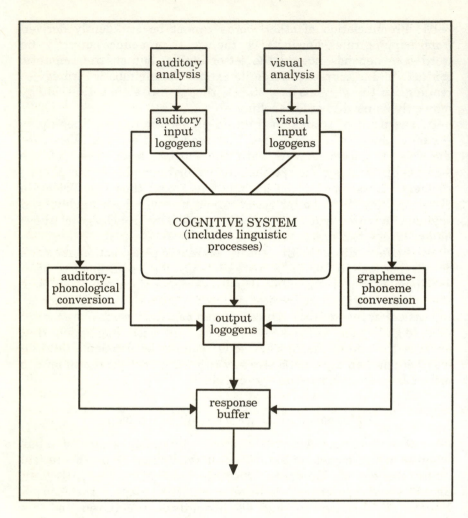

FIG. 5.2. Morton and Patterson's (1980) model of word recognition. (Reproduced with permission.)

once again, there is one for each familiar word. The *cognitive system* handles the processing of semantic information. Specialised linguistic processes are located within this system, too. The *grapheme–phoneme* conversion (GPC) process applies rules which map phonology onto graphemes or letter clusters, and can be used to pronounce unfamiliar words. Note that there is also a route by which the spoken forms of words can be recognised in this model. Access to the word recognition system for these is achieved via the *auditory input logogens*, a set of recognition   devices   analogous   to   visual   input   logogens   (but independent of them) that are specialised for detecting the occurrence of spoken forms of familiar words.

This architecture provides three separate routes by which the appropriate phonology of a printed letter string can be achieved by the reader. If the printed form of a word is detected by the appropriate visual input logogen, contact with the corresponding output logogen that specifies its phonological form can be achieved either directly, or via the cognitive system. Alternatively, the reader can generate the phonological forms of words by following the GPC route. This route involves parsing the input letter string into its constituent graphemes, mapping these onto corresponding phonological specifications using correspondence rules, and then blending the generated phonological segments in order to provide an appropriate phonological string (although see Kay & Marcel, 1981, and Shallice & Warrington, 1980, for alternative views). The GPC pathway is believed to be used for reading unfamiliar words and nonwords, but is of little use with irregular or exception words, whose phonology cannot reliably be generated by applying grapheme–phoneme mapping rules.

There are therefore two different ways of deriving phonology from print in this model: direct detection by the visual input logogens, and indirect generation of phonology by the grapheme–phoneme conversion process. The first procedure corresponds to some extent to the logographic strategy described by Frith (1985), in which the child learns to recognise words by their salient graphic features. This initial reading strategy could therefore be characterised in terms of the development of visual input logogens. During the logographic phase, the child is presumably learning to discriminate the feature conjunctions corresponding to letters, and so continually updates the visual specifications of the input logogens (Seymour & Elder, 1986). In the process of doing so, abstract letter identities will also be acquired and will eventually be used to mediate skilled word recognition via the visual input logogen route.

Does, then, the indirect route to word recognition, which involves applying grapheme–phoneme correspondence rules, correspond to the alphabetic or orthographic strategies for reading? Not as the model shown in Fig. 4.2 stands, as this does not provide any way that the meaning of letter strings can be accessed if their phonology is generated via GPC. This problem can, however, be remedied if it is assumed that the phonological product of this route can activate auditory input logogens, and hence contact the cognitive system through the auditory input route (Coltheart, Masterson, Byng, Prior, & Riddoch, 1983). It is by this route that the reader can gain access to the meaning of words that have been phonologically recoded.

A major weakness of such information processing models of reading is their failure to capture the dynamic nature of children's reading development (see Frith, 1985, for discussion of this point). This is hardly surprising: Being models of skilled adult reading behaviour, they were not designed to do so. It may well be appropriate to suggest that an adult patient with highly localised brain damage is reading normally except that the phonological recoding mechanism is not functional (e.g. Marshall & Newcombe, 1973). However, the same sort of argument becomes implausible when extended to reading development. As we shall discover in Chapter 6, a child who experiences particular difficulty in learning a phonological recoding strategy will be unlikely to learn to read in the same way as normal children. Children with severe and specific deficits typically rely more heavily on other strategies to compensate for shortcomings in recoding, and so develop unusual methods for reading, which may be more consistent with their cognitive capacities.

Information processing models of reading based on the study of adult readers therefore inevitably fall some way short of providing complete accounts of the development of reading in children. The shortcomings of this approach have not, however, gone unnoted by some of the researchers working within this tradition (e.g. Temple, 1988). Others have overcome these limitations by using a judicious combination of developmental and psycholinguistic models to guide theoretical interpretation (e.g. Seymour & Elder, 1986).

Psycholinguistic research on reading development has also significantly extended the body of knowledge concerning reading development. In particular, it has provided careful documentation of the reading characteristics of children with reading impairments—an issue that receives surprisingly scant attention in the cognitive developmental literature more generally. The data have been particularly valuable in casting light on the issue of whether dyslexia arises from single or multiple deficits, and whether all dyslexic children have a common disorder. These points are covered in more detail in the following section, which focuses on methodologies for studying reading development.

METHODOLOGIES FOR STUDYING READING DEVELOPMENT

Given the sustained interest over many decades in how children learn to read, and in why some children fail to develop reading abilities as readily as others, it is perhaps unsurprising that there are so many different ways of studying reading development. And in many respects, the diversity of the approaches to literacy acquisition is beneficial: The database on the cognitive factors affecting reading development is now extensive. The abundance of research in reading development does, however, have its downside. The major problem is that although it is possible to compile a list of cognitive skills that have consistently been found to be related to reading achievement, the list is long, and it is not clear which skills are contributors to reading success, which skills are beneficiaries, and which develop reciprocally with reading ability. The task facing psychologists is to detect the patterns of causality underlying the well-established empirical relationships, and to incorporate these into theories of reading development.

There has been considerable debate in recent years as to which methodologies are most appropriate for identifying causal factors in reading development. Here we briefly outline the principal methodologies in current usage, and note some of the advantages and disadvantages of each approach. Issues concerning methodologies in the study of reading development are covered more extensively by Goswami and Bryant (1990), Jorm (1983), and Wagner and Torgesen (1987). Techniques commonly used in the study of "normal" reading populations are considered first. We then consider the special methodological and interpretational issues that arise from the study of children with reading impairments that are sufficiently severe to be classed as developmental dyslexics.

Normal Reading Populations

Consider the 30 or so children in a typical classroom situated in a state primary school. The children will vary in almost any measure which one cares to take: in physical measures (height, weight, etc.), and in intellectual measures, too (vocabulary knowledge, arithmetic, reading, etc.). Provided that the test administered to the children is appropriately sensitive (for example, the tape measure should not be too short for measuring the height of the children, and the reading test should not be too easy), their scores on each measure should approximate fairly closely to a normal distribution. Our interest here is with the nature of the individual differences between the children in this class on the reading measure. Why do they differ in reading ability? One simple theory is that the best readers are the oldest children, who will generally be more intellectually mature, or possibly may have attended school for a longer period.

Closer scrutiny however, rapidly demonstrates that age and time in school do not give a very good account of the data. Some children pick up reading rapidly and apparently effortlessly, while others, not necessarily less intelligent, find great difficulty, despite a supportive background and good teaching.

If we return to Frith's (1985) developmental theory of reading acquisition considered earlier in the chapter, we can see that there are many possible cognitive sources of the individual variation in reading achievement of children within a particular year at school. Specifically, the children may vary in a number of cognitive skills that contribute to reading development. They may differ in their visual discrimination abilities, in their abilities to learn visual patterns, in their grasp of what is meant by "a word". They may also differ in their skills at identifying the component sounds in words, and in learning to associate particular letters with sounds. A child who has poor development of any of these component skills may be less successful in learning to read than other children. And indeed, deficits in each of these domains—visual discrimination, visual memory, metalinguistic knowledge, phonological awareness, and phonological memory—have all been found to be associated to some degree with lack of early reading success. How, then, do we assess whether each of the cognitive skills in question contributes directly to reading development? In the following sections we outline the principal different methodologies that have been used to identify the cognitive bases of individual differences in reading ability, and briefly consider the strengths and weaknesses of each approach.

Reading Group Designs

One straightforward approach is to compare the performance of children with good and poor reading abilities in tasks tapping cognitive skills that may contribute to reading development. Researchers employing this design have established a variety of differences between the high and low reading ability groups, particularly in tests of language processing. Examples of language processing deficits in poor readers include poor phonological memory for sequences of familiar words (Mann, Liberman, & Shankweiler, 1980), and impairments in both the speed and accuracy of producing familiar words (Denckla & Rudel, 1976; Rapala & Brady, 1990). Good and poor readers are also distinguished in terms of their awareness of the sound structure of spoken words (e.g. Liberman, Shankweiler, Fischer, & Carter, 1974). These findings have been used as the basis for theories linking reading ability with phonological processing skills, and are the main focus of Chapter 6.

The problem with this kind of evidence is that differences between the performance of good and poor readers of the same age in nonreading tasks may reflect a variety of causal and non-causal relationships. The low scores of the poor readers may indeed reflect impairments in a cognitive skill that is critical for successful reading development. Performance differences between reading groups are, however, equally consistent with the converse causal hypothesis, which is that reading ability influences the nonreading skill. It is entirely plausible that there are many beneficiaries of success in reading development.

Yet another possibility is that the reading and nonreading abilities of the children may bear no causal relation to one another, but may both be influenced by a third, unidentified, variable, such as general intelligence. Although experimenters can and do match groups of good and poor readers on obvious possible confounding factors such as intelligence, the possibility remains that another unknown cognitive resource is responsible for both the reading and nonreading differences between the two groups of children.

Performance differences between good and poor readers of the same age therefore do not provide sufficient grounds to distinguish between specific causal hypotheses. For this reason, some reading researchers have argued that the adoption of such designs for studying the basis of individual differences in reading development is worthless, as any differences found between the reading ability groups are uninterpretable (e.g. Bryant, 1986; Goswami & Bryant, 1990). Although there are obvious problems with relying on evidence only from studies using this reading group design, we consider that data obtained from such studies are of considerable value. Null results arising from comparisons of good and poor readers of the same age can be effective in ruling out specific causal hypotheses.

Consider a fictional hypothesis, that reading development is critically influenced by a child's weight. If we compare the good and poor readers in a class of eight-year-old children, and find that the weights of the two groups do not differ, the hypothesis can be rejected. A positive finding that the good and poor readers differed significantly in weight would be consistent with the experimental hypothesis, and so too with a number of different causal and noncausal hypotheses. Following a positive group difference, therefore, the researcher would have to design a more informative study in order to distinguish between the alternative interpretations. The result from the reading group study is nonetheless useful in identifying whether a hypothesis is worth pursuing further.

Because of the problems in interpreting the causal status of group differences established using this design, many researchers have chosen instead to compare the performance of poor readers with normal younger children who are matched on a measure of reading ability. Both of these groups of children have achieved similar levels of reading skill. Using this methodology, known as the matched reading age design, the possibility that any differences between the groups that emerge in nonreading measures are consequences of differences in their level of reading achievement can therefore be ruled out. Where differences between poor reading and their reading-age controls have been found (e.g. Bradley & Bryant, 1978; Snowling, 1981), they are especially informative. For example, the observation that good and poor readers of the same age differ in the skill such as phonological awareness or memory leaves open the possibility that this may be the result, rather than cause, of the reading difference. On the other hand, if poor readers show a lower level of phonological awareness than younger children who are matched with them on reading level, then it is much more plausible to assume that awareness is responsible for reading development than the reverse.

Differences between poor readers and their reading-age controls are, however, relatively unusual. The more commonly reported pattern of findings consists of no differences between the two groups (e.g. Johnston, Rugg, & Scott, 1987). Null effects in this design are, unfortunately, difficult to interpret. Some researchers favour developmental lag interpretations when poor readers perform at equivalent levels to their younger reading-age controls. Beech and Harding (1984), for example, found few differences between poor readers and their reading-age controls in a wide range of phonological processing measures. Relative to normal readers of the same age, though, the poor readers were deficient in many phonological processing tasks. Similarly, Stanovich, Nathan, and Zolman (1988) found that the performance on both reading and nonreading tasks of poor readers and their reading-age controls was more or less indistinguishable. In both cases, the authors argued that because the performance of the poor readers in cognitive tasks was generally appropriate for their reading ability, these children are best characterised not in terms of abnormal cognitive and reading development, but as lagging behind in the component cognitive skills necessary for reading development.

There are problems with this interpretation of null effects in studies using reading-age matches. Although the level of reading ability attained by the poor readers and their reading-age controls is equated, they differ considerably in terms both of amount of educational experience and of intellectual maturity. The poor readers are older than the control children, and so are more intellectually advanced. The poor readers have also had greater experience of instruction in reading and writing skills, although their actual achievements may be comparable with the reading-age control children. For these reasons, the absence of a difference between the two groups does not rule out the possibility that the poor readers are deficient in a particular cognitive skill, and that this deficit is the basis of their difficulties in learning to read.

Correlational Designs

An alternative approach to the study of individual differences in reading development is provided by correlational studies of normal children. In a typical correlational study, the researchers aim to test a causal hypothesis that identifies particular cognitive skills as significant contributors to reading development. Measures of these skills and of reading performance are obtained from a sample of unselected children. The causal hypothesis is tested by assessing the strength of the correlations between the hypothesised causal cognitive skills and the measures of reading ability. If a particular skill is critical to normal reading development, a high correlation would be expected.

In fact, reading-group designs in which good readers are compared with poor readers of the same age represent a special case of the correlational study, in which only children who occupy extreme positions in the distribution of reading ability are given the tests of nonreading skills. In some cases, researchers use a single correlational database as the basis both for correlational analysis and for extracting reading groups for comparison (e.g. Rapala & Brady, 1990). The two analyses, although drawn from a common database, address hypotheses that differ subtly. The full correlational analysis assesses whether there is a significant relationship between cognitive skills and reading development across the whole range of normal reading ability for a particular age range. The reading-group design explores whether the cognitive skills of children who occupy extreme positions in the distribution of reading ability differ.

Although typically motivated by a specific causal hypothesis, the correlational approach (like the related-reading group design) cannot distinguish between alternative causal interpretations of significant associations. The approach has, nonetheless, provided a rich database of the complex interrelationships between reading ability and other cognitive skills. Work in this tradition has provided much basic information about the domains of reading and reading-related abilities, and in particular about the close links between reading success and phonological processing skills. One useful approach within this tradition has been to compare correlations between reading abilities and other cognitive capacities at different stages in reading development. Studies that have adopted this approach have, for example, established that the associations between reading and other intellectual abilities, such as general intelligence and vocabulary knowledge, become increasingly strong as reading skills develop through the school years (Gathercole, Willis, Emslie, & Baddeley, 1991; Stanovich, Cunningham, & Feeman, 1984b). The most likely explanation for this phenomenon is that it reflects mutual facilitation between reading and other intellectual abilities.

Many researchers use multiple regression techniques, such as fixed-order regressions and hierarchical regressions, as a means of testing hypotheses in complex correlational databases. These techniques provide ways of conservatively estimating the strength of the unique relationship between reading scores and a hypothesised predictor of reading, controlling for differences due to factors, such as intelligence and age, which may artifactually inflate simple correlations. Of course, the possibility remains that any residual correlations between variables that remain after partialling out variance due to other factors might still arise from intercorrelations with a further unidentified variable. By careful planning of the studies, however, it should be possible to rule out at least the most obvious intervening factors.

Longitudinal Designs
With each of the methodologies outlined so far, the underlying pattern of causality between empirical associations is ambiguous. The longitudinal approach provides a stronger test of causal hypotheses. In a longitudinal study, a sample of children is selected for study, and is tested and retested at further intervals. In this way, it is possible to determine whether early (sometimes, prereading) cognitive skills effectively predict later reading development. The longitudinal design is demanding of research resources, but it can provide a powerful tool for testing causal theories of the contributors to reading development. It offers a way of exploring whether measures of the hypothesised causal skill do significantly predict later reading development.

The longitudinal approach has provided a particularly effective means of testing the hypothesis that children's phonological processing skills before learning to read directly influence their later success in learning to read and write (e.g. Bradley & Bryant, 1983). It always, of course, remains possible that the developmental relationship is mediated by another identified factor. (There is, however, no design that can avoid this possibility.) Longitudinal studies that test children initially when they are prereaders are relatively unusual, though. More typically, researchers select children in the first year of receiving formal reading instruction, and retest them either once or after a number of further intervals (e.g. Ellis & Large, 1988; Lundberg, Olofsson, & Wall, 1980; Mann & Liberman, 1984). Interpreting longitudinal associations in such studies is problematic (see Wagner & Torgesen, 1987, for discussion of this point). If a measure taken during early reading development predicts later reading achievement, the possibility cannot be ruled out that the early performance measure was itself influenced by the child's early reading experience. If so, the apparently predictive link between the nonreading measure and later reading scores merely reflect the well-established interactive relationship in reading development. Longitudinal studies of post-reading children therefore do not provide strong tests of unidirectional causal hypotheses. Such studies are not, however, uninformative on other issues. Multiwave longitudinal studies, which explore the changing predictors and beneficiaries of reading as reading abilities develop, can provide a rich and useful picture of the development of the skill (e.g. Ellis & Cataldo, in press; Ellis & Large, 1988).

There are also problems of a more technical nature associated with the design of longitudinal studies. The studies are exceptionally demanding of research resources: The children need to be tested at least on two occasions, preferably separated by a considerable period of time. Subject attrition is an inevitable associated problem: A substantial minority of the children tested at the first wave may not be available subsequently, so that some of the initial investment of time can seem wasted. Selection of test material is also particularly problematic. Many studies repeat the same test at different waves of the study, thereby providing comparability of the measures. For some tests, though, the consequences of practice effects that may arise could result in reduced sensitivity of measures over the time course of the study. Finally, there is no going back in a longitudinal study: By the time the first wave of testing children is completed, it is too late to realise that a critical control measure is missing. There is no opportunity to run an extra experiment testing a particular alternative hypothesis.

It should be clear by this point that longitudinal studies take a lot of time and require considerable careful planning. The benefits potential are, however, great: There really is no other way of identifying whether abilities develop independently from one another, or are genuinely and indissociably linked.

Designing Research Programmes

It should be clear by this point that none of these main methodologies for studying cognitive contributors to reading development—reading-group designs, cross-sectional correlational studies and longitudinal studies—can provide watertight tests of causal hypotheses. In combination, however, the alternative methodologies can provide an effective means of testing causal hypotheses.

On balance, the best strategy for designing a research programme to test a particular causal hypothesis seems to be to adopt a convergent methods approach, starting with a reading group study. It takes relatively little time to compare the best and worst readers within a particular age range on measures of a cognitive skill that may contribute to reading development. If no group differences are found, the hypothesis can be ruled out at an early stage, and without too much investment of time. If a positive result is found, an appropriate next step may be to pursue the hypothesis further using a cross-sectional correlational approach. This methodology provides the opportunity of taking measures from a range of tasks believed to reflect different abilities, in addition to the predictor variable and reading measures of primary interest. In this way, it is possible to determine whether the relationship between the predictor variable and reading achievement holds after other potentially confounding factors, such as, for example, general intelligence, have been taken into account. It would generally only be advisable to embark on a longitudinal study of the hypothesis, which would inevitably place heavy demands in terms of time and research resources, if these other approaches yielded positive results.

One further methodology which we have not yet considered involves training children in the cognitive skill believed to contribute causally to literacy development. A number of researchers have been keen to pursue this approach as, it has been argued, a training study can provide the most direct test of a causal hypothesis (e.g. Goswami & Bryant, 1990). If reading achievement is boosted as a direct consequence of a training programme directed at improving specific cognitive skills in the child, a directional causal hypothesis is strongly supported.

Several programmes have been designed to promote in prereading children the phonological processing skills believed to contribute to reading development. All of the programmes successfully trained the target skills; the important issue is whether by doing so, literacy achievement was also promoted. The results have been mixed. Although positive effects of training in literacy have been found

(Lundberg, Frost, & Petersen, 1988), results from other training studies have been more ambiguous (Bryant & Bradley, 1985; Olofsson & Lundberg, 1985). These studies are considered in more detail in Chapter 6. The important point here is that training prereading phonological skills has not always boosted the ease of subsequently learning to read and spell.

In fact, there are problems associated with the interpretation of both positive and null results in training studies. One problem with a positive result is identifying which component of the training programme was instrumental in promoting literacy development. It is entirely possible that the training task may promote cognitive skills other than the target skill intended by the researcher. A training programme directed at accelerating one type of phonological processing skill may well, for example, promote another phonological ability too, and it could be the latter ability that facilitates reading development. This possibility could be evaluated by retesting a range of cognitive skills at the end of training schedules, but is rarely done. If it were, the assumption that the training programme results in highly specific cognitive gains might well turn out to be unjustified.

Null results in a training study can also be problematic. Failure of training in a target cognitive skill to boost later reading development could lead to the rejection of the hypothesis that these skills are critical for reading development. The null result may not, however, necessarily be inconsistent with the causal hypothesis. The researcher may not, for example, have trained a particular ability to a sufficient extent to enhance significantly later reading achievement. Alternatively, more than one ability or skill may be necessary for reading to improve (Byrne & Fielding-Barnsley, 1989).

In summary, the costly and risky combination of longitudinal and training studies advocated by some researchers as the best way of testing causal hypotheses relating to reading should not be seen as guaranteeing the answers to a reading researcher's dreams. Although positive results from training studies provide good support for a causal hypothesis, claims that they are able to provide unequivocal support should be dismissed. There is no single answer to the issue of how to test causal developmental hypotheses. In recognition of this, we would argue that consistent results across different paradigms should be the only basis for retaining confidence in a particular hypothesis.

Developmental Dyslexia

The Problem of Definition

So far in our discussion of methods for studying reading development, we have focused only on comparisons of good and poor readers within normal populations of children. A related tradition in the study of reading development involves the investigation of children with more severe and unexpected reading problems. These children are often described as having developmental dyslexia. How dyslexia should be defined is, however, still a matter of spirited debate. Many experimenters depend on clinical assessments and referrals by educational psychologists and speech therapists to specialised dyslexia units as a means of selecting dyslexic subjects for study. This pragmatic approach has the benefit of ensuring that psychologists study the children who are viewed by educationalists as genuinely having severe disorders of reading development.

More frequently, researchers define dyslexia as the failure to acquire literacy at a normal rate in the absence of any obvious factors, such as emotional disorder, serious socioeconomic disadvantage or low intelligence (e.g. Rutter & Yule, 1975; Vellutino, 1979). Researchers using such definitions of dyslexia have estimated its incidence in the general population at around 5% (Lundberg, 1988).

This discrepancy definition of dyslexia has recently been criticised. In a study that included children with reading disabilities and normal readers, Siegel (1988) found no evidence that the basic reading, spelling, memory, and language skills were different for the dyslexic readers of high or low intelligence scores. Also, some of the children with normal reading development had low IQs. Siegel argued that a discrepancy criterion, according to which reading ability has to be some way below general IQ, should not be used to identify dyslexic children. She suggested instead that a more valuable approach to studying the nature of reading disability in children is to analyse the component skills involved in developmental impairments of reading, irrespective of their intelligence level.

This controversy has at times been very heated; in particular, the discrepancy definition might seem to suggest that only intelligent children from good homes should receive treatment, a view that is clearly unacceptable. We believe that the controversy stems from an injudicious mix of criteria for quite different purposes. From a research viewpoint, it is important to try to select a group of dyslexic subjects whose reading problems are as homogeneous as possible. The causes of reading difficulty are sufficiently complex in children with normal intelligence and good parental support, without needing to add other factors such as social deprivation. From the viewpoint of an educationalist working in a deprived community, however, it would be quite wrong to concentrate efforts principally on a minority of children with a specific reading or language problem despite coming from a supportive home. It is important to recognise that, whereas dyslexia may be most fruitfully studied in children of high intelligence, it is at least as likely that equivalent deficits will occur in less fortunate children, who, from a practical viewpoint, are likely to need even more support and help.

Poor Readers and Dyslexics: Disordered, or Just Extreme?
Another important issue concerns whether children who experience severe difficulties in learning to read and write are qualitatively different from the children of poor reading ability, who presumably represent the lower end of a normal distribution of reading abilities. One view is that the children with the most serious reading problems merely represent the extreme lower end of the normal distribution of reading ability (Rodgers, 1983). This position is supported by results from some experimental studies which have failed to yield any qualitative differences in the reading characteristics of dyslexic children and normal readers (Baddeley, Logie, & Ellis, 1988; Seidenberg, Bruck, Fornarolo, & Backman, 1985; Treiman & Hirsch-Pasek, 1985).

Others, though, have claimed that dyslexic children are different from poor readers. In particular, Stanovich, Nathan, and Vala-Rossi (1986) distinguish between "garden variety" poor readers who are developmentally lagging behind normal readers as a consequence of their generally weak cognitive profiles, and genuinely dyslexic subjects. They argue that many studies have reported that poor readers perform equivalently with reading-age matched controls in both reading and nonreading tasks. In contrast, Stanovich et al. propose that true dyslexic readers are distinctive in terms of their cognitive profiles, and should be characterised as disordered rather than lagging in developmental terms. Their view is that dyslexic readers have specific deficits in phonological skills, which lead to difficulties in decoding words, but that they have cognitive skills and knowledge superior to their reading-age matches because they are older. Thus, they are able to some extent to compensate for their relatively low-level reading difficulties by employing more sophisticated comprehension strategies.

One Dyslexia or Many?
A further debate concerns whether all children with severe reading disorders should be classed as dyslexic and as having the same

disorder. There is considerable evidence pointing to the existence of identifiable subgroups of dyslexia. In an early influential study in this area, Boder (1973) investigated 107 dyslexic children. Of these, 67% were classified as having phonological deficits. Ten per cent of the sample, however, had specific problems in recognising the printed forms of words, and were termed by Boder "dyseidetic" dyslexics. The remaining 20% or so of the children were classified as having both visual and phonological deficits in reading. Frith (1985) has suggested that reading difficulties of the dyseidetic dyslexics reflect failures to develop a normal logographic strategy. The more commonly observed pattern of phonological deficits in dyslexic children (and indeed adults) were attributed to problems in applying the subsequent alphabetic strategy for reading.

Single-case studies of developmentally dyslexic children have provided particularly clear evidence for the heterogeneous nature of their reading problems. These studies have been largely motivated by the psycholinguistic tradition outlined in an earlier section in this chapter, which uses models of skilled reading to characterise developmental disorders of reading. A number of different types of reading deficits have been found in studies of developmental dyslexics. One class of reading deficit has been termed developmental phonological dyslexia. Temple and Marshall (1983), for example, studied a 17-year-old dyslexic girl with a reading age of about 10 years. She made reading errors characteristic of an acquired disorder of reading known as *phonological dyslexia* (Beauvois & Dérouesné, 1979). Her symptoms included difficulty with reading nonwords and long regular words, and insensitivity to the orthographic regularity of the words. It was suggested that the extreme difficulty experienced by this developmental dyslexic in reading unfamiliar letter strings may arise from impaired development of the grapheme–phoneme conversion route to pronunciation shown in Fig. 5.2 (see also, Temple, 1988).

Contrast these reading errors with those reported by Coltheart et al. (1983) in a study of a 16-year-old dyslexic with a reading age of 10 years. Her reading performance appeared to correspond to an excessive reliance on the grapheme–phoneme conversion route, which relies on a phonological recoding strategy. Thus, she had particular difficulty with irregular words (which can only be effectively recognised via the direct route involving the visual input logogens). The problem for this individual appeared to be in developing adequate visual input logogens to enable her to read via the direct route. By analogy with a corresponding pattern of reading errors arising in acquired disorders of adults, Coltheart et al. termed this disorder developmental *surface dyslexia*.

Seymour and MacGregor (1984) conducted a detailed analysis of the reading errors made by four developmentally dyslexic readers, who ranged in age between 13 and 21 years. The details of the reading performance of the different cases need not concern us here. The important point is that each of the cases showed qualitatively different profiles of reading errors. One dyslexic appeared to be impaired in using the phonological route for reading (Temple & Marshall, 1983). Another of the cases appeared to have a deficit in visual processing that resulted in poor development of visual input logogens (Coltheart et al., 1983). One further case appeared to have multiple impairments, revealing deficits in both phonological and visual strategies for reading.

Proponents of this information processing approach to developmental dyslexia have been criticised for drawing strong conclusions about the *disordered* nature of the reading of these developmental dyslexics. Bryant and Impey (1986) studied the reading behaviour of 16 normal children with reading ages of about 10 years. Within this normal sample, some children displayed patterns of errors which corresponded very closely to those of the developmental dyslexics reported by Temple and Marshall (1983) and Coltheart et al. (1983). Some children made predominantly "phonological" errors, whereas others tended to make "surface" errors, to an equivalent extent to the dyslexic cases. On this basis, Bryant and Impey posited it is not appropriate to argue that there is anything unusual or disordered about the reading mechanisms of the dyslexic cases. This interpretation has itself been hotly contested (Temple, 1987).

The controversy over how the reading characteristics of developmental dyslexics should be interpreted is unlikely to be easily resolved, as the advocates of the two alternatives positions are firmly rooted in distinct traditions of reading research. Bryant and colleagues have long been of the opinion that "dyslexic" children and adults represent the extreme end of the normal distribution of reading ability (e.g. Bryant & Bradley, 1985). According to this view, dyslexics are just poor readers. Given this approach, the resistance to interpreting developmental difficulties in literacy acquisition as reflecting disordered or disturbed cognitive mechanisms is unsurprising. Similarly, it is only to be expected that the cognitive neuropsychologists who have extended their models of reading from acquired dyslexia to developmental dyslexia attempt to identify clear dissociations between normal and disordered reading development. Empirical dissociations are currently viewed as providing cognitive neuropsychologists with their most powerful theoretical tool (e.g. Ellis & Young, 1988; Shallice, 1988), and have been used to particularly good effect in the development of models of adult word recognition. Viewing developmental dyslexics as distinct from normal children follows naturally from this perspective.

A FRAMEWORK FOR READING DEVELOPMENT

In this section we present a framework for characterising reading development that draws together many of the theoretical positions outlined in this chapter, and which is sufficiently broad to incorporate both "normal" individual variation in reading ability and "dyslexic" reading. Our aim in presenting this framework is to provide a relatively simple characterisation of the way that reading develops, which can be used as the basis for the evaluation of the links between phonological processing and reading development in Chapter 6.

According to this framework, normal literacy acquisition involves the successful development of three principal strategies for reading. A printed letter string is recognised by the *visual* strategy when it directly matches a stored visual specification that corresponds to a familiar word. Once this direct visual match has been made, knowledge of that word, including its phonological form, becomes available. Words whose visual forms are stored are said to be members of an individuals' sight vocabulary. Most word recognition by adults is probably mediated by this strategy.

A word is recognised by a second strategy, that of *phonological recoding*, when the reader uses knowledge about the correspondences between letters and sounds to generate a full or partial phonological specification that matches the phonology of a familiar word. The third strategy involves use of *context*. A word can be "guessed" on the basis of a variety of sources of information—from the picture accompanying it in the book, from the sentence in which it is embedded, and from the child's expectations. Such contextual factors will in fact influence the generation of a word in combination with a child's attempt at reading, with the influence ranging from the speeding of fluent reading at one extreme to a complete guess at the other.

These three strategies for reading do not emerge simultaneously as a child starts learning to read. There is a specific developmental sequence. Reading by context occurs long before the child is usually considered to be able to read; young children often respond to text by mimicking someone reading aloud words. The words that they use are often (although not always) appropriate for the context of the page of the book, or for the more general situation of the child's interaction with the book.

When a child correctly identifies a word on the basis of guessing by context alone, though, it is not usually considered to be proper "reading". A child is typically described as having started to read when it can reliably recognise a printed letter string as representing a familiar word, independent of its context. The early words that are recognised this way are usually learned by the visual strategy: The child learns to associate the visual characteristics of the word with the phonology and the concept corresponding to the word. Initially, the visual learning of words is incomplete. The child may often learn only the shape of the initial letter of a word (so that any word beginning with *c* is always read as "cat"). With increasing experience of a word, and increasing familiarity with the letters in the alphabet, the stored visual specifications will become more accurate, and will eventually correspond to the letter sequence.

To learn the printed forms of words at this early stage of reading, it is usually necessary for the child to receive explicit instruction about the word corresponding to the letter string: The child will need to be told that *cat* corresponds to the spoken word "cat". Context may, however, be sufficient on some occasions to allow the child to deduce the correspondence between a letter string and its word.

A strategy of phonological recoding typically emerges after the child has learned to recognise the printed forms of a limited set of words by their visual characteristics. Words that are already present in the child's sight vocabulary will be recognised by a direct match with the stored visual representation, as before. The phonological recoding strategy is used by the child as it attempts to identify unfamiliar letter strings. Successful application of a strategy of phonological recoding provides an opportunity for the child to identify a letter string that has not already been learned. By doing so, the child may learn the letter sequence associated with the word, so that it becomes part of the sight vocabulary. If this learning episode is successful, the child will be able to identify it on subsequent encounters by a direct visual match, and not by the more effortful phonological recoding strategy. Phonological recoding thus provides a useful self-teaching tool.

When a phonological recoding strategy is first adopted by a child, it consists only of applying rudimentary knowledge of simple rules for mapping sounds onto the letters of the alphabet. With increasing experience of reading, the child abstracts more complex correspondence rules that take into account the larger orthographic context of individual letters, and applies these rules in reading. Once again, though, it should be emphasised that once the visual form of a familiar word has been learned, the child is likely to recognise it via a direct match between its printed form and the stored visual representation.

Although most skilled readers can readily generate an appropriate phonological recoding for unfamiliar letter strings, during the early stages of learning to read children's use of phonological recoding is partial and may not be very successful. In particular, early use often appears to be characterised by sounding out only the first one or two letters in a word. One way in which a partial strategy can nonetheless be effective is by combining it with the context strategy. A sophisticated guessing strategy results, in which the child selects candidates which are appropriate for the context, and whose initial phonemes correspond to the unfamiliar letter string. A consequence of this combination of phonological recoding and context strategies to guide reading is that children may sometimes be able to read irregular words successfully, although this is accompanied by the danger of generating errors, especially when contextual support is weak.

In summary, then, the phonological recoding strategy in combination with the context strategy provides a further means by which the word can be correctly "read" by the child. Successful use of this approach then provides the necessary link between the printed word form and the word that the child can learn. The printed forms of new words always require visual learning. Phonological recoding, though, allows the child to read a word without having already learned it, and also provides a self-generated learning episode which may allow the child to learn the visual specification of the word.

We now turn to the issue of individual differences in literacy acquisition. Each of the three research strategies described (contextual, visual, and phonological) requires certain basic cognitive resources for normal development, and children will vary in the adequacy of their resources. What cognitive skills are required for the normal development of each strategy? Adequate visual discrimination and visual learning skills are likely to be minimum requirements for the visual strategy. Correspondingly, the phonological recoding strategy appears to need efficient phonological processing skills for its normal development; more detail on these requirements is provided in Chapter 6. The origins of the contextual "guessing" strategy are less apparent, and have been the subject of relatively little direct research. One possibility is that the use of context in reading may draw upon general intellectual resources; thus, the ease with which the child learns to use context in reading may be related to factors such as intelligence and environmental experience.

As a consequence of the variation between children in the cognitive requisites for the three strategies, the ease with which they acquire and develop each of the three strategies will also vary. However, we suggest that poor skills in a domain necessary for the acquisition of one of the strategies may be compensated to some degree by adequate skills in another domain, provided that the deficits are not too severe. Weak visual processing skills may be tolerated without any apparent cost to overall reading ability if the child can both use context effectively and develop a phonological recoding strategy. Poor phonological skills may also be offset by effective use of context and good visual processing skills, although possibly to a lesser extent (discussed later). This could explain why the children in Bryant and Impey's (1986) study all had reading ages of about 10 years, yet some depended primarily on a strategy of direct visual recognition in reading, whereas others relied to a greater extent on a phonological strategy for reading. It also fits well with Stanovich's (1980) convincing evidence of the compensatory use of context by dyslexic children.

For moderate deficits, then, there can be some degree of developmental compensation between the extent to which the three strategies support reading. The consequences of poor development of the context strategy may have the least catastrophic consequences of all for the child's overall reading development. Provided that the child has phonological and visual processing skills that are sufficient to enable it to develop the necessary word decoding skills furnished by the phonological recoding and visual strategies, there may be no serious consequences of poor use of context. Combined with inadequate visual and phonological recoding strategies, though, a child with poor use of context is likely to be notably handicapped in reading development. Children with this low profile of cognitive skills are likely to be children of poor intelligence who have general problems in all learning tasks.

Compensatory strategy use will also be insufficient to maintain a normal rate of reading development in two other groups of children. The first group consists of children whose deficits of critical cognitive skills are sufficiently severe that they fail to acquire more than a rudimentary grasp of the strategy. The second group are those children with poor processing skills in both the visual and phonological domains: Although compensatory use of context may be useful in minimising the problems faced by such children in word decoding, it is not sufficient to maintain a normal rate of reading development. It is these three classes of children—those with generalised intellectual deficits, those with severe deficits in either the visual or phonological domains, and those with both visual and phonological impairments—whose reading development is likely to be handicapped to such an extent that they will be considered dyslexic.

One reason for the prevalence of phonological deficits in developmental dyslexics may be that the phonological recoding strategy is relatively more important for reading development than the visual strategy for an alphabetic script such as English. Perhaps the printed forms of most words are learned via the phonological recoding strategy. This seems likely: Given the enormous number of words that each child learns to read during the early school years, it seems implausible that any more than a small proportion of these words have been explicitly and successfully "taught". It is more likely that children repeatedly encounter the same orthographic fragments that combine to make up printed words, and through phonological recoding provide themselves with many opportunities to learn the links between the printed form of the letter cluster and its spoken equivalent. There may therefore be more tolerance within the developing reading system of poor visual processing skills than there is of inadequate phonological skills: as long as children can phonologically recode with some degree of success, their slow rates of learning visual forms may not matter very much.

A consequence of the dominance of phonologically based reading difficulties in the dyslexic population is that group studies of dyslexics will typically reveal phonological deficits. At an individual level, though, we should not be surprised to find occasionally children whose poor reading development appears to arise from severe problems in developing a sight vocabulary (e.g, Seymour & McGregor, 1984; Temple & Marshall, 1983).

This framework for reading development makes no simple qualitative distinctions between the "normal" poor readers—the children who constitute the bottom 25% or so of the range of normal reading ability—and children whose reading problems are sufficiently severe to be classed dyslexic. The principal characteristics likely to distinguish the typical poor reader from the typical dyslexic are the severity and the breadth of their cognitive deficits, in the ways outlined earlier. The consequences of cognitive impairments that are either more severe within a particular domain or more pervasive across domains may well be catastrophic for reading development. Thus, although the average poor reader and dyslexic may differ in their reading ages by several years, the roots of their reading problems may be rather similar. The principal difference between the two types of reader is that whereas the poor reader may be able to survive at a reasonable level of reading ability by developing strategies to compensate for specific cognitive deficits, the deficits of the dyslexic child are either too severe or too widespread for adequate compensatory strategies to develop.

This chapter provides an overview of reading development. The summary framework for literacy acquisition outlined in the previous section assigns an important role to specialised cognitive skills within the phonological domain. Relatively little has been said so far about how these skills relate to working memory, and in particular how they relate to the phonological loop component of working memory. It is to these issues that we turn in Chapter 6.

CHAPTER SIX

Phonological Processing and Reading Development

Although most people learn to read without encountering significant difficulties, it is clear from Chapter 5 that there are important individual differences in the ease with which children become skilled readers. Children vary greatly in their rate of reading development. Some encounter such severe difficulties in learning to read that they lag considerably behind their peers and never attain normal adult levels of reading ability. These individuals are often classified as dyslexic.

One factor, which has consistently been found to be linked with ease of acquiring literacy, and which differentiates normal children from dyslexics, is the ability to process the sound structure of spoken language. There are many different tasks involving phonological processing in which children of low reading ability perform relatively poorly, but two classes of task are of particular interest here. First, poor readers are impaired in a wide range of *phonological awareness* tasks, in which they are required either to make judgements about or to manipulate the sound structures of words. Secondly, reading achievement during childhood is linked with *phonological short-term memory* ability. Poor readers generally do not perform well in short-term memory tasks such as digit span, serial recall of unrelated strings of words, and the repetition of nonwords.

The purpose of this chapter is to evaluate the links between children's reading success and their skills in both phonological awareness and phonological working memory, and to interpret these links in terms of the framework of reading acquisition outlined in Chapter 5. We focus on two related issues. The first issue concerns whether phonological awareness and phonological memory play causal roles in the process of learning to read. If they do, we need to know what the roles are, and how they relate to the development of the different strategies for reading outlined in the previous chapter. The second issue concerns the relationship between phonological awareness and phonological memory. Do the two types of task tap dissociable skills, or do they both arise from a common phonological substrate? The resolution of this issue has important consequences for the way in which the relationships between phonological processing skills and reading development are characterised, and more particularly for identifying the nature of working memory involvement in the acquisition of literacy.

PHONOLOGICAL AWARENESS AND CHILDREN'S READING

There are many different ways of assessing children's phonological awareness, and the links between phonological awareness and reading development vary according to task (see Goswami & Bryant, 1990, for recent review). An important distinction between awareness tasks concerns the size of the sound unit to which subjects must respond. Some tasks require judgements at the *phoneme* level. For example, the task may be to "say cat without the cuh", or to combine a sequence of phonemes "what word do these sounds make—cuh, ah, tuh?". Other tasks involve the subject responding to larger speech segments, such as syllables. For example, the child might be asked "what word does the following sounds make—he-li-cop-ter?". A unit of sound which is smaller than a syllable but larger than a phoneme is the *rime* of a word. Rime refers to the portion of a syllable which follows its onset, which is typically the initial consonant or consonant cluster. Thus the one-syllable word "cat" can be segmented into an onset—c—and a rime—at. A widely used phonological awareness task known as rhyme oddity detection focuses on the rime portion. In this task the child is asked, for example, "which is the odd word out: *pin, cat, hat?*".

Another important dimension along which phonological awareness tasks vary is the *explicitness* of the judgement that the child makes (e.g. Ellis & Cataldo, in press). Some tasks involve the child making explicit judgements about sound structure. An example of this is the phoneme or syllable tapping task, in which the child has to tap out the number of units of sound in a spoken stimulus (Liberman et al., 1974). In other tasks, the judgement of the sound structure is made by the child in a more *implicit* fashion. A representative implicit awareness task is the rhyme oddity detection paradigm described earlier (e.g. "which is the odd word out: *pin, cat, hat?*"). Although to perform at an above-chance level the child has to be able to make comparisons of the phonological structure of the rime portion of (at least) three items, he or she need not have acquired the explicit concept of "rhyme" to make the correct identification. A similar distinction has been made by Morais, Alegria, and Content (1987), who used the terms *segmental awareness* and *segmental analysis* to distinguish necessary cognitive operations underpinning what we have called here explicit and implicit phonological awareness tasks, respectively.

Children do not acquire all of these kinds of phonological awareness at once. Awareness of syllables occurs prior to awareness of phonemes. Implicit phonological awareness emerges before explicit phonological awareness. In reality, though, the two dimensions of awareness task are largely confounded. Most measures of awareness of phonemes require the child to make explicit judgements of a spoken stimulus (i.e. phoneme segmentation). However, the most influential task involving larger speech segments is the rhyme oddity detection paradigm, and it requires the child to make an implicit judgement. By combining the size of the unit of judgement and the nature of the judgement in phonological awareness tasks in this way, researchers effectively maximise the apparent developmental difference between awareness of phonemes and of supra-phonemic units. For the purposes of this chapter, though, we maintain the usual classification of tasks according to the size of the sound unit (phonemes versus larger segments of speech). In anticipation, the distinction is an important one: Awareness of phonemes and of larger segments of speech have different causal relationships with reading development.

The Development of Phonological Awareness

Children's abilities to make judgements about the phonemic structure of speech stimuli emerge much later, in developmental terms, than their abilities to judge supra-phonemic segments such as syllables or rimes. An early study by Liberman et al. (1974) demonstrated the differential ease with which children can judge phonemic and syllabic structures. These researchers tested nursery children (with a mean age of 4:01 years), kindergarten children (mean age of 5:10 years) and first-grade children (mean age of 6:11 years) on a simple "tapping game". In each trial, the experimenter spoke a word or sound, and the child was asked first to repeat the item, and then to tap out the number of segments it contained. Some of the children were trained to respond to the number of syllables in the spoken item. So, the correct response for the word "lollipop" would be to repeat the word and then tap three times. The other children were trained to tap according to the number of phonemes in the item. For the word "cat", for example, the correct response would be to tap three times.

Figure 6.1 shows the percentage of children at each age in the syllable and phoneme segmentation conditions who reached the criterion of six successive correct trials. None of the nursery children could segment the items by phoneme, but 46% learned to segment by syllable. A small proportion of the kindergarten children succeeded in phoneme segmentation (17%), whereas 48% successfully segmented by syllable. Of the first-grade children, 70% learned to segment by phoneme, and nearly all of them (90%) were successful in the syllable task.

The superior performance of young children in tasks involving the manipulation of syllables rather than phonemes is by no means restricted to the tapping paradigm (e.g. Lundberg et al., 1988; Stanovich, Cunningham, & Cramer, 1984a). Why should it be that children find it easier to make judgements about syllables than phonemes? The answer seems likely to lie in the different relationships that syllables and phonemes have with their associated patterns of sound. Whereas the syllabic structure of a word is usually identifiable on the basis of concentrations of acoustic energy across time, there are no simple acoustic correlates of the phonemic structure.

Consider, for example, the sound pattern corresponding to the word "bag". The middle phoneme in this word—the vowel sound /a/—is influenced by both the previous and subsequent phonemes. Thus, information about all three phonemes in the words is being transmitted more or less simultaneously (Liberman, 1970). This is due to the phenomenon of *co-articulation*, whereby the positioning of a speaker's articulators while a particular phoneme is being produced are influenced by preparation for the target position for the next sound, and by the positioning of the articulators when the previous sound was being produced. An important consequence of this parallel transmission of phonemic information in the acoustic message is that the abstract phonological structure of the utterance cannot be transparently "read" on a phoneme-by-phoneme basis from the physical signal.

The mechanisms by which listeners derive phonological structure from these interactive acoustic signals are complex, and seem likely to

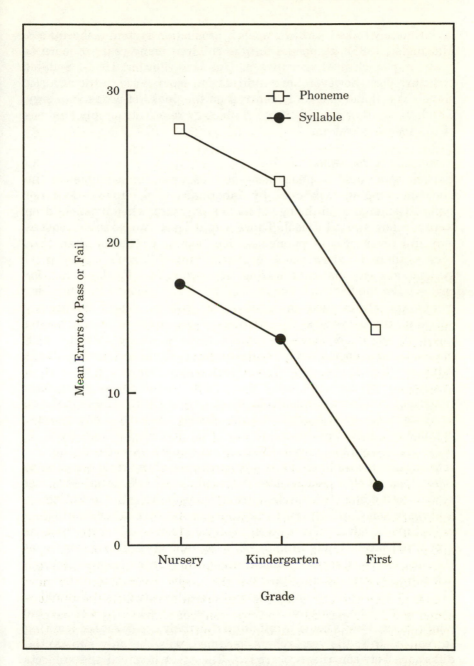

FIG. 6.1. Mean errors of the three age groups to passing or failing criterion of six consecutive trials in the phoneme and syllable segmentation tasks. Adapted from Liberman, Shankweiler, Fischer, and Carter (1974).

be intimately linked with the speech production system (Liberman & Mattingley, 1985). It appears to take children many years to learn to abstract phonological structure in this way (Fowler, 1991). Syllabic structure does, however, have a direct correspondence in the acoustic signal—a syllable is usually centred on the peaks of acoustic energy. Children can therefore identify syllables by relatively simply analysis of the speech waveform.

Awareness of Phonemes
Explicit awareness of phonemes—as measured, for example, in the phoneme tapping task used by Liberman et al. (1974)—does not typically emerge until the age of five or six years, when most children have already started school. There are at least two possible reasons why full awareness of phonemes does not occur earlier than this. Firstly, there is considerable evidence that children's phonological systems are still maturing during this period (see Fowler, 1991, for review). For the first few years of a child's life, it appears that familiar words are represented in a wholistic fashion, based on loosely specified configurations of articulatory gestures. With increasing maturity, the child learns to replace these wholistic patterns with abstract phonological representations of familiar words. It is estimated that this period of phonological development in the speech system is not complete until the age of about seven years (e.g. Nittrouer, Studdert-Kennedy, & MacGowan, 1989). Thus phoneme awareness may emerge when it does—during the early school years—because it is rooted in the child's maturing phonological system.

Secondly, the rapid improvement in phoneme awareness during the school years is also likely to be a consequence of the child learning to read. This point is neatly demonstrated in an influential series of studies by a group of researchers from Brussels. Morais, Cary, Alegria, and Bertelson (1979) studied the phonological segmentation abilities of Portuguese adults who were either illiterate or ex-illiterate. Neither group had received any formal schooling during childhood, for social reasons; the ex-illiterates had subsequently learned to read through attending special adult literacy classes. The issue that interested Morais et al. was whether illiterate and ex-illiterate groups differed in phono- logical segmentation ability. Any advantage of the ex-illiterate adults in such tasks could be attributed to their experience of learning to read as this, the researchers assumed, was the only substantial difference between the two groups. The tests involved the subjects repeating a word or nonword spoken by the experimenter, and then either deleting the initial segment (e.g. "purso" became "urso") or adding a segment at the beginning (e.g. "uva" became "chuva").

Feedback was given during practice trials, but not during the experimental trials.

The differences between the groups were dramatic. For nonwords, the illiterates made on average 19% correct responses in both the deletion and addition tests, and over half failed to make a correct response at all. The ex-illiterates made 71% correct responses for the addition test, and 73% for the deletion trials. None of this group failed every trial. These results suggest that literacy training is indeed instrumental in boosting phonological segmentation ability.

Other findings indicate that this boosting of phonological segmentation skill is a consequence specifically of alphabetic literacy, rather than of literacy *per se*. Read, Zhang, Nie, and Ding (1986) studied the phonological segmentation abilities of two groups of Chinese readers. One group was taught to use the traditional Chinese *logographic* script, in which complex symbols have a nonphonological relationship with words. The other group used the alphabetic orthography for the Chinese language, known as *pinyin*. Using the same measures of phoneme deletion and segmentation that Morais et al. (1979) employed in their study of the Portuguese illiterates, Read et al. found that whereas the subjects who used the nonalphabetic script performed poorly, with a mean performance level of 21%, the pinyin-trained group gained high scores in these measures, with a mean performance level of 83%. The implication of this result is clear: Phonemic segmentation ability is stimulated by learning an alphabetic orthography. It seems likely that this is because such orthographies exploit explicit knowledge of the phonological constitution of words.

What is it about learning to read that promotes explicit phonemic awareness in this way? An important hurdle in literacy development for most children is to grasp the alphabetic principle: printed words contain combinations of visual units (letters, or letter combinations) that are systematically related to the sounds units in the words (phonemes). Thus, the sounds associated with each letter of the English alphabet correspond to single phonemes. The correspondence is not, of course, perfect—there are many irregular words in the printed form of English whose sound pattern could not be derived simply by applying either letter–sound correspondences or higher-level (multiple-letter) mappings of graphemes onto phonemes. Nonetheless, there is a probabilistic relationship between letters (and letter groups) and sounds which can be usefully exploited by the child, via a phonological recoding strategy, in both reading and spelling (see Chapter 5 for a more detailed discussion of phonological recoding in reading development).

It seems likely that early reading development, and in particular the acquisition of the alphabetic principle, boosts the child's abilities to segment speech explicitly at a phonological level. It probably does so by focusing the child on the phonological structure of words. Once the child can identify some or all of the phonemes in a word, a phonological recoding strategy can be adopted. The principal benefit of this strategy is that it provides an opportunity to either read or spell words whose visual characteristics are not already known, and so are not part of the sight vocabulary.

It is not, however, the case that explicit phoneme awareness *only* arises from training in alphabetic literacy. Phoneme segmentation ability can be acquired without the child learning to read. Olofsson and Lundberg (1985) found that a small proportion of prereading kindergarten children were able to segment explicitly at the phoneme level. Note, though, that because children do not enter schools in Sweden until the age of about seven, the prereaders in this sample were older than the typical prereaders in North American or British studies. There is therefore greater opportunity for maturation of the phonological system in the Swedish sample. Nonetheless, the finding does show that some children acquire explicit phonemic awareness without being taught to read.

Explicit phoneme awareness can also be *trained* in prereading children. A number of studies have shown that in an experimental context segmentation ability is boosted by direct practice at a phoneme segmentation task (Content, Kolinsky, Morais, & Bertelson, 1986; Fox & Routh, 1975). More importantly, though, phonological awareness has been shown to be trainable over much longer periods as a consequence of training given in the preschool period. Once again, it is notable that the best example of preschool phoneme awareness comes from a study of prereading children in a country—this time, Denmark—in which school entry is delayed until the age of seven.

Lundberg et al. (1988) designed a training program to stimulate phonological awareness in 235 six-year-old Danish children. The training programme started initially at the beginning of the children's preschool year. During this year, the children were given daily sessions of meta-linguistic games and exercises; these included a variety of rhyming games, followed by practice in segmenting speech utterances into progressively smaller units, from identifying individual words in sentences to isolating phonemes within words. Thus the programme was structured to focus children on increasingly fine-grained components of speech—starting at the level of words, and differentiating progressively through to the syllabic and subsyllabic (phoneme) level.

Measures of reading, spelling, and mathematical ability were taken approximately one and a half years, and two years, later. Tests of the children's performance in various tasks of explicit awareness of sound structure were also given at a number of intervals during the longitudinal study. The performance of the experimental group at each stage was compared with a control group of children who followed the regular Danish preschool programme, which did not provide a notable emphasis on metalinguistic development.

Figure 6.2 shows the mean scores of the two groups before and after the programme, derived by combining the scores across the three phoneme segmentation tests (phoneme deletion, phoneme segmentation, and phoneme synthesis). The experimental group showed a dramatic increase in explicit phoneme awareness after the training programme, relative to the control children. Much more modest (although significant) improvements in word and syllable segmentation tasks were found for the experimental group at posttest. Performance was, however, much better in these tasks than the phoneme level segmentation measures; the absence of a dramatic promotion of syllable segmentation in the experimental group may therefore be due to a ceiling effect.

The important point is that these results show that phoneme segmentation skills can be trained in prereading children, and hence that segmentation ability is not simply a consequence of early reading experience. It should be noted, however, that the same kind of training programme might well not be successful if directed at four-year-old prereaders from other countries. It seems possible that due to the process of increasing phonological maturation of the speech systems, which proceeds up to the age of seven years at least, programmes designed to boost explicit phoneme awareness will be maximally effective when targeted at children at the upper end of this age range, whose basic speech representations are themselves likely to be more analytic.

Returning to the Lundberg et al. (1988) training study, the most important finding concerned the impact of the training in phonological awareness on the children's subsequent literacy achievement. Scores in both reading and spelling measures were substantially greater in the experimental group two years after the training programme had commenced. The impact of the programme, though, was restricted to literacy development. In fact, in measures of mathematical attainment, the control group outperformed the experimental group.

In summary, the findings from Lundberg et al.'s training study establish an important causal link between explicit phoneme

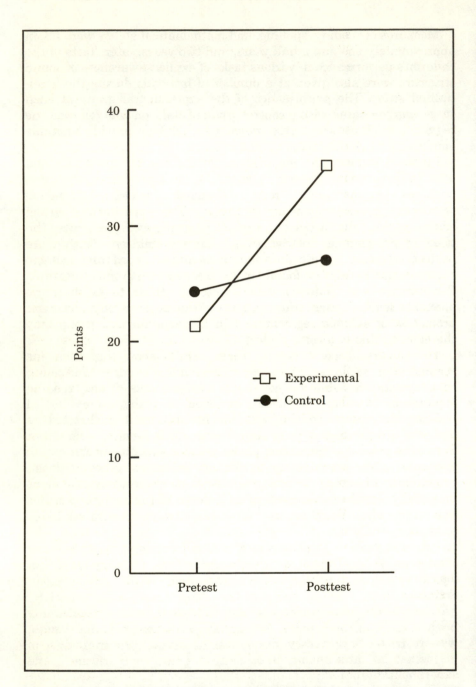

FIG. 6.2. Scores combined across all metaphonological tasks for both groups at pretest and posttest. Adapted from Lundberg, Frost, and Petersen (1988).

awareness and subsequent literacy development. The findings of Morais et al. (1979) and Read et al. (1986), however, appeared to favour the converse causal connection, which is that learning an alphabetic orthography itself promotes explicit awareness at the phoneme level. Despite supporting two opposing causal hypotheses concerning the links between awareness of phonemes and reading development, these two sets of findings are not incompatible with one another. Phoneme awareness and reading ability probably develop reciprocally during the early school years (e.g. Bertelson, Morais, Alegria, & Content, 1985).

What, then, is the developmental sequence of this interactive relationship between reading and phoneme awareness? It seems likely that for children learning to read at a relatively young age, the initial pacemaker in the reciprocal relationship is the activity of learning to read. Once children start to learn that letters are associated, they need to be able to identify the constituent phonemes in spoken words if they are to apply successfully a phonological recoding strategy. Thus, early reading development will stimulate the development of explicit awareness of phonemes. The extent to which children are successful in developing their phonemic awareness will then influence their ease of acquiring an alphabetic strategy for reading and spelling. Thus, after the initial stages of reading development, reading ability and phonemic awareness are likely to facilitate one another.

This characterisation of reading as the initial pacemaker in the interactive relationship may not always hold. It is clear from Lundberg et al.'s (1988) training study that explicit awareness of phonemes can be stimulated without direct reference to the alphabetic principle, by providing the children with a rich linguistic environment in which they are encouraged to differentiate progressively smaller units of sound. Whether this type of activity would work with prereading children who are considerably younger than the six-year-old Danish subjects participating in this study, though, is open to question. The rapid gains made by this relatively old group may be due in part at least to the near maturity of their phonological systems.

This maturational position is also supported by the results of a further study by the Brussels group with Portuguese illiterate adults. Morais, Content, Bertelson, Cary, and Kolinsky (1988) trained their subjects in an initial phoneme deletion task (e.g. "fak" became "ak"). Despite poor initial performance in these explicit phoneme awareness measures, many of the illiterates rapidly learned to make the required phoneme deletion. The group was 69% accurate in the final block of trials. It therefore appears to be much easier to acquire explicit awareness of phonemes in adulthood rather than during the prereading years. Again, this result points to phoneme awareness depending to some extent at least on the maturation of the speech system.

There is a great deal of evidence that individual differences in awareness of phonemes and reading ability are closely linked, in line with this interactive framework. Poor readers have been found to perform at a consistently lower level in phoneme segmentation tasks than good readers of the same age, and the same nonverbal intelligence level (e.g. Mann & Liberman, 1984). Similar findings of a close relationship between the two sets of measures emerge from correlational studies. Reading ability and performance in phoneme awareness tasks have been found on many occasions to be highly related to one another during the early school years, even after more general factors, such as age and general intelligence, have been taken into account (e.g. Stanovich et al., 1984a,b; Tunmer & Nesdale, 1985).

Our account earlier of a reciprocal relationship between phonological awareness and reading development identified the point at which the child "cracks the alphabetic code" as the catalyst for the development of phoneme awareness. According to most theories of reading development, the alphabetic strategy follows the initial logographic strategy for reading, in which the child learns new words simply in terms of their visual configurations. It should therefore be the case that the relationship between measures of phoneme awareness and reading should become increasingly close as reading ability develops. There is considerable support for this view. A number of longitudinal studies have shown that scores in tests that assess explicit phoneme segmentation during the first year or so of schooling are not particularly effective predictors of very early reading development (e.g. Ellis & Large, 1988; Stuart & Coltheart, 1988). The major contribution of explicit phoneme awareness to reading development appears to emerge at about the second year of reading (Ellis & Large, 1988; Ellis & Cataldo, in press). Beyond this point, phonological awareness and reading ability maintain a close relationship that appears to be interactive rather than unidirectional.

The study by Ellis and Cataldo is particularly interesting, as it focuses on the causal relationship that phonological awareness has with both spelling and reading. The detailed aspects of their results need not concern us here. The important point to emerge from their causal analyses of their longitudinal database is that spelling is the major catalyst for the emergence of explicit awareness of phonemes, which in turn predicts subsequent reading development. Early spelling ability itself was predicted by the children's performance in a measure of implicit phonological awareness which focused on multiple-phoneme segments. As Ellis and Cataldo point out, this interactive developmental sequence fits well with the characterisations of reading development provided by Frith (1985). According to this theory, children start to use a rudimentary alphabetic strategy to guide their spelling attempts. Once the strategy has become established, it is then applied to reading.

So far, we have not considered the basis of the shared individual differences found in measures of explicit awareness of phonemes and in reading development. One view is that the roots of significant differences between children in terms of their phonological awareness and their reading ability lie in the quality of their phonological representations. Specifically, it has been suggested that the central deficit in children who make poor reading progress is weak or inadequate phonological coding within the speech system (e.g. Liberman, 1989; Shankweiler & Crain, 1986). As a consequence of their poor speech coding, these children will be less able to segment speech strings than others, and so will be handicapped in their attempts to apply a phonological recoding strategy for reading. Morais et al. (1987) take a similar stance, suggesting that the causes of developmental reading difficulties lie in the perceptual representations of speech.

Awareness of Larger Sound Segments

Even before starting school, many children show some knowledge of the syllabic structure of spoken stimuli. Half of the nursery children tested by Liberman et al. (1974) could tap out the number of syllables in words. Some preschool children can also perform reliably in tasks that involve implicit judgements of the rime portion of words. For example, Bryant, Bradley, MacLean, and Crossland (1989) tested children at the ages of three and four years on a measure of rhyme detection, in which they had to detect the word that did not share the same ending as the other two in a spoken sequence (e.g. "peg", "leg", "sun"). Of the 64 three-year-olds tested, 14 performed at an above-chance level in this task. Fifteen months later, almost half of the children performed reliably in this task. This developmental improvement between three and four years of age was not a consequence of early reading development, as even at the later time most of the children had still not started school.

Measures of awareness of rhyme and syllables can therefore be obtained from children *before* they start learning to read, in contrast to phoneme awareness, which appears to be stimulated initially *as a consequence* of early reading experience. Two hypotheses concerning the developmental role of awareness of rhyme have been considered. The first hypothesis is that awareness of rhyme makes a causal contribution to early reading development. The second hypothesis is that rhyme awareness is an important precursor of the later, more analytic, phoneme awareness ability. Findings from longitudinal studies have provided support for both of these hypotheses.

This issue has been studied extensively by Bradley, Bryant and colleagues from Oxford. They have conducted several longitudinal studies in which measures of rhyme awareness were given to children before they started school or to read (Bradley & Bryant, 1983; Bryant, MacLean, Bradley, & Crossland, 1990). These measures were then used as predictors of the children's later reading and spelling achievements some years later.

In each study, a significant and specific relationship was found between preschool rhyme awareness and later scores in literacy measures. Bradley and Bryant (1983) obtained a combined awareness measure that tapped the children's sensitivity to rhyme and alliteration (in which the first two phonemes in the words were shared) at the ages of four and five years. This measure accounted for significant portions of unique variance in reading and spelling achievement four years later (between 4 and 10%, across measures), even after differences due to the children's vocabulary and short-term memory skills had been controlled. Similar results were obtained by Bryant et al. (1990). Rhyme oddity detection scores at age four acted as significant predictors of reading and spelling scores two years later, after age, mother's educational level, vocabulary, and IQ had been partialled out.

These longitudinal predictive relationships between early awareness of rhyme and later literacy achievements are certainly consistent with the hypothesis that children's awareness of sound structure plays a causal role in their reading. Bradley and Bryant (1983) attempted to address this hypothesis more directly, by training phonological awareness in subjects from their longitudinal sample whose scores in their sound categorisation measures were unusually low. The results from the training study were generally supportive of the hypothesis that rhyme awareness is important for reading development. The group trained in sound categorisation showed a three- to four-month superiority in reading and spelling measures ahead of a control group trained in conceptual categorisation. The difference was not, however, significant. A group of children trained in both sound categorisation and simple alphabetic correspondences (with the aid of plastic letters) did show significant gains in terms of reading and spelling achievement, though.

The results from this training study are therefore ambiguous. Training in both categorisation of sounds and familiarising the children with letters seems to promote literacy development. It is, however, well-established that prereading children's knowledge of letters is an excellent predictor of later reading achievement (e.g. Ellis & Large, 1988; Tunmer, Herriman, & Nesdale, 1988). It may therefore be unsurprising that promoting familiarity with the alphabet will result in gains in reading development.

So far we have not considered the nature of the relationship between awareness of intrasyllabic units, such as the rhyming portions of words, and awareness of phonemes. Are the two skills completely independent of one another, or are they related? One plausible version of the second alternative is that awareness of rhyme is the developmental precursor of explicit phoneme segmentation ability. Progress in differentiating the larger units of sound corresponding to rimes and syllables, which is probably based on analysis of acoustic features such as the amplitude envelope of the speech stream, may be achieved before the child can start identifying and representing the abstract phonological structure of speech stimuli. Another level of description of this developmental relationship is that phonological awareness becomes increasingly explicit with time (Ellis & Cataldo, in press).

The longitudinal study reported by Bryant et al. (1990) provides some important data on the nature of the developmental relationship between rhyme awareness and phoneme awareness, and on the links of each with reading success. In addition to taking measures of rhyme oddity detection from their sample at initial testing, when the children were aged four years, these researchers assessed explicit phoneme segmentation one year later. Three tasks were used— deletion of the first phoneme, deletion of the second phoneme, and phoneme tapping. (The explicit phoneme awareness tests could not be administered at the earlier time of testing, as the children would have found them too difficult). The outcome measures were two tests of reading and one test of spelling, administered when the children were six and a half years old.

By taking this range of measures, Bryant et al. (1990) were able to determine whether or not rhyme awareness and phoneme awareness have independent links with reading development. Firstly, they established that both the rhyme detection measure and the scores in the three phoneme awareness tasks were significantly related to later reading and spelling achievement. Scores in the first phoneme deletion task, the phoneme tapping task, and the rhyme detection tasks were all significantly linked with subsequent reading and spelling scores, even after age, mother's educational level, vocabulary scores, and IQ had been taken into account. These findings are consistent with the view that phoneme awareness and earlier awareness of rhyme are related.

Secondly, Bryant et al. (1990) tested whether rhyme detection ability was a significant predictor of later literacy attainment after the variance accounted for by phoneme awareness had been taken into account. This was indeed found to be the case: Scores in the rhyme detection test significantly predicted reading and spelling achievement even when entered after the phoneme awareness measures into the multiple regression equations.

On the basis of these results, Bryant et al. (1990) concluded that there are two causal connections between awareness of rhyme and literacy acquisition (see Fig. 6.3). The first is an indirect link between rhyme awareness and later reading and spelling, which is mediated by phoneme awareness. These authors suggest that the contribution made by sensitivity to phonemes is to help the child learn grapheme–phoneme correspondences and hence acquire a phonological recoding strategy. The second causal route runs directly from rhyme awareness to spelling and reading. Bryant et al. (1990) proposed that this route has nothing to do with the development of a phonological recoding strategy in reading. Instead, they speculated that it reflects the influence of sensitivity to rhyme on children's learning of spelling patterns. Specifically, they pointed to Goswami's (1986) research, which showed that children quickly learn that words with the same

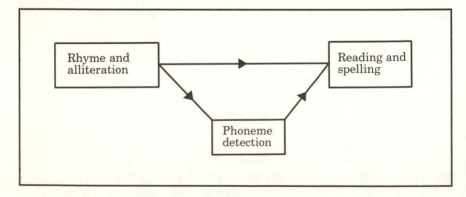

FIG. 6.3. The hypothesised causal relationships between rhyme and alliteration abilities, phoneme detection skills, and the development of reading and spelling. Adapted from Bryant, Maclean, Bradley, and Crossland (1990).

ending (rhyme) often share a common spelling pattern, and that they use this knowledge in their attempts to spell words that are not in their sight vocabulary. The idea, then, is that the adequacy of children's skills at detecting common rhyme segments in words will be determine the utility of this strategy of spelling by analogy, and so will influence the rate of development of reading and spelling ability.

This suggestion that there are two ways in which young children's awareness of the sound structure of spoken stimuli influences the acquisition of literacy is an interesting and influential one. It should be noted, though, that the direct causal link between phoneme awareness and both reading and spelling one year later may be overestimated. By the age of five and a half years, most British children will have started to read. Thus their performance on the phoneme awareness tests at this time may be a consequence in part at least of their early reading success. In the absence of measures of reading at the same time as the phoneme awareness measures, it is unfortunately impossible to rule out this possibility that reading is influencing performance in the phoneme manipulation tasks, rather than vice versa.

Returning to the relationship between prereading sensitivity to rhyme and later success in learning to read and spell, a primary theoretical issue concerns the *origins* of individual differences in rhyme awareness. Why can some children more easily detect shared rhyme portions of words than others? There are a number of obvious possibilities. The children may differ in the adequacy of their representations of speech stimuli. This account corresponds closely to the one proposed by Liberman (1989), according to which the basis of the defective performance of poor readers on phonological processing tasks is their weak phonological encoding. This account seems particularly plausible if, as Bryant et al. (1990) suggest, sensitivity to rhyme is a developmental precursor to phoneme awareness.

There is evidence that sensitivity to rhyme in prereading children can be stimulated by a rich linguistic environment. Bryant, Bradley, MacLean, and Crossland (1989) tested the nursery rhyme knowledge of three-year-old children participating in their longitudinal study, and found that this factor was a significant predictor of later reading. Obvious differences in socio-economic status of the children, and of parental educational achievement, were controlled in this analysis. Most importantly, once nursery rhyme knowledge had been included in the regression analysis, the measure of rhyme awareness taken when the children were four years old no longer accounted for significant portions of variance in the reading and spelling scores taken two years later. This suggests that children's sensitivity to rhyme emerges from their experience and knowledge of linguistic material, and in particular that it is rooted in familiarity with nursery rhymes, whose prosodic structure emphasises shared sounds in words.

A final point here is that the relationship between knowledge of nursery rhymes and later achievement in literacy skills may be due to either environmental or constitutional factors. An obvious possibility is that the children with best knowledge of nursery rhymes at the age of three years were those children who had had most exposure to that kind of rich linguistic experience. Alternatively, though, these children may simply be most effective at representing and learning phonological material. A project currently underway in our laboratory is investigating these alternative hypotheses, by providing a longitudinal study of the developmental relationships between awareness of rhyme, phonological memory, and nursery rhyme knowledge in preschool children. Measures are also being obtained of the emphasis placed by parents on providing the child with different types of linguistic experience. In this way, we hope shortly to be able to identify the relative contribution of environmental and phonological factors in the emergence of cultural linguistic knowledge such as nursery rhymes.

Phonological Awareness and Phonological Recoding

There is little doubt that children's awareness of the sound structure of spoken language is related to the ease with which they learn to read and to spell during the early school years. There are, however, a number of different levels of knowledge about the structure of language that can be distinguished, and each of these levels shares a complex developmental relationship with literacy acquisition. An early form of phonological awareness involves awareness of syllables and intra-syllabic segments such as rimes, which emerges for many children in the preschool years, and before reading starts. Many four-year-old prereading children can, for example, judge which words rhyme and which do not. Sensitivity to rhyme during this preschool period is a good predictor of later success in learning to read and write. It has been suggested that one important reason for this is that words that rhyme often share common spelling patterns. Thus, an ability to detect rhyme will allow the child the opportunity to spell, and to read, by analogy.

Skills at segmenting spoken words at the level of individual phonemes typically emerge later, at about five or six years of age. At this time, most children are already learning to read. Reading skill and phoneme awareness appear to have a reciprocal relationship, developing in a mutually facilitative manner. There are, however, important individual differences in the ease with which children learn to segment speech into phonemes. Some theorists have suggested that children who have difficulty in developing phoneme segmentation skills have basic deficiencies in the way in which they represent phonological information.

Phoneme awareness skills in young children are closely associated with reading development. What, then, is the specific nature of the relationship? It seems most likely that awareness of phonemes is critical for the successful development of the phonological recoding strategy for reading and spelling. A child attempting to spell a word by phonological recoding will need to identify the component sounds of the target word ("cat" is /k/ /æ/ /t/) and then to map each phoneme onto its associated letter if the attempt is to be successful. It is therefore unsurprising that the child's skills at decomposing the phonemic structure of spoken stimuli—as indexed by measures of phoneme segmentation—are positively associated with its abilities to use a phonological recoding strategy for reading and spelling.

Although phoneme awareness appears to be necessary for the successful development of a phonological recoding strategy, some recent results indicate that it is not a sufficient condition. In order to capitalise on their phonological segmentation abilities in reading and spelling, young children also appear to need basic knowledge of letter-sound correspondences. Byrne and Fielding-Barnsley (1989) trained a group of prereading four-year-old children in phoneme segmentation, but found that even the children who did learn to segment at this level also needed to have explicit knowledge of the associations between individual letters and phonemes in order to be able to recode phonologically an unfamiliar letter string. Children appear not to readily infer these alphabetic correspondences, and need to be explicitly taught them in order to be able to apply their phonemic awareness skills in the development of a phonological recoding strategy.

Similar conclusions emerge from a rather different kind of study reported by Tunmer et al. (1988). These researchers conducted a two-year longitudinal study of children that started in the first year of school. Measures of reading, phonological awareness, and letter identification were taken. Both phonological awareness and letter knowledge were found to be significant predictors of reading ability at the end of the first year. The awareness measures accounted for 23% of variance in the pseudoword reading scores, and letter knowledge accounted for a further 16% of reading variance. Most importantly, though, the interaction between the phonological awareness and letter knowledge measures (obtained by multiplying one with the other) itself accounted for a further significant 4% of variance in the reading scores. It appears that this interaction is due to the fact that good reading scores were only achieved when the children had high levels of both phoneme awareness and letter knowledge. Poor performance of either of these types of measure were associated with much lower levels of pseudoword reading accuracy.

In summary, then, the development of a phonological recoding strategy for reading and spelling appears to require both phonemic awareness and specific knowledge about alphabetic correspondences. Why, though, do some children fail to develop adequate phonemic awareness and alphabetic knowledge? No clear answer is available as yet. The view currently favoured by theorists, though, is that the root causes of reading difficulties lie in weak or inadequate phonological encoding. Although there is some evidence that such inadequacies may be genetic in origin (Olson, Wise, Connors, & Rack, 1990), there are also clear indications that environmental and cultural experiences may be critical to the development of children's representations of the speech code.

PHONOLOGICAL WORKING MEMORY AND CHILDREN'S READING

Although phonological awareness probably represents the phonological processing ability that has been most closely linked with reading development, there is substantial evidence too that the ease with which children learn to read is associated with their skills in *phonological short-term memory tasks*. The remainder of this chapter focuses on this developmental association between phonological memory and literacy. In the first part, we evaluate the evidence linking reading ability with phonological memory skills. In the second part, we consider whether phonological awareness and phonological memory are independent of one another, and whether they play differentiable roles during the years when children are learning to read and to spell.

Detailed reviews of a wide range of studies exploring phonological working memory in children of different reading abilities are provided by Jorm (1983), Torgesen (1978) and Wagner and Torgesen (1987). Here we will not attempt an extensive review, but focus instead on some representative studies, which investigate the relationship between reading ability and phonological memory.

Group Studies of Good and Poor Readers

The earliest links between reading and phonological memory emerged from studies comparing the short-term memory characteristics of groups of children of good and poor reading ability. In a series of influential experiments, I. Liberman, Mann, Shankweiler, and colleagues from Haskins Laboratories demonstrated that poor readers have specific deficits of short-term memory. One of the principal paradigms that this research group used to explore the phonological memory characteristics of children of different reading abilities involved comparing their serial recall of lists of memory items that were either phonologically confusable (e.g. *b, c, d, g*) or phonologically distinct (e.g. *h, k, q, w*). The effects on immediate memory of varying the phonological similarity of a memory sequence was outlined in Chapter 1. Serial recall is disrupted when lists contain items that are phonologically similar, in both adults (e.g. Conrad & Hull, 1964) and children (e.g. Hitch & Halliday, 1983). According to the current model of working memory, the phonological similarity effect reflects the contribution to immediate memory of the phonological storage component of the phonological loop.

Shankweiler et al. (1979) tested eight-year-old children who were either superior, marginal or poor readers. The children in each group were matched for IQ, which was well above normal level. In Experiment 2, sequences of five letter sequences that were either phonologically distinct or phonologically confusable were presented visually to the children in each group, for immediate written recall. Results were scored in terms of the number of errors made across all list positions for each subject, and the findings are shown in Fig. 6.4.

Two important findings emerged from this experiment. Firstly, the good readers made fewer recall errors than either the marginal or the poor readers. Secondly, although there was a general increase in recall when nonconfusable as opposed to confusable list items were used, the beneficial effect of phonological distinctiveness was significantly greater for the good readers than for the other two groups. The superior readers made fewer errors in recall of the phonologically nonconfusable lists (e.g. *h, k, l, q*) than either the marginal or the poor readers.

Similar results were found in a corresponding experiment in this series that used auditorily presented consonant sequences. This replication across presentation modality establishes that the inferior phonological memory performance of the children of poorer reading skill is not simply a consequence of their problems in reading the to-be-remembered items, but instead reflects a general characteristic

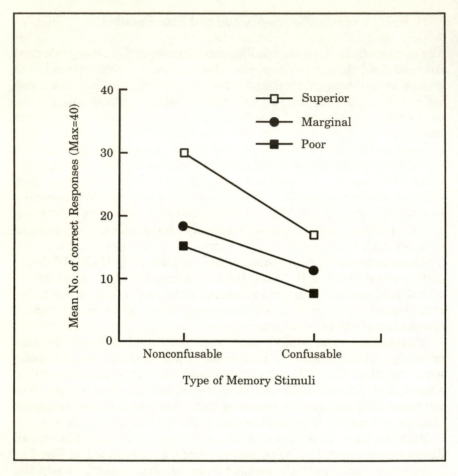

FIG. 6.4. Performance of the reading ability groups in tests of memory for visually presented acoustically confusable and nonfusable letter sequences. Adapted from Shankweiler, Liberman, Mark, Fowler, and Fischer (1979).

of their phonological memory skills. Specifically, the findings suggest that the phonological store component of the phonological loop is impaired in children with poor reading development. If the phonological store was reduced in capacity in these children, it would indeed be expected that they would show lower overall immediate memory performance. The reduced phonological similarity effect of the poor readers suggests that these children might have been relying instead on some other form of memory coding. Accordingly, Shankweiler et al. (1979) interpreted the results as suggesting weak or defective coding in the phonological working memory of inferior readers.

This interpretation has been supported and extended by findings of further studies reported by this research group. The poorer serial recall performance and the reduced sensitivity to phonological similarity of poor readers found by Shankweiler et al. (1979) has also been found with more meaningful memory lists. Mann, Liberman, and Shankweiler (1980) compared the effects of phonological similarity on good and poor readers' recall of meaningful and meaningless sentences. An example of a phonologically confusable meaningful sentence used in this study was "Don't roar any more at the store's door or Miss Moore will get sore". The matched meaningless sentence, also highly confusable, was "Don't sing at the ring's sting or the king will get winged". For both meaningful and meaningless memory sequences, good readers accurately recalled more items than a group of poor readers, and were more disrupted by the highly confusable memory lists.

Results reported by Liberman, Mann, Shankweiler, and Werfelman (1982) suggest that the immediate memory deficit is confined to verbal material, as we would expect if the locus of the deficit is phonological working memory. Liberman et al. used a continuous recognition paradigm, in which the children were presented with a long series of visual stimuli, and had to respond to each item by saying "yes" if they thought the item had been presented earlier in the sequence, and "no" if they thought it had not. The stimuli consisted either of nonsense syllables, unfamiliar faces, or nonsense line drawings. The mean performance of the eight-year-old good and poor readers on each set of stimuli is shown in Fig. 6.5.

No significant differences in recognition performance were found across reading ability groups for either the nonsense designs or the faces, but the good readers were significantly better at recognising the nonsense syllables than the poor readers. The memory deficit associated with low reading ability is therefore restricted to linguistic stimuli, and does not reflect a general memory deficit. The generalisation of poor phonological memory performance in children of low reading attainment from the more usual serial recall procedure to a continuous recognition paradigm also indicates that the deficit is not restricted to tasks explicitly requiring the retention of order information.

The general pattern of findings reported by these researchers have been replicated by other research groups (e.g. Olson, Davidson, Kliegl, & Davies, 1984; Siegel & Linder, 1984). The studies have, however, relied largely on comparisons of the phonological memory characteristics of good and poor readers of the same chronological age. But, as we discussed in Chapter 5, differences in reading group

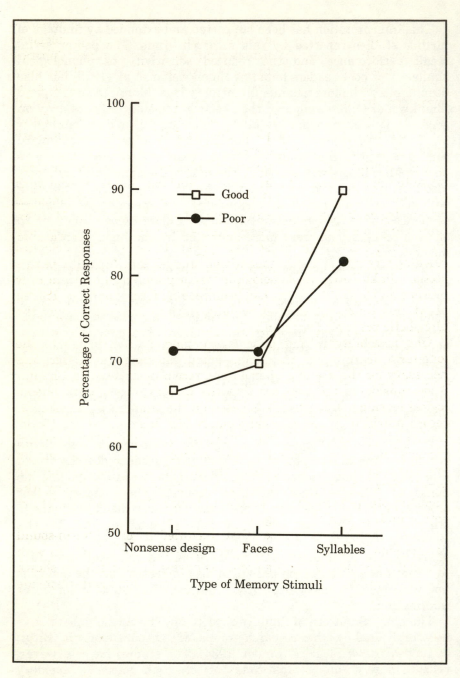

FIG. 6.5. Mean recall performance of good and poor readers as a function of type of memory stimuli. Adapted from Liberman, Mann, Shankweiler, and Werfelman (1982).

designs of this type are consistent with many different causal (and indeed, noncausal) hypotheses. Specifically, the poor phonological memory skills of poor readers could be on the one hand the underlying cause of their reading difficulties, or alternatively a consequence of their lesser reading attainment. In order to uncover the causal structure of the relationship between phonological memory and reading development, it is necessary to turn to alternative methodologies.

A number of studies have compared the phonological memory performance of poor readers with younger control children of matched reading age, and have obtained mixed results. Following the procedure used by Shankweiler et al. (1979), Johnston (1982) compared serial recall of lists of phonologically confusable or nonconfusable consonants in groups of 9-, 12- and 14-year-old children classified as dyslexic. The memory sequences were presented auditorily, and the children attempted to repeat them at recall. The performance of these children was compared with both chronological age controls and reading-age-matched controls.

Although the dyslexic children performed more poorly overall in this serial recall task than their age-matched controls, there was no difference in memory performance between the dyslexic groups and their reading-age matches. Moreover in this study, all groups—normal readers and dyslexics—were equivalently disrupted by highly confusable sequences. These findings appear to conflict with Shankweiler et al.'s earlier findings that poor readers are less sensitive to phonological similarity than good readers (of the same age). One possible reason for the apparent conflict may arise from the age differences of the dyslexic subjects across different studies. Older children were tested by Johnston (1982) than by Shankweiler et al. (1979), and there is some independent evidence suggesting that poor readers do become more sensitive to phonological similarity in memory tasks as they grow older (Olson et al., 1984).

More importantly, though, the dyslexic children did not have poorer serial recall than the younger children of matched reading ability. Null results in this type of design, where poor readers are matched with younger normal readers of the same overall reading ability, are ambiguous, as we discussed in Chapter 5. The equivalence of phonological memory skills of the two groups is equally consistent with two converse causal hypotheses: That phonological memory skills contribute to reading development, and in contrast that reading success stimulates memory development.

Subsequent work has confirmed both the equivalence in overall phonological memory performance of poor readers and younger reading-matched controls, and the sensitivity of the poor readers to phonological similarity of memory items. Hall, Wilson, Humphreys, Tinzmann, and Bowyer (1983) investigated the possibility that the interaction between reading ability and phonological confusability found by Shankweiler et al. (1979) and Mann et al. (1980) could reflect a floor effect in the level of memory performance of the poor readers. Hall et al. tested the sensitivity to phonological confusability of a memory list of eight-year-old poor readers of either normal or low general intellectual ability, using relatively short lists of either four or five items. The mean level of memory performance in all three relevant experiments reported in this paper was between 30% and 60% for the confusable sequences for each group. The simple results to emerge from these studies was that the poor readers of normal IQ were not impaired in recall of the visually presented letter strings, and that each group was disrupted to a similar extent with the phonologically confusable lists. Only the poor readers of low general ability showed impaired recall performance, but even this group was found to be sensitive to phonological confusability.

Findings reported more recently by Johnston, Rugg, and Scott (1987) are also consistent with the view that the interaction between reading ability and phonological confusability in short-term memory tasks reflects scaling problems in the data. They report an experiment using a meticulous methodology in which the span of each subject was determined individually and list length for the experimental memory test was set at one item less than span for each child. No correlation was obtained between reading ability and the size of the phonological similarity effect in serial recall ($r = 0.01$). Poor readers of average intelligence were found to have lower levels of recall than normal readers of the same age, but equivalent to younger reading-matched controls. Low ability poor readers were, however, impaired relative to even the younger reading-matched controls.

The findings of both Hall et al. (1983) and Johnston et al. (1987) indicate that earlier findings of relative insensitivity of children with low reading attainment to phonological confusability of memory strings are probably artifacts of floor effects in the recall levels of poor readers. Johnston et al. plausibly suggest that the independence of poor readers' recall of phonological factors in these early studies may reflect their abandonment of a phonological strategy in favour of a nonphonological one at levels of very low performance. There have been other cases too where subjects appear to have shifted to nonphonological strategies under conditions where the memory lists are very long (Gathercole & Baddeley, 1990a; Salamé & Baddeley, 1986).

On balance, then, it appears that low ability readers do have an overall phonological memory deficit: Their memory performance is generally poorer than that of good readers of the same age, and equivalent to that of younger children of matched reading abilities. Nonetheless, poor readers do seem to represent memory items in the phonological loop, so long as the task is not too hard. Recent findings from the Haskins group, which show that poor readers are influenced by phonetic factors such as similarity and phonetic adjacency in memory tasks to an equivalent extent to good readers (Brady, Mann, & Schmidt, 1987), concur with this view.

The research considered so far has relied largely on the serial recall paradigm to explore phonological memory characteristics in children with varying levels of reading ability. Another technique, which we consider to be a useful and sensitive indicator of phonological memory skills in young children, is nonword repetition (see Chapter 3 for discussion of the use of nonword repetition as a measure of phonological memory). In each trial in this task, the child immediately repeats the unfamiliar item spoken to it by the experimenter. We have found that nonword repetition performance was a particularly effective discriminator of language disordered children from younger language-matched controls (Gathercole & Baddeley, 1990b; see Chapter 3). Are, then, poor readers also impaired in this phonological memory task?

The answer appears to be that children of low reading ability are indeed impaired in repeating nonwords. The first demonstration of this deficit was provided by Snowling (1981). She compared the performance of a group of 20 dyslexic children aged between 9 and 17 years with a group of normal readers matched for reading age in a task involving the immediate repetition of single spoken items. The items were either words or nonwords. The dyslexics and the normal controls did not differ in their ability to repeat real words. The dyslexic children were, however, significantly impaired in their repetition of the longest (four-syllable) nonwords, compared even with the younger controls of matched reading ability. Similar findings of impaired nonword repetition by poor readers have also been reported by Brady, Shankweiler, and Mann (1983) and Snowling, Goulandris, Bowlby, and Howell (1986).

In tests of nonword repetition, therefore, children with poor reading ability perform at an even lower level than younger children matched on reading ability. One interpretation of this finding is that the low reading achievement of some children arises as a consequence of central impairments in phonological memory function, possibly as a consequence of having a phonological loop of reduced capacity or efficiency. At present, however, the evidence is not sufficiently unambiguous to support this contention strongly. Factors other than phonological memory may underlie the association between nonword repetition and reading ability: The basis for this link therefore needs to be analysed in much more detail before any firm conclusions are drawn.

Longitudinal Studies

Findings from group studies indicate that poor readers typically have less adequate phonological memory skills than most children of their age. In serial recall tasks, poor readers usually perform at about the same level as younger reading-age-matched controls. There is, however, some evidence that poor readers are even worse in another measure of phonological memory—nonword repetition—than reading age controls.

The pattern of causality underpinning these developmental associations between reading ability and measures of phonological memory is unclear. The associations are consistent with the view that phonological memory skills play a critical role in the development of reading skills during the early school years. The evidence from reading group studies is, however, equally consistent with the converse view, namely that phonological memory skills are influenced by early reading success. One effective way of discriminating between these alternative causal hypotheses is to adopt a longitudinal approach, and to ask the question: Do phonological memory skills in prereading children predict their later reading achievement? If they do, the relationship cannot be attributed to the influences of reading achievement on phonological memory skills, as the children could not read when the first measures of phonological memory were taken.

The Cambridge Study

We have just completed one such longitudinal study (Gathercole & Baddeley, in press). About 150 four-year-old children were tested within six weeks of school entry, and given a battery of tests including measures of reading, vocabulary, general intelligence, and phonological memory. The children were retested again at ages five, six and eight years. Of interest here are the children who could not read when they were initially tested at school entry. Would their phonological memory skills predict their reading achievement at age eight?

Three reading tests were administered to the 70 eight-year-old children who were unable to read at age four, and who were still

TABLE 6.1
Examples from the Reading Tests used in Cambridge Longitudinal Study

Test	Example of a line from the test
British Abilities Scales[1]	said water bird wood running
Neale Test[2]	The bird hopped up to my window
Primary Reading Test[3]	He opened his ———— to shout
	(asleep chest mouth ears pocket)

[1] Elliott (1983), [2] Neale (1989), [3] France (1981)

available to participate in the study four years later. A brief summary of the tests is provided in Table 6.1. The reading test from the British Abilities Scales (Elliott, 1983) provides a measure of word decoding ability—the child has to read single words without any context. In the Neale Reading Test (1989), the child is required to read aloud a short passage, which corresponds to a picture shown on the facing page. We took two measures from this test. The accuracy measure corresponded to the number of words correctly read by the child. Only 46 children in the longitudinal sample were given the Neale test. Finally, the children were given the Primary Reading Test (France, 1981). In the later items of this test, the child was shown a sentence with a missing word, such as *It began to* _____ *so we put on our coats.* The test administrator read aloud the sentence omitting the missing word, and the child had to ring which of five alternative words was the missing one. For this example, the alternative words were *rain, bucket, collar, dance, spare.* The number of correct words selected by the child provided the word recognition score in this test. The test administrator then repeated the test, this time saying the missing word, rather than omitting it. The child was asked to look again at the five options, and to select the printed word which it thought corresponded to the spoken one. The number of correct choices in this second administration of the test was calculated for each child, providing the comprehension score. In addition to the reading tests, two measures of arithmetical ability were given, in order to provide a test of the specificity of any relation found between phonological memory and subsequent reading development.

The main phonological memory test given to the children at age four, when they were prereaders, was nonword repetition. Nonword repetition scores reflected the number of correct repetitions of 40 nonwords, each of which contained between one and four syllables. Here we report the associations between the children's prereading nonword repetition scores and their reading test scores four years later. A series of fixed-order multiple regression analyses were performed, with reading score at age eight providing the criterion variable in each case. Table 6.2 shows the additional percentage variance in each of the reading measures accounted for by age four nonword repetition scores, after the contributions of chronological age and nonverbal intelligence (Raven's Progressive Coloured Matrices) had been taken into account. The numbers in parentheses show the additional variance after vocabulary, as well as age and nonverbal intelligence, had been partialled out.

Age four phonological memory skills—as indexed by nonword repetition scores—significantly predicted the children's performance four years later in the Primary Reading Test. Prereading nonword repetition scores accounted for between 8% and 11% of variance in the two scores taken from this test, after adjustments had been made for age and nonverbal intelligence. When vocabulary at age four was also taken into account, nonword repetition scores still accounted for a significant portion of variance in the recognition scores (4.4%). This degree of unique association is comparable to that obtained by Bradley and Bryant (1983) in their longitudinal study, using prereading phonological awareness as a predictor of later reading achievement in similar fixed-order multiple regressions.

It should be noted, though, that adjusting for vocabulary scores here may result in an overly conservative estimate of the contribution of phonological memory to later reading scores. Evidence from this longitudinal database has already established that nonword repetition scores and vocabulary knowledge are closely related during the early school years, and that during the earliest period of the study, the phonological memory measure appears to be the pacemaker in the developmental relationship (Gathercole et al., 1992; see Chapter 3). By controlling for individual differences in vocabulary knowledge, therefore, we are to some extent also controlling for phonological memory differences.

TABLE 6.2

Additional Variance in Outcome Measures (Taken at Age Eight) Accounted for by Nonword Repetition Scores Four Years Earlier, after Adjustments for Age and Nonverbal Intelligences Scores (and Vocabulary Scores too Shown in Parentheses)

Outcome Measure	Additional r^2	
Reading:		
Primary Reading	0.09**	(0.04*)
Neale Accuracy	0.01	(0.00)
BAS	0.01	(0.00)
WISC[†] Arithmetic	0.00	(0.00)
Vocabulary	0.10**	(0.00)

$*p < 0.05$ $**p < 0.01$ [†]Wechsler (1974).

There were no significant associations between prereading nonword repetition scores and the measures derived from either of the other two reading tests. In each case, the additional variance accounted for by repetition scores was less than 2%, and was nearly zero when adjusted for vocabulary scores. Similarly, the links between age four repetition scores and the arithmetic measure taken at age eight were not significant in the corresponding fixed-order multiple regressions analyses.

Prereading phonological memory skills therefore appear to be highly specific predictors of later achievement in one type of reading test only—the Primary Reading Test. Why should this be? To answer this question, it is necessary to compare the nature of the different reading tests. Consider first the single-word reading test, taken from the British Ability Scales. As there is no context for the words in the test, it provides a relatively pure measure of the child's word decoding skills. Moreover, many of the words in the test involve irregular or inconsistent spelling patterns—by our calculations, at least 50% of even the early words in the test (the first 30) are irregular. A phonological recoding strategy will therefore not be at all effective for many of the words in the test. And even for the regular words, a recoding strategy would have to be very efficient to allow the child to recognise the words, as there is no context to enable the child to generate candidates based on partial phonological recoding. Performance in this reading measure therefore seems likely to reflect largely the child's sight vocabulary—the words whose visual configurations were already known to the child at the time of the test.

The Neale test provides a measures of reading in context—the child reads aloud a story corresponding to a picture. In this test, then, the child is likely to be able to use context to guide its recognition of unfamiliar words. However, many of the words in the sentences are not highly predictable from the preceding context, so that a sophisticated guessing strategy (in which the child matches a partial phonological code with plausible candidates for the word) may not be very useful unless either the word is regular or the child's use of this strategy is very effective. Once again, it seems likely that successful reading in this test will mainly be guided by direct recognition of words in the child's sight vocabulary.

The demands of the Primary Reading Test are quite different. The child is provided with the phonological form of the target word— generated either by the context (the rest of the sentence) or by the test administrator. The task is to select which of the five optional words corresponds to the target word. For half of the items, none of the foils share the same initial letter (or phoneme) of the target words. The degree of letter overlap between the target and foils in the remaining items is variable, but in no cases would the child have to recode graphemically more than the first three phonemes of the target (or, phonologically recode more than the first three letters in the five words) in order to make the correct selection. We are not suggesting here that the children only perform this task by a phonological recoding strategy—when the target word is within a child's sight vocabulary, it is presumably recognised relatively easily without the need for phonological recoding. But a partial recoding strategy would be very effective in this test as a way of enabling the child to choose target words that are not within the sight vocabulary. Our claim, then, is that this test encourages children to use letter–sound correspondences as a way of identifying words whose visual forms are not familiar to them. It therefore seems likely that there is a substantial component of the scores derived from this test which reflects the children's skills at applying a (possibly partial) phonological recoding strategy.

This analysis of the three reading tests suggests that phonological recoding is more likely to be effective in helping the child identify unfamiliar words in the Primary Reading Test than either the BAS test or the Neale test. The predictive and highly specific relation between prereading nonword repetition scores and later performance in the Primary Reading Test is consistent with the view that phonological memory skills are necessary for the development of a phonological recoding strategy. The better the prereading memory skills, the more effective the child is four years later in this test, which places heavy demands on phonological recoding.

There appears, though, to be no significant association between phonological memory and the rate with which a child establishes a sight vocabulary. This conclusion may seem rather surprising, given that phonological recoding is typically viewed as a self-teaching mechanism: The idea is that if the child successfully identifies a word by recoding it, the visual configuration of the word may be learned by the child. Thus, the next time the word is encountered, the child may not need to recode, as it may be represented within the sight vocabulary. According to this argument, good phonological recoding skills should promote development of the sight vocabulary. Our data suggests that this is not the case. One possible reason for this concerns the words included in reading tests. A large proportion of the words in reading tests have irregular spelling patterns. A phonological recoding strategy is likely to be less successful for such words. If measures were derived of the children's reading only of the regular words in the test, a link with earlier phonological memory skills may indeed be found.

We have focused here on the differences between the reading measures taken in this study, motivated by the differential links between prereading phonological memory skills and subsequent scores across the reading tests. It should, however, be noted that each of the reading scores was highly and positively correlated with the scores from the other tests—the correlations coefficients varied between 0.7 and 0.95. Clearly, there is a substantial common substrate to performance across different reading tests. The point here is simply that tests that provide the child with the phonology of the target word and a number of optional letter strings will be more likely to reflect current phonological recoding ability than single-word reading tests.

Other Longitudinal Studies
Although other longitudinal studies have taken measures of phonological memory skills, to our knowledge none of them have initially tested children prior to the emergence of reading skills. One widely cited study was reported by Mann and Liberman (1984). The children were first tested towards the end of their kindergarten year, when they were aged just under six years, and were then retested one year later. The aim of this study was to investigate whether phonological memory skills could be used to predict later reading achievement. At initial testing, the children were tested on their immediate serial recall of rhyming and nonrhyming strings of words, on a receptive vocabulary test, a nonverbal ordering test, and a task involving the children making judgements about the syllabic structure of words spoken by the experimenter. One year later, the children's reading skills were assessed using standardised reading tests.

In order to explore the relationship between early phonological memory ability and later reading attainment, Mann and Liberman divided the 62 children participating in the study into three reading ability groups on the basis of teachers' recommendations at the second time of testing. The children in the good, average, and poor reading groups did not differ significantly in vocabulary knowledge. They were, however, distinguished on the basis of their immediate memory performance one year earlier. Serial recall scores increased significantly with the groups of higher reading proficiency, and the group differences were greatest for the nonrhyming lists. The correlation between reading scores and memory for the nonrhyming sequences was significant ($r = 0.39$). The reading ability groups were not, however, distinguished in their earlier nonverbal memory skills, suggesting a degree of specificity to the link between reading ability and phonological working memory.

These results indicate that phonological memory measures taken within a year of starting school can effectively predict individual variation in reading attainment one year later, even for unselected groups of children. Moreover, the specificity of the memory deficits associated with poor reading development to linguistic material of low inter-item phonological confusability directly supports the contention that the poor readers have defective phonological memory function. The results are therefore consistent with the view that phonological memory skills may play a causal role in the development of a phonological recoding strategy.

There are, however, a number of methodological concerns with this study that warrant caution in theoretical interpretation. Firstly, the children were not tested for their reading skills at initial testing, thus leaving open the possibility that very early reading attainment in some of the children might have influenced both their phonological memory skills and their subsequent reading sophistication, rather than vice versa. Secondly, no measure of nonverbal intelligence was obtained or taken into account, raising the possibility that the children with low reading ability also had poorer general intellectual ability. This is particularly important, as the studies of Hall et al. (1983) and Johnston et al. (1987) have demonstrated that children with poor reading development and low general ability have immediate memory deficits that may not be linked with their reading difficulties. Thus, although the results of Mann and Liberman (1984) are certainly consistent with the notion that there is a causal association between phonological memory skills and reading development, the data are also compatible with other interpretations. A further longitudinal study reported by Mann (1984) falls prey to the same ambiguity of interpretation.

A more extensive longitudinal study charting the developmental association between phonological memory skills and reading achievement is reported by Ellis and Large (1988; see also, Ellis, 1989). Forty children were studied at three points in time between the ages of five and seven years. Only eight of the subjects were prereaders at the initial time of testing. Three phonological memory measures were obtained at each wave—auditory digit span, auditory word span, and auditory sentence span. At each of ages five, six and seven years, there was evidence for a close association between the phonological memory measures and reading achievement. Auditory sentence span correlated significantly with age five reading measures even after IQ had been controlled, and all three phonological memory tests had significant partial correlations with age six and age seven reading measures. These results therefore provide further confirmation of a developmental association between phonological memory skills and reading ability.

Ellis and Large explored the causal underpinnings of this developmental association by comparing cross-lagged correlations between the phonological memory measures and one of the reading measures—the Schonell Reading Test (see Chapter 2 for a discussion of the logic of cross-lagged correlations). The comparisons that they reported were consistent with the view that reading achievement was the pacemaker for later phonological memory development, rather than vice versa. Reading at age five was more strongly correlated with age six auditory digit span than age five span was with reading at age six. The correlations were about equivalent in the two directions one year later, when age six and seven measures were compared. On this basis, Ellis and Large proposed that reading achievement stimulates phonological memory skills at this time, and that beyond age six or so, the two abilities develop in a reciprocal relationship. Essentially similar conclusions were drawn by Ellis (1989) on the basis of a causal analysis of this longitudinal database.

It should be noted, however, that for the two other phonological memory measures taken at age five in this study—auditory word span and auditory sentence span—the correlations with age six reading are slightly greater (although not significantly so) than the converse links between age five reading and the age six memory measure. Thus, two out of three of the cross-lagged correlations run counter to Ellis and Large's characterisation of auditory short-term memory being a beneficiary of early reading development, and indicate instead either an interactive relationship between the two abilities, or possibly an indeterminate one reflecting the influence of another common factor on them both. Furthermore, the age five data are confounded by consisting primarily of test results from early readers rather than prereaders. An unbiased estimate of the contribution of phonological memory to early reading development cannot be obtained within this design. For these reasons, the findings of this particular longitudinal study of phonological memory and reading development are not at all clear cut.

We obtained data in our Cambridge longitudinal study that allowed us to compute comparable cross-lagged correlations to those reported by Ellis and Large (1988), but which in contrast were based on data only from children who were prereaders (Gathercole et al., in prep.). Both the nonword repetition tests and the single-word reading test (BAS) were administered at each of the four waves of our study, which allowed us to compare the correlations between the pairs of measures across the one-year time intervals. Only children who were prereaders at initial time of testing were included in these analyses.

Our results were quite different to those reported by Ellis and Large. Comparisons can only be made between waves two and three (ages five and six years), and waves three and four (ages six and eight years), as there were no positive reading scores at age four. The correlation between age five nonword repetition scores and age six reading scores was 0.521; the converse correlation between age five reading and age six nonword repetition was 0.399. Although the difference was not significant, there is certainly no indication that reading was the pacemaker of phonological memory development at this time. Rather, the insignificant difference favours a reciprocal relationship between the two abilities. The correlation between age six repetition scores and age eight reading was 0.225, and the converse correlation between early reading and later repetition scores was 0.258. Again, the difference was not significant, suggesting mutual facilitation between reading and phonological memory. During the final two waves of the study, measures of auditory digit span were also taken from each child. The correlation between age six digit span and age eight reading was 0.057; the converse correlation between age six reading and age eight digit span was 0.033. Both of these sets of cross-lagged comparisons between ages six and eight indicate that there was no important developmental relationship between phonological memory and reading during this period.

Quite different conclusions emerge, though, when scores in the Primary Reading Test are used as the reading measure. Nonword repetition scores at age six account for a further significant 6% of variance in age eight reading scores, even after age, nonverbal intelligence, and vocabulary scores at the earlier point in time have been taken into account. The Primary Reading Test is the test in which the child is shown a printed sentence containing a missing word (e.g. *It has been a long time ____ we met*); the task is to circle which of the five optional words is the missing one. We argued earlier that a strategy of partial phonological recoding of unfamiliar words is very useful in this task: The children know which is the missing word, and have to choose which of the five letter strings could correspond to that series of sounds. The significant link between age six nonword repetition and later Primary Reading Test scores, and the absence of a significant corresponding association between the memory measure and later single-word reading, support our earlier contention that phonological memory is important for developing a phonological recoding strategy for reading.

It is notable that Ellis and Large (1988) used the Schonell Reading Test, which, like the reading test of the British Abilities Scales that we used, is a test of single-word decoding ability. It therefore appears that inconsistencies in the relationships of phonological memory with different reading measures, both within our study and between our study and that of Ellis and Large, may reflect the fact that not all reading tests, and in particular ones that require single-word reading, depend to the same extent on phonological recoding. Instead, performance in such tasks probably largely reflects recognition of words that are already within a child's sight vocabulary. The results suggest that the development of a sight vocabulary may proceed independently of phonological memory factors.

We do not wish to rule out the possibility that reading achievement can influence the development of phonological memory, and that the two abilities develop in a mutually facilitative manner. This seems entirely plausible. At present, however, evidence suggests that prereading phonological memory skills genuinely do contribute causally to early reading development. Once reading has begun, a reciprocal relationship may then develop.

PHONOLOGICAL MEMORY, PHONOLOGICAL AWARENESS, AND LEARNING TO READ

Our reviews of the research focusing on phonological memory and reading development, and on phonological awareness and reading development, have resulted in two converging conclusions. Both types of phonological processing ability appear to play causal roles in the acquisition of literacy skills. More specifically, both phonological memory and phonological awareness appear to be linked with the development of a phonological recoding strategy for reading and spelling.

What, then, is the nature of the contributions of phonological awareness and phonological memory to the development of reading and spelling abilities? Do individual differences in phonological awareness and phonological memory draw on a common domain of phonological processing skill, in which case their links with reading development may plausibly have a common basis? Or do memory and awareness reflect fundamentally different abilities which accordingly play differential roles in learning to read and spell?

Earlier in the chapter, we considered the theoretical accounts that have been advanced to explain the apparently causal relationship between phonemic awareness and reading. One dominant perspective is that children's metalinguistic abilities reflect the adequacy of their phonological coding in the language system (e.g. Liberman, 1989;

Shankweiler & Crain, 1986; Vellutino, 1979). According to this type of account, poor readers have weak and poorly specified phonetic codes that impair their abilities to make explicit judgements about, for example, phonetic structure. Shankweiler and Crain (1986) and Crain, Shankweiler, Macaruso, and Bar-Shalom (1990) have developed this perspective in some detail, and propose that as a consequence of their deficits in constructing low-level phonological representations of linguistic stimuli, poor readers fail to proceed at a normal rate through the hierarchy of increasingly abstract and meaningful representations of speech events. Thus, a result of the low-level phonological deficits of poor readers is that they encounter difficulties in processing syntactic and semantic structures of both spoken and written language. According to this view, then, there are far-reaching information-processing consequences of weak and inadequate phonetic coding.

Many proponents of this view also interpret the inferior phonological memory skills of children with low reading ability in terms of weak phonetic coding in the language system (e.g. Brady, 1991; Fowler, 1991; Liberman et al., 1982). The position of these researchers, then, is that both phonological memory and awareness tasks draw upon the child's phonological representations of linguistic stimuli: for both kinds of task, the less adequate the basic representational system, the poorer the performance of the child.

This perspective—that phonological memory and phonological awareness reflect a common phonological skills domain—certainly accounts for a number of established empirical findings. It explains why phonological memory skills are closely related to children's abilities in basic phonological processing measures, such as the accuracy and speed of producing words and phrases (Rapala & Brady, 1990). It explains why children with low reading ability are typically poor at both phonological memory tasks and at tasks involving phonological awareness (e.g. Mann, 1984; Mann & Liberman, 1984). It also provides a plausible account of why both phonological memory and phonological awareness abilities are implicated in the development of a phonological recoding strategy in reading.

More direct investigations of memory and awareness skills, however, have failed to reveal an equivalence relationship. There appears to be some degree of independence in the skills which form the basis for phonological awareness and phonological memory tasks. There are a few relevant findings. Firstly, the early longitudinal study of Bradley and Bryant (1983), in which children's awareness of rhyme at age four was found to predict later reading achievement, included a measure of phonological memory. The task involved recall of lists of unrelated words, and was included as a necessary control for the oddity detection paradigm, in which the child had to identify which word of a set of three did not share a common sound. Clearly, children may fail the oddity detection task because they cannot recall the three words sufficiently well to compare their phonological structure. Bradley and Bryant attempted to avoid this ambiguity of interpretation by assessing the significance of the links between early detection scores and later reading achievement after scores in the memory test had been taken into account. The residual association between detection performance and scores in the literacy tests after memory differences had been controlled remained significant.

The independence of the predictive relationship between rhyme awareness and later literacy attainment from earlier phonological memory scores is important, as it suggests that the two classes of task should not be viewed as equivalent. However, it should be noted that the reading outcome measures used in this study were a single-word reading test and the Neale Test. In our longitudinal study, we found that prereading phonological memory skills did not significantly predict achievement in either of these types of test, both of which, we have argued, encourage children to read only words within their sight vocabulary. The findings from this study, then, do not rule out a contribution of phonological memory to the development of a phonological recoding strategy. They do, however, suggest a degree of independence between rhyme awareness and phonological memory skills.

We have recently looked more directly into the relationship between rhyme awareness and phonological memory skills in children of early school age, with the aim of identifying whether or not the two types of measure tap dissociable cognitive domains (Gathercole et al., 1991a). In this study, a battery of phonological and nonphonological tests was given to 57 children in their first year at school (mean age 4:09) and 51 children in their second year (mean age 5:09). The phonological tests included two measures of phonological memory— nonword repetition and auditory digit span. In addition, the rhyme oddity detection task used by Bryant et al. (1990) was given to all of the children. Other more general measures that were taken included two reading tests, a vocabulary test, and a measure of nonverbal intelligence.

In both age groups, the three phonological measures were significantly correlated with one another, although the two memory tests (digit span and nonword repetition) were more closely associated with one another than rhyme awareness. More specifically, though, we were interested in addressing two particular issues concerning the relationship between phonological memory and phonological awareness in this study. Firstly, we wanted to know whether equivalent associations would be found between rhyme awareness and reading, and phonological memory and reading. Secondly, we wanted to know whether there was any specific association between awareness of rhyme and vocabulary knowledge. In several studies described in Chapter 3, vocabulary and nonword repetition performance have been found to be closely related to one another. If the awareness measure and nonword repetition draw upon a common phonological processing domain, vocabulary should also be found to be significantly associated with rhyme awareness.

The findings pointed to a clear dissociation between the phonological memory and rhyme awareness measures. Consider first the analyses of the vocabulary data. Although the established link between vocabulary knowledge and nonword repetition was replicated for both the four- and five-year-olds, there was no specific significant association between the vocabulary scores and the rhyme detection scores. Thus, the memory–vocabulary link does not appear to reflect simply a general phonological processing factor. We take this finding as good support for our proposal that during the early school years, phonological memory abilities *per se* may significantly constrain the long-term phonological learning of new words (see Chapter 3).

The memory and awareness measures also had distinctive relationships with the scores in the two reading measures. The measures were the single-word reading test of the British Abilities Scales, and the Primary Reading Test (see Table 6.1). Scores in both of the phonological memory tests were significantly linked with both reading measures in the five-year-old group, but not for the four-year-old children. Rhyme awareness scores, however, were significantly associated with performance in the Primary Reading Test in both age groups, but were not linked with performance in the single-word reading test.

Thus, although all three phonological processing measures had significant links with reading achievement, the patterns of association are quite distinct. Cross-sectional correlational studies of this kind clearly cannot establish the causal underpinnings of empirical relationships, but they do nonetheless provide snapshots of how skills interrelate at specific points in time. The data indicate that phonological memory skills become most closely related to reading achievement after the children have been reading for a year or so, but not initially. Rhyme awareness, on the other hand, is linked with reading even when children have only been reading for a few months, but this relationship is restricted to the Primary Reading Test.

These results suggest that we need distinct theories of the developmental links of reading with phonological memory and phonological awareness; thus accounts which attribute an undifferentiated "phonological" substrate to them both are likely to be inadequate. There may well be a common phonological processing component of the kind suggested by Shankweiler and Crain (1986)—indeed, we found evidence for such a phonological factor in factor analyses of our data—but there are also unique attributes of the two types of measure which need theoretical explanation.

What distinctive contribution might phonological working memory make to reading development? The available data are consistent with the notion that the locus of the contribution is in the development of a phonological recoding strategy. In the Cambridge longitudinal study, prereading phonological memory scores only predict reading four years later, but only in a test that appears to favour a phonological recoding strategy. In the cross-sectional study described earlier in this section, links between phonological memory and reading were only present for the children that had been reading for a year or so. It is at about this time that children usually start to learn and apply the alphabetic principle in reading.

One possibility is that phonological memory contributes to the long-term learning of the letter–sound mapping rules that are necessary for the use of a phonological recoding strategy. In Chapter 3 we considered the evidence that the process of long-term phonological learning of new words is based on the temporary phonological record provided by phonological memory (e.g. Baddeley et al., 1988b; Gathercole & Baddeley, 1989b). The idea here is that phonological memory may play a similar role in the long-term learning of grapheme–phoneme correspondences: Children with poor phonological memory skills may encounter difficulties in building the requisite stable associations that would enable them to map letters onto sounds in word decoding.

There is clear evidence that knowledge of letter-to-sound associations is critical to normal reading development. Children with severe developmental reading problems have consistently been shown to have poor knowledge and use of grapheme–phoneme correspondence rules, as illustrated in their attempts at spelling nonwords (e.g. Snowling, 1980). Furthermore, research by Tunmer et al. (1988) and Byrne and Fielding-Barnsley (1989) considered earlier in this chapter indicates that a child can only proceed with a strategy of phonological recoding if it has both adequate knowledge of letter–sound relationships, and phonemic awareness. Perhaps, then, this is the point at which phonological memory and phonological awareness skills combine in promoting reading development: Awareness of sound structure enables the child to strip off phonemes from familiar words, and adequate phonological memory skills facilitate learning of letter–sound rules, which can then be applied to the segmented phonemes.

There are other ways in which good phonological memory skills may help the development of a phonological recoding strategy. In order to identify a target word by applying grapheme–phoneme rules to an unfamiliar letter string, the child has to store the generated sound segments, and then to blend them phonologically. This process appears to require a buffer storage medium akin to the phonological loop component of working memory (Baddeley, 1978). If the phonological loop is used for this purpose, we might indeed expect that children with very poor phonological memory function will not be very successful in sounding out unfamiliar letter strings and blending them to produce a word.

Both of these suggestions—that phonological memory contributes to the learning of letter–sound correspondences, and that it may store sound segments generated during phonological recoding—provide the possible basis for the causal link between prereading phonological memory and later achievement in reading and spelling. In both cases, the nature of the contributions to reading development can be distinguished from that of phonological awareness. Both accounts are, however, necessarily speculative. More direct evidence of the nature of memory contribution to reading development is clearly needed to advance our theoretical understanding of this relationship.

HOW DOES READING PROGRESS WITHOUT ADEQUATE PHONOLOGICAL SKILLS?

Phonological processing skills and reading ability are intimately linked. The developmental course of the associations between two important types of phonological processing—phonological awareness and phonological memory—and literacy acquisition are complex and interactive. Despite the complexity of the developmental relationships, though, it is fairly clear that adequate phonological awareness and phonological memory skills are *prerequisites* for normal reading development. Although the two types of skill are related to one another, they appear to make distinctive contributions to reading development.

In terms of the framework for reading development presented in Chapter 5, it appears that a phonological recoding strategy for reading and spelling will only emerge and develop normally if the child has adequate phonological awareness and phonological memory skills. What happens if these conditions are not satisfied? Some insight as to the consequences of impoverished phonological processing skills on literacy acquisition are provided by a recent single-case study.

Campbell and Butterworth (1985) studied RE, an undergraduate psychology student who experienced extreme difficulty in reading nonwords. Despite this deficit, reading of words was at a normal level for her educational background. Spelling was, however, a problem—RE made more errors in a spelling test than matched controls, and produced a greater proportion of misspellings that were not phonologically plausible.

Apart from experiencing problems with phonics instruction during early school years, RE appears to have had a fairly normal educational background. Exploration of her phonological processing skills, however, revealed dramatic cognitive deficits. RE had very poor immediate memory for phonological stimuli, with a span for auditorily presented lists of between three and four items. Performance was better, although still impaired, with visual presentation procedures. Further experiments showed that she was sensitive to neither phonological similarity nor word length in tests of immediate serial recall. In this respect, she differs even from patients with severe acquired phonological memory deficits such as PV (e.g. Vallar & Baddeley, 1984a), whose diminished memory span is nonetheless influenced by phonological similarity. The complete absence of either similarity or word-length effects indicates that neither subcomponent of the phonological loop—the phonological store or the subvocal rehearsal process—is being used normally.

This interpretation was also supported by RE's poor performance in other phonological processing tests. Although she had normal acoustic discrimination, RE was found to perform poorly in tests of phonological awareness. She had great difficulty in a "Spoonerising" task, which involved transposing the first phonemes of familiar word pairs such as "Chuck Berry" into "Buck Cherry". Similarly, her performance was poor in a task involving counting phonemes.

It is evident from RE's academic achievements that she has been able to use sophisticated compensatory strategies to overcome her deficits in phonological processing. Analysis of her performance in tasks requiring phonological judgements for written words, in particular, revealed a dependence upon orthographic and visual processing strategies, seemingly in compensation for phonological impairments. Nonetheless, RE's reading skills are quite clearly not normal, and the reading problems seem to be more or less squarely located within the application of grapheme–phoneme correspondences in spelling nonwords. Correspondingly, her spelling problems seem largely to reflect impaired phonological recoding, resulting in increased frequency of phonologically implausible spellings relative to controls. This interpretation receives direct support from the findings that RE was even unreliable at generating the correct sounds for letters of the alphabet (e.g. "duh"), although she was give the letter names (e.g. "dee"). This deficit provides support for our earlier claim that temporary phonological memory may be important in the long-term learning of letter–sound correspondences.

The co-occurrence in RE of impaired phonological processing skills and problems in reading unfamiliar letter strings is certainly consistent with the view that both phonological awareness and phonological memory contribute to the development of a phonological recoding strategy (for a similar case, see Funnell & Davison, 1989). Note, though, that despite these severe deficits of phonological awareness and phonological memory, RE attained a normal level of reading ability for words, although her capacity to read unfamiliar nonwords remains poor, supporting the view that she has failed to develop a capacity for phonological recoding. Given that her level of general intelligence is clearly very high, it seems likely that she managed to achieve her reading performance by depending largely on compensatory dependence on a visual learning strategy. This case is clearly an important one, as it puts phonological skills into perspective. Although phonological processing appears to be necessary for *normal* reading development, children can learn to read in other ways, too.

OVERVIEW

The evidence reviewed in this chapter testifies to strong and genuine developmental links of reading with both phonological awareness and phonological memory. Both phonological skills appear to have reciprocal associations with reading, such that reading and phonological awareness, and reading and phonological memory, develop in mutually facilitative fashions. Both of the phonological skills do, however, appear to contribute causally to the development of a phonological recoding strategy for reading and spelling. Without adequate phonological processing skills, children do not appear to be able to develop a normal phonological recoding strategy, and this will typically impair their reading development unless they can develop effective compensatory strategies.

Despite the corresponding relationships of both phonological aware-ness and phonological memory with reading development, they do not appear to reflect a single phonological factor. When the fine grain of the developmental relationships is studied (in particular, by varying the nature of the reading task), phonological awareness and phonological memory appear to have distinctive separate links with reading development. The reason may be that the two types of skill make differential contributions to the development of a phonological recoding strategy. An effective recoding strategy involves mastery of several subprocesses: At the very least, it requires analysis of the spoken forms of words into their component sounds, the abstraction and application of letter–sound correspondence rules, and blending of component sounds generated by the application of these rules. Perhaps phonological memory and phonological awareness contribute to different subprocesses. It certainly seems likely that children's abilities to analyse words into their constituent sounds will depend on their phonological awareness. Phonological working memory, on the other hand, is known to mediate long-term phonological learning (see Chapter 3), and so may be critical in the long-term learning of the correspondence rules. Clearly, these speculations require further substantiation. The general notion that phonological memory and awareness skills both make distinctive contributions, which converge in promoting the development of phonological recoding does, however, seem to make good sense of the current body of evidence.

CHAPTER SEVEN

Visual Word Recognition

So far we have considered the ways in which the phonological component of working memory (the phonological loop) contributes to the *development* of reading ability during childhood. The evidence reviewed in Chapter 6 points to a specific link between children's phonological working memory skills and the ease with which they develop a strategy of phonologically recoding unfamiliar words. We now turn to a related issue, which is whether the phonological component of working memory plays a role in *on-line reading* in adults and children. In this chapter, the focus is on the psychological processes involved in reading single words (an activity that is also often described as word decoding). The nature of possible working memory involvement in the *comprehension* of connected text is considered in detail in Chapter 8.

The study of the psychological mechanisms involved on recognising individual words is beset with both empirical inconsistencies and theoretical debate. Many years of intensive research on word recognition have established that the psychological processes involved are exceptionally complex. In particular, it has become clear that the way in which people read words can change dramatically according to the task being required of them, and also as a function of the kind of written material involved. Even more importantly for the present concerns, the involvement of phonological working memory in single-word reading appears to depend critically on the nature of the reading task.

Working memory involvement in word recognition has been the subject of systematic study in three reading populations—skilled adult readers, neuropsychological patients, and children. The principal findings in each of these areas of research are reviewed in this chapter. Before considering this evidence, though, we provide a brief overview of current thinking about the psychological processes involved in reading single words. In particular, we focus on the contentious issue of how, and under what conditions, phonological recoding occurs during reading.

PHONOLOGICAL RECODING DURING READING

Although the irregularity of the spelling–sound patterns of English is often emphasised by psychologists and linguists, many English words do have regular spelling–sound correspondences. Such words can be read in two ways, in what are often termed the "direct visual" and "indirect" routes to word recognition. Morton and Patterson's (1980) dual-route model of reading was discussed in detail in Chapter 5 (see Fig. 5.2). The direct visual route involves the word being detected by the visual input logogen specialised for the visual form of that lexical item. The phonological form of the word is made available after the word has been recognised by the input logogen, via activation of the corresponding output logogen. The indirect route, in which the reader phonologically recodes the letter string, is represented by the grapheme–phoneme conversion route.

The presence of an indirect nonlexical route to word recognition is implicated by our abilities to pronounce unfamiliar letter strings (e.g. *slint* and *trin*), and to make silent judgements about the phonology of nonwords (thus, we find it relatively easy to decide that the letter string *phoks* sounds like a real word whereas *phoths* does not). Readers also appear to generate phonology for nonwords even when the task does not explicitly require it. Evidence for this view comes from the lexical decision paradigm, in which the task is to decide whether letter strings are familiar words or not. Subjects take longer to reject nonwords if they are homophonic with real words (as in *phoks*) than if they are not (Besner & Davelaar, 1983; Rubenstein, Lewis, & Rubenstein, 1971). This finding, which is known as the pseudohomophone effect, has been widely interpreted as reflecting automatic phonological recoding of unfamiliar letter strings.

Despite our obvious capacity to derive pronunciations from unfamiliar letter strings, there is a consensus view that most skilled readers rely on the direct visual route when reading familiar text under normal conditions (see reviews by Carr & Pollatsek, 1985, and Patterson & Coltheart, 1987). One of the most convincing arguments in favour of this position concerns the structure of the English orthography, in which the relationships between graphemes (letters, or groups of letters) and phonemes are often opaque. Many English words contain letter sequences which bear highly irregular relationships with the phonology of the word. Exception words such as *yacht* and *aisle*, for example, must be recognised on the basis of their visual characteristics (i.e. via the direct visual route) as their pronunciations could not possibly be generated by the application of even the most sophisticated grapheme–phoneme correspondence rules.

Similarly, some words with different pronunciations and meanings share the same spelling pattern. Such words are termed "heterophonic homographs", and when they occur in text it is impossible to derive reliably the appropriate meaning and pronunciation by applying letter–sound correspondence rules. Take, for example, the heterophonic homograph *bow*. Readers can only recognise the correct lexical form on the basis of the context of the letter string (e.g. *The ribbon was tied in a bow*, and *The conductor took a bow*). There is no way in which simple phonological recoding of the identical letter string *bow* in the two cases could yield different pronunciations. The phonology of at least this class of words must therefore be accessed *after* the meaning of the word had been activated.

Related to this point is a recent study testing Chinese readers on identification of logographic Chinese characters. The phonology of Chinese characters can only be accessed *after* they have been recognised as familiar words, because the visual features of the logographs provide only minimal cues as to the phonetic structures of the words. Despite this, Perfetti and Zhang (1991) found that characters were recognised more rapidly if they had been primed by homophonic characters—that is, by different visual forms that shared the same phonology. In this orthography, of course, no one could argue that this phonological priming arises as a consequence of phonological recoding, as there does not exist a rule-like relationship between the visual characteristics of the character and its name. The finding therefore provides a cautionary demonstration that evidence that the reader has generated a phonological representation is not a sufficient basis for inferring prelexical phonological recoding.

Returning to the written form of the English language, it appears that given the structure of the orthography, recognition of the printed forms of familiar words by phonologically decoding them is unlikely to be as effective a reading strategy as recognition by the direct visual route. There is both experimental and neuropsychological evidence to support this view. Firstly, the regularity of the spelling–sound correspondences within words does not influence either the speed or accuracy with which subjects can recognise the printed forms of high frequency words in a lexical decision tasks (Parkin, 1982; Seidenberg, Waters, Barnes, & Tanenhaus, 1984). Thus, words with irregular spelling patterns are recognised as readily as regular items. Secondly, several neuropsychological patients (known as "deep dyslexics") have been studied who have apparently lost the ability to use the indirect route to reading; such patients are completely unable to pronounce nonwords. They are, however, capable of recognising and pronouncing many words (Patterson, 1982; Funnell, 1983). The reading of familiar words therefore can proceed without support from the indirect route involving phonological coding.

The current view, then, is that in normal reading situations, skilled readers recognise the printed forms of familiar words by directly matching the letter string with a stored visual specification. The phonological form of the word only becomes activated after lexical contact has been achieved. A word's pronunciation derived in this way is termed "postlexical phonology". This contrasts with "prelexical phonology", which refers to pronunciations achieved in the course of lexical access via the indirect route to word recognition.

PHONOLOGICAL LOOP INVOLVEMENT IN WORD RECOGNITION

The indirect route to reading has a number of features in common with the phonological loop component of working memory. Both mechanisms operate on a visual representation of language, and convert it into a phonological code. In the case of the indirect route to reading, this conversion of information from the visual domain into the phonological one is achieved by applying grapheme–phoneme correspondences rules (Morton & Patterson, 1980), or look-up routines (Shallice & McCarthy, 1985). In the phonological loop, the visual form is translated into a subvocal articulatory sequence, which then generates a phonological specification to be held in the phonological store. When familiar words are involved, the reader presumably accesses and activates a stored articulatory specification of the word. With unfamiliar words and nonwords, however, some kind of mapping rules are required to convert the letter sequence into an articulatory form.

The degree of overlap in the information processing procedures that are necessarily involved in (1) the indirect route to reading, and (2) the recoding of visual information into the phonological loop, have not gone unnoted: A number of researchers have asked whether the two mechanisms are one and the same. In other words, is the phonological loop used to achieve prelexical phonology? In the following section we consider experimental, developmental, and neuropsychological evidence that is directly relevant to this hypothesis.

Skilled Adult Readers

A variety of reading-based tasks have been used to test the hypothesis that phonological recoding during reading is mediated by the phonological loop. These tasks include judgements of rhyme, homophony, and stress structure. Across the full range of tasks, the findings have been notably inconsistent. When results are classified according to reading task, however, a relatively consistent pattern of findings emerges. In the following section we consider reading tasks that have been used to address the phonological loop hypothesis.

Homophony Tasks
A paradigm that has proved useful in testing this hypothesis involves subjects making judgements about the sound structure of a printed letter string. Baddeley and Lewis (1981) asked subjects to make three different kinds of decisions about the phonological forms of nonwords, across a series of experiments. In one task, subjects decided whether a printed nonword sounded like a real word or not (e.g. *cayoss*). In another task, the nonword was paired with a familiar word for comparison: The question to subjects was, "Do these two letter strings sound the same?" (e.g. *ocean–oshun*). A further task involved a phonological comparison of two nonword letter strings; subjects had to decide whether they sounded the same (e.g. *kerm–curm*). The rationale behind using nonwords in these different silent phonology tasks was that access to phonology for these stimuli must be via the indirect prelexical route (i.e. assembled phonology); being nonwords, there would be no stored (addressed) phonological specification for the reader to access.

A straightforward test of the phonological loop hypothesis was provided across this series of experiments. Engaging the subjects in irrelevant articulation during reading (e.g. repeatedly saying "hiya" without pause) is extremely disruptive for immediate memory of the sequence of the visually presented items (Baddeley et al., 1975; see Chapter 1). This phenomenon, known as the articulatory suppression effect, appears to be a consequence of blocking the subvocal articulation process that is necessary to translate visual material into phonological form, within the phonological loop. It therefore follows that if the generation of phonology for unfamiliar letter sequences is mediated by the subvocal articulation component of the phonological loop, performance on the pseudohomophony tasks used by Baddeley and Lewis (1981) should be disturbed by irrelevant articulation.

In each of the experiments, this prediction received no support. There was no effect of articulatory suppression on either the speed or the accuracy with which subjects made pseudohomophony judgements. Similarly, Besner, Davies, and Daniels (1981) asked subjects to judge whether a printed nonword sounded like a familiar word (e.g. *kammel*), and found no significant effect of suppression on performance. These results establish that nonlexical phonology can be derived from print, presumably by the indirect nonlexical route to reading, while the articulatory activity of the phonological loop activity is suppressed. On these grounds, it looks as though the simple hypothesis that the phonological loop is necessary for the phonological recoding of unfamiliar print should be rejected.

Similar conclusions were recently reached by Daneman and Stainton (1991) in which subjects encountered homophones in a very different kind of reading task. They devised a "comprehension-sensitive proofreading task", in which subjects had to detect typographical errors in natural text. The aim of the experiment was to determine whether readers activate phonological codes during silent reading. To test this, they replaced selected words in the text with their homophones. Thus, *idle* and *bored* became either (a) *idle* and *board* or (b) *idle* and *beard*. If subjects were recoding the text into phonological representations, they should have greater difficulty in detecting the error in the case of (a) than (b). Consistent with previous research using more artificial laboratory reading tasks (e.g. Van Orden, 1987), Daneman and Stainton found in Experiment 1 that subjects made 12% more errors in detecting homophonic errors (example (a)) than nonhomophonic errors (example (b)), providing that they were familiarised with the content of the text. Thus, subjects appeared to be misled by words that sounded like the target words, even though they were spelled differently.

The possible involvement of phonological working memory in this activation of phonological representations during silent reading was tested in Experiment 2. Subjects in this experiment proofread the same materials either under conditions of concurrent irrelevant articulation (repeating a word such as "dromedary" or "correlation" without pause) or maintaining a six-item digit load. In both cases, there remained a significantly greater error rate in detecting homophonic than nonhomophonic errors, and this difference was not significantly reduced relative to the control condition in the earlier study. Daneman and Stainton accordingly conclude that "the results argue strongly *against* [our italics] a phonologically based working memory as the primary source of the homophone confusion effect" (p. 624).

More direct evidence that articulatory suppression has dissociable influences on the phonological recoding of pseudohomophones and on short-term memory for printed letter strings is provided by Besner and Davelaar (1982). Experiment 2 employed a serial recall paradigm in which subjects recalled lists of four visually presented nonwords. There were three critical experimental manipulations. The nonwords varied in length—they were either one or three syllables in length—and while they were presented subjects either engaged in articulatory suppression or did nothing (the control condition). On the basis of previous work with familiar words (e.g. Baddeley et al., 1975), it was expected that recall would be better for long than short nonwords, and that this length effect would be abolished by articulatory suppression. The third experimental manipulation, though, was new. Within each of the length and suppression conditions, the nonwords were either pseudohomophones (e.g. *chirch*, *streat*, *sqair*, *kaught*) or were not (e.g. *chiltch*, *sprean*, *squoal*, *kaunch*).

The results of this experiment are summarised in Table 7.1. There are two noteworthy aspects of the results. Firstly, the usual finding that articulatory suppression eliminates the word-length effect with visual presentation was found. Secondly, there was a significant pseudohomophone effect in recall—the nonwords that sounded like real words were much better recalled than the ones that did not. But

TABLE 7.1

Mean % Recall as a Function of Length of Words, Pseudohomophony, and Concurrent Task Condition

	Quiet	
No. of syllables	Pseudohomophones	Controls
One	72.9	90.1
Three	82.4	57.8
	Articulatory Suppression	
No. of syllables	Pseudohomophones	Controls
One	55.1	46.3
Three	58.9	43.6

Adapted from Besner and Davelaar (1982).

in contrast to the word-length effect (attributed to the operation of the subvocal rehearsal process in the phonological loop), the pseudo-homophone advantage was not diminished by concurrent articulation. A similar pattern of results was obtained in Experiment 1 of this paper, which varied phonological similarity of the nonwords rather than the number of syllables. Suppression completely eliminated the phonological similarity effect in recall, but the recall advantage to pseudohomophones was undiminished. Thus in both experiments, subjects were able to take full advantage of the phonological structure of the pseudohomophones in the articulatory suppression conditions. The same suppression conditions were, however, sufficiently destructive of phonological loop activity to completely abolish the word-length and phonological similarity effects.

Thus, the speed and accuracy with which subjects make decisions about homophony of letter strings is uninfluenced by articulatory suppression. This finding, consistent over tasks requiring explicit judgements about homophony and also in the "proofreading" paradigm of Daneman and Stainton (1991), points to independence of homophony judgements from the phonological loop component of working memory. We return to theoretical accounts of this independence later in the chapter.

More Complex Judgements of Phonology and Prosody

Judgements about homophony simply require the subject to decide if two letter strings share the same phonological structure. In this section, we consider research which has used more complex phonological tasks, such as rhyme judgement and judgements of stress structure, to address the phonological loop hypothesis. As we shall see, different results and conclusions emerge with an increase in the complexity of the judgements concerning the sound structure of printed letter strings increases.

Rhyme Judgements. In a rhyme judgement task, subjects decide whether a pair of stimuli share the same final vowel–consonant segment. Besner et al. (1981), for example, asked subjects to make speeded judgements about which printed letter strings rhymed (e.g. *drought–flout*, and *stawn–jorn*) and which did not (e.g. *give–jerk*, and *troct–jesh*). Thus, even in the "yes" trials, the two phonological representation will be different prior to the final vowel–consonant segment. The subject's task, then, is to judge whether the two representations share the appropriate phonological segments. The segmental analysis procedures involved in rhyme judgement are therefore much more complex than those required in decisions about homophony, where a global judgement about whether two phonological specifications are identical is sufficient for accurate performance.

Rhyme judgement performance has been found across several independent studies to be disrupted by articulatory suppression. Besner et al. (Experiment III) found that rhyme judgements became significantly more inaccurate under conditions of articulatory suppression, for both word pairs (e.g. *freight–slate, canoe–choose*) and nonword pairs (e.g. *swoin–toyne, quoz–fint*). Using the same materials, Wilding and White (1985) found across a series of experiments that both the speed and the accuracy of rhyme judgements about pairs of words were impaired under articulatory suppression.

Johnston and McDermott (1986) carried out a systematic evaluation of the effects of articulatory suppression on rhyme judgement decisions about pairs of words. Across a series of experiments using the same materials, they varied both the rate of articulatory suppression and the manner of presentation of the word (simultaneous versus successive). Irrespective of these procedural variations, articulatory suppression impaired subjects' accuracy in making rhyme judgements.

Results from different studies requiring rhyme judgement are therefore consistent: Articulatory suppressions impairs subjects' abilities to make silent comparisons of rhymes for printed items. In interpreting these findings, however, it is necessary to take account of the fact that the suppression effects observed are relatively small in magnitude: Rhyme judgements can still be made during irrelevant articulation, although typically at some cost to accuracy.

Stress Judgements.   Recent work has explored whether the articulatory component of the phonological loop is responsible for representing the syllabic stress structure of words during reading. All multisyllabic words contain both strongly and weakly stressed syllables, and this distinctive prosodic dimension appears to function as an important aid to the perception of spoken words.

Within the English language, the stress patterns of words cannot be transparently derived from the corresponding printed word form. Indeed, words known as stress homographs share the same phonological form but differ in both their stress assignment and their meaning (e.g. *permit* and *permit*). For these words, the distinctive stress patterns associated with the different lexical forms provide important cues to comprehension for the listener. On the basis of a variety of kinds of evidence, including the presence of stress homographs, it is believed that the stress pattern of a word must be stored as part of its phonological and prosodic specification (e.g. Cutler & Isard, 1980; Selkirk, 1980).

Two recent studies have investigated whether the subvocal articulation component of the articulatory loop is involved in making judgements about the stress structure of familiar words. Campbell, Rosen, Solis-Macias, and White (1991) required subjects to compare the internal stress structure of pairs of printed words. All of the words contained two syllables, and were not phonologically similar to one another. Half of the pairs shared the same stress structure (e.g. *supper/robber*), whereas the other half did not (*abyss/malice*). Subjects worked through two lists of such word pairs as fast as possible, ticking pairs that shared stress structure. Speed of completing the lists and accuracy on individual pairs was calculated.

Each of the lists was tested under a control condition and under two different concurrent task conditions. Subjects either heard the experimenter continually saying "ba-ba-ba" throughout the experiment (concurrent audition), or were required to say "ba-ba-ba" themselves (concurrent articulation). If subvocal articulation within the phonological loop is required for subjects to make comparisons of stress structure, performance should be disrupted significantly in the concurrent articulation condition.

This prediction was supported. Subjects were both slower and less accurate in making stress comparisons under concurrent articulation than concurrent audition. Similar results in Italian have been obtained by Burani, Vallar, and Bottini (1991). Both speed and accuracy of subjects' decisions about the stress markings of printed word pairs, and of their initial sounds, were significantly impaired by articulatory suppression. In contrast, concurrent articulation of a nonspeech kind—chewing—did not influence either kind of judgement. Thus, as with the rhyme judgements tasks considered above, it appears that stress assignment during silent reading is disrupted by articulatory suppression.

Summary
There is consistent evidence of phonological loop involvement in silent reading tasks that require the comparisons of complex physical structure, such as judgements of rhyme and of stress markings. Simpler decisions about the sound structure of letter strings, such as homophony judgement, however, show no evidence of loop contribution.

Why should this be? The most widely accepted explanation of this inconsistency across tasks is that it is due to variations in the complexity of the segmental processes that are demanded by the different judgements. Both rhyme and stress judgements involve complex analysis and comparisons of the phonological representations of two items. Deciding whether one item sounds like another, in contrast, is a relatively straightforward equivalence judgement which does not require segmental analysis. So, do rhyme and stress judgements require a temporary phonological memory representation of the two items in order that the reader can perform the necessary segmental analyses and comparisons? It seems plausible that this is the case (Baddeley, 1986; Besner, 1987).

There is rather less agreement about the nature of the phonological code used to make the simpler homophony judgements. Why is it uninfluenced by suppression? One possibility discussed by Baddeley (1986) is that traces may be set up directly in the phonological store from long-term memory. The visual form of words or nonwords may activate either addressed phonology (in the case of words) or assembled phonology (for unfamiliar letter strings), via the long-term memory system specialised for word recognition. The activated phonology may then be automatically represented in the phonological store. So by this account, a phonological representation can be set up in the phonological loop without subvocal articulation.

Baddeley speculated that the phonological trace set up via this route may be adequate to sustain an immediate phonological decision, such as a homophony judgement, and will not be disturbed by irrelevant articulatory activity. The trace may not, however, be sufficiently durable to support either delayed output in span-type procedure or further segmental analysis, such as required by more complex phonological tasks.

Another possibility is that the demands placed on the phonological loop in generating the phonology for a single (fairly short) letter string are sufficiently light that subjects can perform the necessary subvocal articulation and generate a phonological code for the store despite irrelevant articulatory activity. One way that this could be achieved is by time-sharing between the irrelevant articulatory activity required of suppression and the articulatory coding of the target letter string. This hypothesis receives some support from data reported by Besner et al. (1981). Two experiments (IV and V) used a pseudohomophone judgement paradigm in which subjects decided whether letter strings (such as *kraydel*) sound like real words. When subjects suppressed in time with a metronome ticking at a rate of 170 beats per minute (Experiment V), performance in this task was unimpaired by suppression, as we reported earlier. Error rates increased significantly in the articulatory suppression condition in Experiment IV, however, when subjects were instructed to suppress "as quickly as you can".

Interpretation of this result depends on understanding the difference in the cognitive demands of paced suppression and maximum suppression rate, but as yet the nature of this difference is not clear. The result is, nonetheless, intriguing. Consider first the hypothesis that the "fast as you can" suppression condition led to the *complete* suppression of phonological loop activity, rather than just partial involvement in the paced suppression condition. By this account, the impaired accuracy of pseudohomophone judgement in the former condition is entirely consistent with the view that prelexical phonology is maintained in the phonological loop, but that its storage demands are sufficiently light that via strategic time-sharing, homophone judgements can be made during typical (and less complete) articulatory suppression activity.

An alternative account of these findings is that central executive involvement is necessary to maintain a very fast rate of suppression. Thus, the decrease in accuracy of pseudohomophone judgements may merely be a consequence of generalised cognitive load, rather than of specific phonological loop involvement. This problem in untangling the true origins of concurrent task effects is a persistent one in this literature, largely because of the reliance on only one concurrent task condition (typically, articulatory suppression). So, it appears that the Besner et al. (1981) result is an interesting one, but that unambiguous interpretation will have to await further experimentation that distinguishes the generalised cognitive demands imposed by doing two things at once from more specific suppression of phonological loop activity.

A contrasting position taken by Besner and colleagues (Besner & Davelaar, 1982; Besner, 1987) is that two kinds of phonological code are derived from print. The first corresponds to a trace in the phonological loop, and is disrupted by articulatory suppression. The second phonological code is *not* sensitive to suppression, and appears to correspond to Baddeley and Lewis's (1981) description of the *inner ear* (contrasting with the phonological loop system, which was colloquially termed the *inner voice*). Besner has little further to say about the nature of the putative code. Baddeley and Lewis, though, suggested that it may correspond to an acoustic image that could be generated without any subvocal articulatory activity, but which was not sufficiently robust to be useful in either memory tasks or tasks requiring complex segmental analyses and comparisons.

These alternative accounts of the apparently selective influence of articulatory suppression on complex phonological comparisons rest largely on experimental comparisons between one concurrent task condition (articulatory suppression) and a control condition of no concurrent activity. Unfortunately, many of the studies reviewed in this chapter have not included a further concurrent task that does not involve articulation, so that there is no control for the generalised consequences on task performance of doing two things at once. It is possible that subjects' abilities to make complex comparisons of rhyme and stress structure deteriorate under articulatory suppression simply because of a generalised increase in cognitive load, rather than more particularly as a consequence of suppression of the phonological loop. This explanation is made all the more plausible by the fact that silent phonology tasks that are not disturbed by suppression—such as pseudohomophone judgements—are easier and so may call less upon more general processing resources than tasks such as rhyme judgement.

Reassuringly, Wilding and White (1985, Experiment 2) found that neither the speed nor the accuracy of rhyme judgements were affected by a concurrent task that involved foot-tapping. Both performance measures were, however, disrupted by articulatory suppression. This result lends some credence to interpretations of the articulatory suppression effect in terms of phonological loop activity. Without the inclusion of such experimental controls, though, there is a danger that detailed theorising about phonological loop involvement in the derivation of phonology from print may turn out to be premature.

Neuropsychological Studies

There has not been an extensive amount of neuropsychological work relevant to the links between phonological working memory and visual word recognition, but the available findings do complement the conclusions drawn from work with normal skilled readers. The evidence from patients with highly specific phonological memory deficits is largely consistent with the claim that the phonological loop is not involved in deriving phonology from print via the prelexical route. Neuropsychological findings also implicate the subvocal articulatory component of the phonological loop in making complex segmental and supra-segmental comparisons, such as rhyme judgements and stress assignment. In other words, patients with deficits in subvocal articulation appear to behave more or less like normal skilled readers under conditions of articulatory suppression.

For illustration here we outline the case of BO, studied by Waters, Caplan, and Hildebrandt (1991); similar conclusions also emerge from the study of MK (Howard & Franklin, 1990). BO is a neuro-psychological patient with a severe deficit of immediate verbal memory (with a span of two or three items only). Her performance across a range of phonological memory tasks suggests impaired operation of the articulatory rehearsal component, possibly accompanied by a deficit of the phonological store. How good, then, is BO's single-word reading? She appeared to be able to derive reliably meaning from print. Although BO read rather more slowly than the control subjects, her accuracy at judging whether pairs of words were synonyms or not (e.g. *odour–smell*, and *pearl–forty*) was well within the normal range. Similarly, BO performed exceptionally accurately, although once again slowly, in a written lexical decision task in which she had to judge whether letter strings were words or not.

It also appears that BO was able to generate phonology from print prelexically. Individual nonwords were presented visually, and BO was asked to judge whether they were homophonic with real words (e.g. *grean*) or not (e.g. *freat*). She was not perfect at this task—her overall level of accuracy was 85% compared with 95% for an age-matched control group. Nonetheless, her performance was well above chance level. Similarly, BO was able to perform at a reliably high level in a task that required making homophony judgements about pairs of printed familiar words.

A deficit in subvocal rehearsal therefore did not prevent the patient from either reading familiar words or making simple homophony judgements about familiar and unfamiliar letter strings. This profile of intact reading ability accompanied by defective phonological memory skills is entirely consistent with the view, based on work with normal skilled readers, that both the direct visual route and the indirect phonological recoding route to word recognition are independent of the phonological loop component of working memory.

Waters et al. (1991) did not test whether BO was able to make rhyme or stress judgements about pairs of letter strings. On the basis of findings from normal subjects indicating that such decisions are disrupted by articulatory suppression, we would expect her to be deficient in such tasks. This hypothesis was, however, tested in a more extensive study by this group on six further patients with disturbed articulatory planning (Waters, Rochon, & Caplan, 1992b). The deficits in the high-level speech planning of these dyspraxic patients were found to be mirrored by disturbed articulatory rehearsal in standard tests of verbal short-term memory. These findings are of considerable theoretical importance, as they suggest that the subvocal articulation component of the phonological loop is closely linked with the planning of articulatory speech activity (see Chapter 1). For the present purposes, though, the most important experiments conducted with these patients involved them making phonological judgements about printed letter strings. They were required to make judgements about word pairs concerning either homophony (e.g. *poll–pole* [yes], or *spit–spin* [no]) or rhyme (e.g. *door–war* [yes], or *farm–warm* [no]).

If the dyspraxic patients have a deficit in subvocal articulation so that they perform like normal subjects under articulatory suppression, they should be able to make simple phonological judgements that require little segmentation, such as homophony, but not the more complex rhyme judgements. Although the findings are not unequivocal, they are generally consistent with these predictions. Mean accuracy on visual homophone judgements was 86% for the patients, and 95% for the controls. In the rhyme task, the mean performance level of the patients was 75%; the control group averaged 92% correct. In both tasks, the dyspraxic group performed significantly more poorly than the controls. Nonetheless, there is a tendency towards a relatively higher error rate for the patients in the rhyme judgement task. Consistent with this interpretation, Waters et al. (1992b) found that the rhyme judgement performance of the dyspraxic patients declined significantly with visual compared to auditory presentation of the word pairs. No such decrement was observed, though, across corresponding homophony judgement conditions.

Investigations of the STM patient PV, however, failed to yield any sign of deficits even in tasks which involve making very complex judgements about segmental and prosodic structure. Vallar and Baddeley (1984b) tested this patient's abilities to make rhyme judgements about pairs of pictures, word–picture pairs, and nonword–picture pairs. She was completely unimpaired in her ability to make rhyme judgements in each of these conditions. Furthermore, PV performed well in a task that required her to identify the stressed syllable in three-syllable letter strings.

One reason for the apparent discrepancy between the phonological processing abilities of PV and the dyspraxic patients reported by Waters et al. (1992b) may lie in their specific phonological loop impairments. Whereas the dyspraxic patients appear to have deficits in the subvocal articulatory process, PV is believed to have a primary disturbance of the other component of the phonological loop—the phonological short-term store. Vallar and Baddeley (1984b) suggest that she has no articulatory deficit, but that she chooses not to use subvocal mediation as a strategy in short-term memory tasks, probably because the phonological trace resulting from such articulatory activity is very weak. This account leaves open the possibility that PV does strategically use subvocal articulation in other tasks, such as rhyme and stress judgement. Her unimpaired performance in these tasks can then be explained if it is assumed that these judgements are mediated by subvocal articulatory activity, rather than by phonological representations in the phonological store. In favour of this argument, it should be noted that syllabic stress is realised at an articulatory rather than a phonological level. A consequence of this interpretation is that it would indeed be expected that patients with a primary deficit in the articulatory process should be relatively more impaired at judgements of rhyme and stress than those, like PV, with impairments of the phonological store component of the phonological loop.

At this point, speculation is preceding the evidence by some distance, and there is a clear need for further careful experimentation with both normal subjects and individuals with acquired phonological memory deficits before strong theoretical claims can or should be made. More generally, though, there is a reasonable degree of convergence between neuropsychological and experimental data concerning links between the phonological loop and reading single words. Recognition of words by the direct visual route appears to proceed completely independently of the phonological loop, and readers can also readily derive phonological representations from print despite at least partial suppression of loop activity. Capacities to perform more complex segmental and prosodic analyses of letter strings, though, appear to depend to some degree on mediation by speech-based mechanisms shared by the phonological loop.

Developmental Studies

The possible involvement of the phonological loop in phonological recoding during children's reading development has also been explored experimentally. The issue is even more complex in children's reading than in skilled adult reading, due to the developmental changes known to take place in the use of phonological recoding as a reading strategy. Chapters 5 and 6 provide detailed discussions of phonological mediation in reading development. In the section following we outline the role that phonological recoding appears to take in reading development, based on the framework developed in Chapter 5. Experimental evidence concerning phonological mediation at different points during reading development is also considered.

Phonological Recoding during Reading Development
The ease with which children acquire literacy depends critically on their abilities to develop a strategy of using the correspondences between letters and sounds to guide both reading and spelling

attempts. In reading, phonological mediation provides the child with an opportunity to identify printed letter strings whose visual form has not already been learned—that is, words that are not within the child's "sight vocabulary". Even though many of the words in the English language do not have entirely regular spelling–sound patterns, the letter sequences within most words convey sufficient information about sound structure to enable the child, who may also be guided by context, to make successful guesses as to the identity of the letter string.

Recognition of printed words via phonological recoding appears to be most important in the early stages of reading development, when many of the words that the child encounters in text, or wishes to spell, may not be familiar. By correctly sounding out the target item, or using partial phonological information in combination with contextual knowledge, the child can extend its sight vocabulary without being explicitly taught the word. As reading abilities develop, however, the repertoire of words whose visual forms are familiar to the child expands to such an extent that recognition of words by a phonological recoding strategy is likely to become less important. By the time the child becomes a skilled reader, reading under normal circumstances will be based principally on direct visual recognition of words within the (by now extensive) sight vocabulary.

Strong claims about young children's dependence on phonological recoding when reading for meaning have been made on the basis of the sentence reading paradigm developed by Doctor and Coltheart (1980). In a widely cited experiment, groups of children aged between six and ten years were shown printed sentences for silent reading. The task was to judge whether or not the words made sense. Some of the sentences that were meaningless contained homophonic words, which rendered the sentences meaningful when converted into phonological form (such as, *He ran threw the street*). Other sentences remained meaningless when phonologically recoded (e.g. *He ran sew the street*).

The six-year-old children were much more accurate at rejecting the meaningless sentences that sounded meaningless than the ones that sounded meaningful (92% and 29% correct, respectively). The older children, however, were much better than the young at correctly rejecting the sentences that sounded correct but were in fact meaningless; the ten-year-old group were 79% accurate on this sentence type. A very similar developmental trend occurred for sentences that contained nonwords whose phonological forms made sense (e.g. I *noe* him).

Doctor and Coltheart argued that these results demonstrate the greater reliance of beginning readers on a phonological recoding strategy than older, more skilled, children. This interpretation certainly tallies with the view that a phonological recoding strategy is dominant during the early stages of reading development, and that it becomes less important as the readers become more skilled. However, the findings are equally consistent with an alternative interpretation first advanced by Oakhill and Garnham (1988), which does not involve any strong claims about the young children recognising the words via a phonological recoding strategy. The argument is as follows: Less experienced readers may simply be less confident in their spelling abilities. They are therefore less likely to reject sentences that they consider may (or may not) contain words that are wrongly spelled. A similar interpretation can also be extended to reports that young unskilled readers are relatively poor at rejecting nonwords that sound like words in a lexical decision task (Johnston et al., 1987). Although it is possible that the young readers are more reliant on a strategy of phonological recoding for lexical access than older children, it may simply be the case that they are rather less confident about the spelling patterns of words.

Thus, evidence that young readers generate the phonology of printed letter strings does not necessarily mean that the children are either phonologically recoding all printed letter strings, or that the phonology is derived prior to lexical access. It is rather more likely that familiar words that are present within the child's sight vocabulary are recognised directly on the basis of their visual characteristics, and that the phonology of the words is generated postlexically. Returning to the example of the homophonic sentence used by Doctor and Coltheart (*He ran threw the street*), the lexical item *through* may be activated by the phonological form achieved postlexically when the child read its homophonic form *threw*, and so intrudes without any recourse to prelexical phonological recoding.

Some researchers have been puzzled about why, if a phonological recoding strategy is important to early reading and spelling development, children do not use it in this type of experimental situation (Goswami & Bryant, 1990). The answer seems relatively straightforward: Although phonological recoding is undoubtedly an important strategy for attempting to read unfamiliar letter strings, it probably does not represent the dominant, or indeed the most effective, reading strategy for even the young reader. The strategy is likely to be reserved for those letter strings that are not within the child's sight vocabulary; if the words employed in an experiment are familiar, it is easier and faster for the child to recognise them by the direct visual route rather than by phonological recoding (Thorstad, 1991). In studies of children's silent reading, experimenters typically select words that will be familiar to most of the children. Thus the majority of words would indeed be expected to be read via the direct visual route.

In summary, it seems likely that under normal circumstances, such as reading for meaning, even beginning readers recognise familiar words by the process of direct visual recognition, rather than phonological recoding. We suggest that where possible, young children (like skilled readers) access the phonology of a printed word *after* lexical access, rather than *before* it. Words will be recognised by the phonological recoding strategy only if the following two conditions are satisfied: The child is currently applying such a strategy, and the letter string is not a familiar one that can be directly recognised.

The Phonological Loop and Children's Reading
Work on the involvement of the phonological loop in children's visual word recognition has largely been motivated by the pervasive view that younger children read to a greater extent by a phonological recoding strategy than older children and adult skilled readers. From our perspective, there are two difficulties with this approach. Firstly, as we discussed earlier, it is not at all clear that even very early readers recognise familiar words by phonological mediation. And given that experimenters typically select words that will be familiar to the child, "live" phonological recoding is likely to be captured only rarely in experimental sessions.

Secondly, the evidence from studies of normal and brain-damaged adults indicates that both prelexical and postlexical phonology can be accessed without placing significant demands on phonological working memory. The phonological loop only appears to be critical in tasks requiring relatively complex analysis of the sound structure of printed material. Thus, even if young readers were recognising words predominantly by phonological mediation, there is no reason to expect disturbance of this strategy by tasks such as irrelevant articulation, which are designed to suppress phonological loop activity (unless, of course, phonological mediation involves different cognitive processes in unskilled and skilled reading). As with adults, though, we would expect some disturbance by concurrent articulation in tasks such as rhyme judgement.

Consistent with this perspective, the developmental findings have indeed been found to correspond closely to results from studies of normal skilled readers. Kimura and Bryant (1983) studied young readers' abilities to judge whether a printed letter string corresponded to a picture. The children were aged between six and eight years, and their task was to sort word–picture pairs into two piles, according to whether they did or did not match (see Fig. 7.1). Each child carried out this task on two occasions, with different sets of materials. On one occasion, the task was performed in silence. On the other, the child continuously repeated "ice cream" while performing the sorting task.

Articulatory suppression did not influence either the speed or the accuracy with which the children matched the words and pictures. This result indicates that these young readers were able to recognise the visual forms of words without relying on the phonological loop. It does not, of course, rule out the possibility that the children were using phonological mediation to access the word meanings, as work with normal adult readers indicates that even this phonological recoding task is unhampered by articulatory suppression. The Kimura and Bryant result therefore is not relevant to the issue of whether the children in their task were recognising the words on the basis of prelexical phonology. It does, however, appear to rule out the possibility that subvocal articulatory recoding is necessary for children to read familiar words (see also Barron & Baron, 1977).

A rather different conclusion, however, follows from a study reported by Mitterer (1982). In Experiment 2, a group of normal readers from Grade 3 took part in a lexical decision experiment in which they were asked to nod their heads if the displayed letter string was a real letter string and to shake their heads if they thought it was not real. The nonwords were either homophonic with real words (e.g. *fome*) or were not (e.g. *fode*). Lexical decision was tested under two

FIG. 7.1. Examples of picture–word pairs used in Kimura and Bryant's (1983) matching task. (Reproduced with permission.)

conditions: A concurrent vocalisation condition in which the child had to count in series from one, continuing until the lexical decision had been made, or a control condition of no concurrent activity.

In this study, articulatory suppression *was* found significantly to disturb the accuracy of lexical decision in the normal readers. Furthermore, analysis of nonword errors by subtype (pseudo-homophones or not) revealed that the greater frequency of error responses on the nonwords that sounded like real words declined significantly under articulatory suppression. From this result, it appears that the young readers were indeed phonological recoding the nonword letter strings, and moreover that this recoding activity was disrupted by irrelevant articulation. This finding is clearly at odds with findings from studies of normal adult readers, which have shown that judgements of pseudohomophony are unimpaired by articulatory suppression (Baddeley & Lewis, 1981).

One possible explanation for the sensitivity of prelexical phonological recoding in children but not adults to articulatory suppression is that it is simply a consequence of requiring relatively unskilled readers, for whom reading is not yet an automated procedure, to do something else at the same time as reading. In favour of this interpretation, it should be noted that the irrelevant articulatory activity used by Mitterer's subjects (counting in series) was rather more demanding than the usual articulatory suppression procedure of rote repetition of a word. And, as indeed with most studies in this literature, no nonarticulatory concurrent condition was included in order to control for this possibility that the deterioration in task performance was simply due to overload of general processing resources.

It should also be noted that a recent study by Arthur, Hitch, and Halliday (in press) has yielded findings which conflict directly with the Mitterer (1982) result. In Experiment 1, they, too, tested the ability of eight-year-old children to make lexical decisions with and without articulatory suppression. As in the Mitterer study, the nonwords were either pseudohomophones (e.g. *bote*) or not (e.g. *lote*). This time, the child pressed one of two keys according to whether it thought the letter string displayed on the screen was a real word or not. Both the speed and accuracy of the keypresses was recorded. The articulatory suppression activity involved repeatedly counting from one to five.

The children made more errors on the nonwords that sounded like real words than the ones that did not, indicating that some phonological recoding took place in this procedure. The more surprising result, though, was that not only was there no significant effect of articulatory suppression on accuracy of lexical decisions (in contrast to Mitterer's findings), but that the children were actually significantly faster at making lexical decisions under the articulatory suppression condition than under the control no activity condition. So, irrelevant articulation speeded subjects' responses, without any tradeoff in accuracy.

In a further experiment in this paper, Arthur et al. tested children's abilities to make rhyme judgements about pairs of printed words with and without concurrent articulatory suppression. This time, the results corresponded with those reported previously for normal adult readers: Accuracy of rhyme judgements declined significantly under the articulatory suppression condition. This finding replicates an earlier study by Barron and Baron (1977), who found that articulatory suppression impaired judgements about word pairs in children across a wide range of reading ages.

Why might it be that blocking subvocal articulation had beneficial effects on the children's abilities to make lexical decisions but deleterious consequences for rhyme judgement? The answer is likely to lie in the different demands of the two tasks. In a lexical decision experiment, the best strategy for accurately judging lexicality is likely to involve deciding whether a direct visual match is found. Readers may, however, also perform a phonological check subsequent to making (or not making) a visual match. If this late checking procedure is mediated by the phonological loop, suppressing loop activity should therefore save the readers' time at no expense to accuracy. This phonological check must, however, be distinguished by the prelexical phonological recoding, which mediates the higher error rates with pseudohomophones than ordinary nonwords, as this was not disturbed by articulatory suppression. This prelexical phonological recoding therefore appears to take place in children, as in adults, largely independently of the phonological loop.

The contrasting disruptive consequences of articulatory suppression on rhyme judgements, though, can be explained in the same way as the corresponding finding with skilled readers (e.g. Johnston & McDermott, 1986). In order to make explicit comparisons of the segmental structure of two letter strings, the reader appears to need to maintain the phonological representations within phonological working memory; preventing them from doing so by concurrent articulation will therefore impair accuracy of rhyme judgements.

OVERVIEW

In this chapter, we have considered in detail the possibility that the phonological component of working memory is involved in word recognition. The weight of experimental, neuropsychological, and developmental evidence reviewed in the course of the chapter favours the view that the phonological loop plays only a very minor role in reading at the single-word level. The suppression of phonological loop activity has no detectable deleterious effects on reading for meaning in either skilled adult readers, or children of different levels of reading ability. Even in the rather special circumstances in which skilled readers phonologically recode either familiar words or novel letter strings, there is little evidence of significant phonological loop mediation. Two possible accounts of this apparent independence of phonological recoding and phonological working memory have been considered: Either phonological representations can be derived from print without involvement of the loop system (Besner & Davelaar, 1982), or they can be represented within the phonological store directly from long-term memory, without subvocal articulatory mediation (Baddeley, 1986). At present, though, experimental techniques do not appear sufficiently sensitive to allow these two alternatives to be distinguished empirically.

The only reading situations in which phonological loop involvement has been consistently identified have required subjects to make rather complex comparisons about the segmental and prosodic structures associated with letter strings. The two relevant tasks here are rhyme judgement and syllabic stress assignments. Performance in these tasks is significantly and consistently impaired when phonological loop activity is disrupted either by concurrent irrelevant articulatory activity (in both skilled and unskilled readers), or as a consequence of brain damage. The phonological involvement in such tasks may result from the storage demands placed by such judgements—two phonological representations have to be maintained, updated, and compared in order to perform segmental or prosodic analyses. This will impose a significant memory load, with the result that phonological loop constraints become relevant. The nature of phonological memory contribution to performance of such tasks is, however, in need of further exploration and explanation. In particular, recent neuropsychological evidence suggests that subvocal articulatory activity may be more critical than phonological storage to making accurate judgements and comparisons of these kinds. Whether experimental work with normal readers will uphold these implications from neuropsychological data, though, remains to be seen.

CHAPTER EIGHT

Language Comprehension

In recent years, the notion that working memory is involved in the comprehension of spoken and written language has received widespread attention. Part of the reason for the popularity of this view lies in its intuitive plausibility. Our comprehension of the complex syntactic and semantic information conveyed in both spoken language and text often appears to lag behind the sensory input, so that we have the experience of labouring with interpretation of the meaning of a sentence some time after either the speaker has finished speaking, or after the text has been "read". Such constructions, in which the reader chooses the wrong syntactic interpretation of a sentence and is subsequently forced by conflicting semantic or syntactic cues to make a re-interpretation, are termed "garden path" sentences. Consider, for example, the following sentences: *I saw that gasoline can explode. And a brand new gasoline can it was too.* The word *can* is usually initially assigned verb status within the first sentence. If the first sentence is to be integrated with the second, however, the reader is forced to reparse the initial sentence and to interpret *can* as a noun. To do this, it has been argued that the comprehender may use a verbatim representation of the sentence held within working memory as the basis for the syntactic re-interpretation. This buffer facility may be particularly useful in comprehending spoken language, which is physically accessible to the listener for a very brief period only.

This view that working memory provides a buffer storage of the verbatim form of connected language represents only one of a wide range of distinguishable roles assigned to working memory in comprehension. In this chapter, we aim to provide a coherent evaluation of the contributions of two components of the working memory model—the phonological loop and the central executive—to language comprehension. For each component, we will draw on evidence from experimental studies of skilled language users, from neuropsychological case studies of patients with acquired memory and comprehension impairments, and from work on the development of comprehension during childhood. Before considering the empirical findings in detail, though, we briefly preview the principal contrasting roles that have been assigned to working memory in comprehension by psycholinguistic models of language comprehension.

WORKING MEMORY INVOLVEMENT IN MODELS OF LANGUAGE COMPREHENSION

Two models of language understanding have been particularly influential in stimulating psychological research in the involvement of working memory in comprehension. Clark and Clarke (1977) identified a major role for working memory in their four-step model of spoken language comprehension. The first step of the model involves the construction of a phonological representation of the message in working memory. This memory representation is then used as a basis for the identification of the content and function of the constituents of the message. From this information, the underlying propositions are used to build a hierarchical structure of the sentence. Finally, the working memory representation of the raw input form is purged, so that the listener retains the meaning of the message rather than its exact meaning.

According to this model, the working memory representation of the linguistically unprocessed message represents a critical stage in the process of comprehension of any verbal message. Although the specific working memory mechanism that satisfies this buffer function was not identified by Clark and Clarke, it corresponds directly to the phonological loop component of the working memory, which is specialised for the temporary storage of the phonological form of linguistic material.

The strongest version of this model, according to which all understanding is based on analysis of a working memory representation of the sentence, has to be rejected. There is clear evidence that much of our processing of spoken language at least proceeds in real time, or "on-line". Numerous experimental studies have established that spoken words are on average recognised within about 200ms of the onset of the acoustic signal, and that both sensory and contextual information influences this rapid word recognition process (e.g. Marslen-Wilson, 1987; Marslen-Wilson & Tyler, 1980). Given the rapidity of understanding at the single word level at least, it is clearly the case that lexical semantic information can be accessed without reference to a working memory representation. This does not mean that buffer storage of the raw input form of sentences is never necessary. Although words presented in isolation or in syntactically simple sentence structures may be processed on-line, the construction of semantic and syntactic interpretations at the message level may lag behind the input, and so may proceed "off-line". In such situations, the presence of a working memory representation of the message provides a backup both for the higher-level linguistic interpretation and for recognition of words later in the sentence. This position, or variants of it, has been adopted by many theorists concerned with working memory input into language comprehension, and will be discussed in more detail in the next section.

A contrasting role of working memory in language comprehension was assigned by the text comprehension model developed by Kintsch and Van Dijk (1978; see also Van Dijk & Kintsch, 1983). In the model, the linguistic message is processed in cycles, each cycle representing a chunk containing several propositions. A short-term memory buffer is used to retain as many of these propositions as its limited capacity permits, and these stored propositions form the basis of coherence processing. If an overlap in the arguments of the propositions in a particular chunk is found with the propositions from an earlier chunk retained in the buffer, the text is accepted as coherent. In the absence of such a match, inference processes involving search within long-term memory are necessary, making heavy demands on general processing resources.

In this model, capacity limitations within the short-term memory buffer will constrain the efficiency of coherence processing. Kintsch and Van Dijk suggest that the buffer capacity may depend on the processing resources currently available, such that with more difficult messages, capacity may be devoted to aspects of processing other than short-term storage of propositions. According to this model, then, we might expect working memory requirements for sentence processing to vary with the difficulty of the syntactic or semantic structure of the sentence.

The functions fulfilled by working memory across these two models differ considerably. The storage functions attributed by Kintsch and

Van Dijk to working memory (maintenance of the predicate–argument structure of propositions) seem to be more readily satisfied by the general resources of the central executive than the more specialised phonological loop system. In contrast, the Clark and Clarke (1977) model emphasises the importance of a phonological loop-type representation of the phonological form of the message as the basis for language comprehension processes. As we shall see in the remainder of this chapter, the view that the phonological loop and central executive make dissociable contributions to language comprehension is well supported by more direct empirical evidence.

Finally, a less commonly held view is that language comprehension can proceed completely *independently* of phonological working memory (Howard & Butterworth, 1989). This position is supported by evidence of apparently normal development of language comprehension in the presence of severe phonological memory deficits.

THE PHONOLOGICAL LOOP AND
LANGUAGE COMPREHENSION

The notion that working memory provides a temporary verbatim representation of the linguistic message that is used during the comprehension process has been very influential in guiding research on language understanding. As work in this area has progressed, however, it has became clear that this simple notion requires considerable theoretical refinement if it is to provide a reasonable account of the available data. Views have varied on precisely what function in the comprehension process is fulfilled by the phonological loop component of working memory. Before reviewing the relevant literature, we briefly outline the three principal theoretical stances that have been adopted concerning the relationship between phonological working memory and language comprehension.

An assumption shared by all current theories is that comprehension of clauses and sentences with simple syntactical and semantic structures proceeds on-line, and thus without reference to a phonological working memory representation of the message. The first class of view is that phonological working memory is, however, used as a backup store to be consulted during off-line linguistic analysis (e.g. Saffran & Marin, 1975; Baddeley, Vallar, & Wilson, 1987; Martin, 1987). Messages that have been assumed to benefit from off-line language processing include sentences that are semantically reversible, have passive forms, and contain centre-embedded clauses (e.g. *The boy that was carried by the girl had red hair*). In each of these cases it has been argued that the high degree of linguistic complexity of the sentence forms, married with the absence of a simple pragmatic interpretation of the sentence based on the main lexical elements, forces the comprehender to carry out the necessary syntactic and semantic analysis off-line, based on a temporary phonological representation of the sentence (e.g. Caramazza, Basili, Koller, & Berndt, 1981a; Saffran & Marin, 1975). Similar claims have been made about phonological working memory involvement in understanding sentences that contain many content words (e.g. *Touch the small red circle after the large green triangle*), and also long sentences in which the preservation of word order is critical (e.g. *One could reasonably claim that sailors are often lived on by ships of various kinds*). For these kinds of long sentence constructions, it has been argued that the listener (or reader) has to maintain in phonological memory the full word sequence in order to interpret the full sentence form, and so that understanding these forms taxes the limited capacity of phonological working memory (Baddeley et al., 1987; Martin, 1990).

An alternative position that has been argued by Caplan, Waters, and colleagues is that phonological working memory representations do indeed provide an input into the analysis of linguistically complex structures, but that the contribution occurs much later in the information processing sequence than is assumed by the first class of account. Specifically, these researchers claim that phonological memory is used as a postsyntactic checking mechanism for syntactically complex sentences in which the assignment of lexical items to the parsed syntactic structure is not straightforward. Thus by this account, phonological memory representations do not provide the basis for the initial syntactic and semantic analysis, but for subsequently checking the products of syntactic analysis.

Finally, a less commonly held view is that language comprehension does not require phonological memory support at all (Howard & Butterworth, 1989). This position is supported by evidence of apparently normal development of language comprehension in the presence of severe phonological memory deficits.

Studies of Skilled Comprehenders

The contribution of phonological working memory to skilled adult comprehension has been tested directly by investigating the consequences of experimentally disrupting the use of the phonological loop during the performance of language-understanding tasks. Three techniques have been used to manipulate phonological loop contribution: articulatory suppression, phonological similarity, and unattended speech. The disruptive influences of these variables on immediate verbal memory performance are well established, and have been attributed to disturbed operation of the phonological loop component (see Chapter 1). These techniques therefore offer a set of useful tools for investigating whether the phonological loop does contribute significantly to sentence processing in skilled comprehenders.

Articulatory Suppression

Consistent disruptive effects of requiring subjects to engage in irrelevant articulation while reading for meaning have only been found with long and complex sentence structures. In an early study, Baddeley (1978) found that suppressing articulation did not impair either the speed or the accuracy with which subjects could verify simple active sentences such as *Canaries have wings* and *Canaries have gills*. When printed material of greater linguistic complexity has been used, however, the results are quite different. Baddeley, Eldridge, and Lewis (1981) required subjects to make decisions about whether long sentences such as *She doesn't mind going to the dentist to have fillings, but doesn't like the rent when he gives her the injection in the beginning* were semantically anomalous or not. Anomaly involved substituting one word within the sentence (i.e. *rent* for *pain*). As Fig. 8.1 shows, errors in detecting the anomalous sentences increased significantly under the articulatory suppression condition, although there was no corresponding effect on judgements for the control sentences. Speed of making the decision was not, however, compromised by articulatory suppression.

These results were replicated and extended in a further experiment in which the anomalous sentences included either substituted words or pairs of transposed words. Once again, accuracy decreased under conditions of articulatory suppression. The error increase was particularly great for subjects' detection of sentences that contained transposed words. This result fits well with findings from more conventional short-term memory paradigms showing disruptive effects of suppression on the retention of order information (e.g. Baddeley et al., 1975; Levy, 1971). These findings are consistent with neuropsychological evidence that phonological loop support is most important for understanding sentence constructions in which the lexical semantics of the main content words is not sufficient to guide interpretation, and word order is critical to meaning.

Baddeley et al. (1981) also showed that the decrease in accuracy of detecting anomalous words and transpositions in text did not occur when subjects engaged in concurrent tapping. It therefore appears that the disruptive effect of suppression on reading for meaning is not

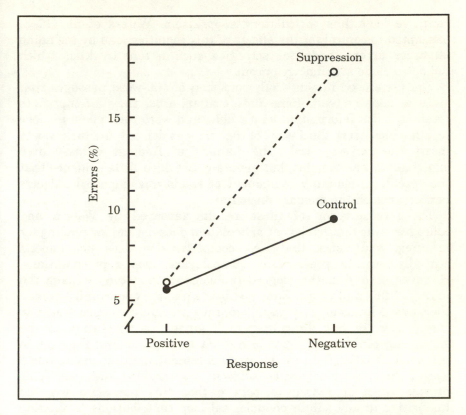

FIG. 8.1. Mean percent errors on positive and negative sentences, as a function of concurrent task. From Baddeley, Eldridge, and Lewis (1981). (Reproduced with permission.)

simply a consequence of carrying out two tasks at once (reading and articulatory suppression), but instead arises from a specific disturbance of the phonological loop component of working memory.

Findings from studies using different types of reading tasks and concurrent verbal activity, however, have led to contrasting theoretical interpretations of the role of phonological working memory in text comprehension. Waters, Komoda, and Arbuckle (1985) investigated the effects of a concurrent shadowing task on reading of prose passages. Shadowing involves the immediate repetition of heard stimuli; in these studies, the stimuli to be shadowed consisted of a random sequence of the digits *one, two* and *three*. Shadowing shares the same component of irrelevant articulation as articulatory suppression, provided the rate is as fast as a typical articulatory suppression condition. In addition, though, it involves the perception of unpredictable spoken stimuli, and so imposes a heavier general cognitive load than articulatory suppression. Waters et al. (1985) attempted to control for the effects of this cognitive load by including other concurrent shadowing activities, such as tone tracking, which did not include articulatory output.

The texts used in this study consisted of 150-word passages that subjects silently read. Immediately afterwards, they attempted to recall as much information as possible, and were then given a Cloze test in which every third word of the text was deleted; the task was to insert the correct word. The pattern of findings across three experiments was complex, but generally provided little evidence that the specific articulatory component of shadowing impaired subjects performance on the memory measures.

The interpretation of these results favoured by Waters and colleagues was that irrelevant articulation does not impair reading for meaning, and hence that text comprehension does not depend critically on the presence of phonological loop representations. However, several methodological problems in this study weaken the impact of this null result. Firstly, subjects had the opportunity to read the passage for as long as they liked, thus providing an opportunity to compensate for any difficulties in linguistic interpretation in the shadowing condition by spending extra time processing the text in this condition. Secondly, the measure of reading comprehension was a very indirect one, involving subjects' *memory* for the text. This provides another reason to believe that this paradigm may be insensitive to any subtle phonological loop contributions to reading comprehension, and so provides an insubstantial basis for rejecting the phonological loop hypothesis.

Waters, Caplan, and Hildebrandt (1987) attempted to test more specifically the nature of the contribution, if any, of the phonological loop to reading comprehension. In Experiment 3 of this paper, subjects made decisions about the semantic acceptability of sentences. While they were carrying out this task, they either engaged in articulatory suppression, tapping, or no concurrent activity. The mean reaction times in the different concurrent task conditions are shown in Table 8.1, as a function of whether the sentences contained one proposition (e.g. *It was the gangsters that broke into the warehouse*) or two propositions (e.g. *The man hit the landlord that requested the money*). Articulatory suppression significantly increased response times relative to the no-task control condition for the sentences containing two propositions, but not for the one-proposition sentence. There was no corresponding influence of tapping, indicating that the suppression effect was not simply a dual-task decrement of a general nature. A similar pattern of findings was obtained on accuracy of the responses.

TABLE 8.1

Mean Reaction Times (ms) as a Function of the Number of Propositions in the Sentences

Concurrent Activity	One Proposition	Two Propositions
None	2204	2730
Tapping	2186	2794
Articulation	2482	3245

Adapted from Waters, Caplan, and Hildebrandt (1987).

These results, then, provide direct support for the notion that the phonological loop does contribute to the linguistic processing of complex sentences. Waters et al. (1987) make strong and specific claims about the selective influence of suppression on recall of the two-proposition sentences only. They argue on the basis of linguistic parsing models (e.g. Berwick & Weinberg, 1985) that increasing the number of propositions in the sentences does not increase the complexity of the syntactic structure of the sentence, but that it does add to the final stage of assigning the semantic values of the main lexical items to the parsed syntactic structure. Thus, the selective influence of suppression on processing of the two-proposition sentences is interpreted as reflecting consultation of phonological loop representations of the original sentence form at a late postsyntactic stage.

Although this interpretation is interestingly specific about phonological loop involvement in comprehension, it is by no means unambiguous. Firstly, it is not clear that competence models of linguistic parsing necessarily apply to performance, and that they correspond to the way in which people actually construct meaning representations from text. Secondly, there are many changes which inevitably result from increasing the number of propositions in a sentence: A concomitant increase in the number of specific nouns, for example. It seems very unlikely that all of the consequent changes in linguistic form which result in "adding" a proposition to a sentence will be cleanly restricted to the postsyntactic checking mechanisms.

Reading sentences for meaning, therefore, does appear to be sensitive to articulatory suppression, providing that the sentence constructions are of a relatively high degree of linguistic complexity or length. The precise linguistic conditions under which phonological loop involvement is implicated in text processing are, however, as yet still a matter for theoretical debate and further empirical investigation.

Phonological Similarity

According to the current working memory model, phonological similarity disrupts phonological loop function by degrading phonological representations in the short-term store component (Salamé & Baddeley, 1982). If this is the case, and the phonological loop does play a role in sentence processing, then comprehension performance should be reduced if the words in sentences have a high degree of phonological similarity. Baddeley and Hitch (1974) tested this hypothesis. They asked subjects to judge whether the word order was correct or not for sentences which were either high in phonological similarity (e.g. *Rude Jude chewed his crude stewed food*) or low in similarity (e.g. *Rude curt Jude ate his plain boiled meal*). As these examples show, the sentences were matched for meaning and number of words across the two conditions. The results were inconclusive. Subjects were significantly slower at judging whether sentences contained word transpositions for similar rather than dissimilar texts. The latency increase with high phonological similarity was not significant across items, however. Also, there were no effects on accuracy of the judgements (see also McCutcheon & Perfetti, 1982).

Further research using this phonological similarity paradigm with sentences has added to the interpretational problems. Baddeley and Lewis (1981) confirmed that the phonological similarity effect was restricted to speed of processing rather than accuracy, and also found no significant interaction between phonological similarity and articulatory suppression in semantic anomaly judgements. In more traditional short-term memory tasks, the interaction between phonological similarity and articulatory suppression is of course well established (e.g. Levy, 1971; Peterson & Johnson, 1971), so the apparently independent effects of the two variables in this sentence processing task represent a puzzle. There is some evidence that the slowing down in processing with texts that are high in phonological similarity is due to the accompanying high degree of visual similarity of the sentences. Baddeley and Lewis (1981) found a substantial correlation between the time taken to verify sentences and a measure of visual similarity based on digram overlap between words. Distinguishing which of the kinds of similarity—phonological or visual—is the critical factor in these studies would require further careful experimentation. On this basis, a cautious interpretation of the phonological similarity results is that they do not lend further independent support to the notion that the phonological loop contributes to text processing.

Unattended Speech

In common with the phonological similarity effect, the disruptive influences of unattended speech on immediate recall appear to arise from degradation of representations of memory items in the phonological short-term store (see Chapter 1). If the phonological loop does contribute to the linguistic processing of text, unattended speech should also disturb sentence processing.

A recent experimental series reported by Martin, Wogalter, and Forlano (1988) set out to test this hypothesis. The primary task involved subjects silently reading text, completing a distractor test, and then answering questions on the text. The main dependent variable was comprehension accuracy. A variety of secondary tasks were compared across a series of five experiments—in addition to the control condition, subjects variously listened to jazz music, vocal music, white noise, prose, and random word lists. The results were clear. There was a decrement in reading comprehension when the concurrent noise contained meaningful verbal material, whether in text or in music. There was, however, no further effect on comprehension of a meaningless speech background consisting of nonwords than of concurrent white noise (Experiment 5; see also Baddeley et al., 1981). These results point directly to the locus of concurrent speech interference on the processing of text being located at a semantic, and not phonological, level, and certainly merit replication and further investigation.

Summary

For long and syntactically complex material, there is clear evidence of consultation of the phonological loop at some stage during linguistic processing. Across several experiments, subjects' reading of these types of material for meaning has been found to be selectively impaired by articulatory suppression. Two main theoretical interpretations of the results have been advanced. Baddeley and Lewis (1981) interpreted their results as reflecting the use of a verbatim record of the phonological form of a sentence in complex syntactic analysis, and for retention of word order where it is critical to meaning. Waters et al. (1987), in contrast, claim that the evidence is more consistent with reference to the phonological memory representation of the sentence after syntactic parsing has been completed, when lexical items are mapped onto the parsed syntactic constituents. At present, however, it seems fair to say that the limited amount of relevant data available is consistent with either position.

Results using other techniques designed to disturb phonological loop contribution, such as varying the phonological similarity of the sentences or listening to irrelevant speech, have yielded much less consistent results than the suppression studies. There are a number of reasons why the absence of effects of phonological similarity and unattended speech on reading for meaning does not necessarily challenge the conclusions drawn from the suppression studies. One possibility is that articulatory suppression disturbs the operation of the phonological loop to a greater extent than the other variables; certainly, research with immediate recall tasks suggests that the unattended speech effect is relatively weak. An alternative explanation is that the types of sentences used in the similarity and unattended speech studies have generally been less lengthy and syntactically complex than the ones that have consistently been shown to be sensitive to articulatory suppression.

Finally, it should be noted that whereas the locus of the articulatory suppression effect appears to be the subvocal rehearsal component of the phonological loop, the disruptive influences of phonological similarity and unattended speech are usually attributed to the passive phonological store component. A final interpretation of the findings reviewed in this section that may be worth exploring is therefore that it is the subvocal rehearsal process used to maintain phonological representations that is consulted in the course of complex language processing, rather than the phonological record of the sentence.

Neuropsychological Investigations

Patients with acquired brain damage resulting in severe phonological working memory deficits have provided a particularly fruitful source of "natural" data concerning working memory involvement in language processing. The typical profile of a STM patient is of very poor performance in immediate verbal memory tests, with a greater memory decrement for auditorily than visually presented material. Despite the severe short-term memory deficits of these patients, spontaneous speech production can be quite normal (e.g. Shallice & Butterworth, 1977; see Chapter 4) and language comprehension appears to be relatively intact on informal testing. On the basis of the research with skilled language users reviewed in the previous section, though, we would expect these patients to experience difficulties when their understanding of long and syntactically complex sentences is tested.

The available neuropsychological evidence has in general supported this prediction. Saffran and Marin (1975) published an early influential paper in this area. They reported a single case study of a patient IL who had poor immediate memory skills corresponding to a deficit of the phonological loop. A sentence repetition task was used. IL could frequently correctly paraphrase a sentence which she could not correctly repeat verbatim; this indicates that for some sentence types at least, an intact phonological loop is not necessary for understanding. For two particular sentence types, however, IL frequently produced paraphrases of the sentences that were semantically incorrect—passive constructions (e.g. "The boy was pushed by the girl"), and centre-embedded sentences (e.g. "The man the boy hit carried the box"). The paraphrase errors in both cases seemed to be due to dependence on a simple pragmatic strategy in which syntactic relations between elements were assigned in a simple Subject–Verb–Object sequence. Such a strategy would be expected to yield consistent errors with both passive and centre-embedded sentences.

Saffran and Marin linked the systematic semantic misinterpretations of IL with her severe phonological memory deficit. They commented that "having the phonemic record around for a while does seem useful ... when there is need to reconsider the first or ongoing interpretation: when syntax is tortuous ... and when messages are garbled or otherwise noisy" (p. 432). This interpretation of phonological working memory involvement in language comprehension clearly fits well with the idea discussed earlier in the context of studies with normal adults, that the phonological loop system is useful for retaining order information in long and syntactically complex sentences.

Similar results were obtained by Friedrich, Martin, and Kemper (1985) in their study of another STM patient, EA. The sentence repetition of this patient once again showed a dependence on Subject–Verb–Object interpretation in place of full syntactic analysis, resulting in subject–object role reversals in passive sentences. In general, EA's repetition accuracy declined as sentences increased in syntactic complexity, showing a pronounced dependence on the interpretation of sentences in terms of pragmatic plausibility rather than syntactic structure.

Further exploration of the language comprehension capacities of a conduction aphasic patient was provided by Caramazza, Basili, Koller, and Berndt (1981a; see also Caramazza et al., 1981b). MC had normal speech production, but a severe repetition deficit for auditory material. His comprehension was tested for sentences that were either semantically reversible (e.g. "The cat is chased by the dog") or semantically constrained (e.g. "The bone is being eaten by the dog"). With both auditory and visual sentences, MC performed more poorly on the reversible sentences than the semantically constrained ones, suggesting once again dependence on a pragmatic strategy of semantic interpretation rather than full syntactic analysis. When errors were made, they were more likely to involve choosing a foil corresponding to a syntactic misinterpretation of the sentence rather than a lexical substitution. Again, the result suggests inadequate syntactic analysis.

The language comprehension abilities of the STM patient PV have also been explored (Vallar & Baddeley, 1984b; 1987). Her immediate memory deficits (discussed also in Chapters 1 and 3) appear to reflect a highly specific impairment of the phonological store (Vallar & Baddeley, 1984a). PV does appear to have language comprehension deficits, but as with other patients, they arise only for the more syntactically complex sentence constructions. With simple active and passive constructions, and semantically reversible sentences, PV was unimpaired. She did, however, perform below the level of controls in Part 6 of the Token Test, which involves following long and complex instructions such as "If there is a black circle than pick up the red square".

The effects of sentence type on PV's comprehension were explored more systematically in a sentence verification task (Vallar & Baddeley, 1984b). PV and controls were required to judge whether sentences were true or false. The sentences were of three types. In Condition A, active and passive sentences ranging between five and nine words in length were used (e.g. "Prime ministers are mountainous"). In Condition B, additional words were added to the sentence types used in Condition A so that the original propositional structure was maintained (e.g. "It is true that physicians comprise a profession that is manufactured in factories, from time to time"). The length of these sentences ranged between 13 and 22 words. The sentences in Condition C shared the same length range, but were constructed so as to require maintenance of the surface form over intervening words for comprehension. In these sentences, it is never possible to reject a sentence because the subject and predicate were simply semantically incompatible. The false items in Condition C were typically constructed by reversing two relevant items from true sentences (e.g. "The world divides the equator into two halves, the northern and the southern").

In Conditions A and B, PV performed well, at a level just below the range of the control subjects. In Condition C, however, PV was no better than chance on either the auditory or the visual versions of the test. So, her impairments appeared to be largely restricted to the long sentences where word order was critical. She was, however, able to cope with short sentences of a syntactically equivalent type.

Furthermore, when long sentences in which the false items contained a semantic mismatch were presented, no notable performance decrement was found.

On further investigation, PV's syntactic comprehension was found to have the following characteristics (Vallar & Baddeley, 1987; Baddeley et al., 1987). She performed well on short sentences with a wide range of syntactic constructions and, unlike other STM patients, had no problems with semantically reversible items. PV showed a substantial improvement in accuracy when shortened versions of the complex sentences containing word reversals (Condition C in Vallar & Baddeley, 1984b) were employed. Finally, PV performed poorly when a semantic error involved an anaphoric reference to a token that occurred more than one sentence earlier.

Other recent explorations of the sentence processing abilities of STM patients have yielded broadly similar findings. Four chapters by independent research teams published in Vallar and Shallice's (1990) book *Neuropsychological impairments of short-term memory* focus exclusively on the issue of phonological loop involvement in the language comprehension of STM patients. The data reported in these papers consistently reveal that STM patients have problems in understanding long and syntactically complex sentences, such as passive constructions and sentences containing embedded clauses that cannot be pragmatically interpreted (Caplan & Waters, 1990; Martin, 1990; Saffran & Martin, 1990; Vallar, Basso, & Bottini, 1990). Nonetheless, it should be noted that the specific profiles of comprehension deficits vary considerably from patient to patient, and as yet it is far from clear how the theoretical accounts linking phonological memory and comprehension considered later can convincingly embrace this degree of variability.

One class of theoretical account attributes a significant role to the phonological loop in first-pass language processing, in which the comprehender carries out the initial syntactic analysis of the linguistic information. Baddeley et al. (1987) suggested that the phonological loop acts as a "mnemonic window" during sentence processing, providing a phonological representation that can be used to support off-line analysis and integration of the incoming discourse. Meanings of individual words are assumed to be accessed immediately, although the order of wording will need to be retained for full syntactic analysis for some kinds of linguistic constructions. The idea is that the size of the chunk that needs to be retained in the mnemonic window will vary with material and structure. Only when the size of the chunk needed to support accurate interpretation exceeds the capacity of an individual's phonological loop will comprehension deficits be found. So with simple sentence structures, even the very limited phonological working memory capacities of an STM patient will be sufficient to support full comprehension.

A slightly different position has been proposed by Caramazza and colleagues (e.g. Caramazza & Berndt, 1985). They have proposed that the phonological loop stores the *intermediate products* of syntactic analysis generated during the course of linguistic analysis, so that "morphologically interpreted phonological representations are placed in phonological working memory for syntactic parsing" (p. 46).

A third first-pass account is provided by Martin (1987). She has suggested that the phonological loop may buffer spoken language that is heard *after* the listener engages in off-line language processing, for example following an embedded clause within a sentence. According to this "downstream hypothesis", the listener can use the phonological loop representation to catch up with the sentence after analysis of the linguistically complex part of the sentence has been completed. The suggestion is that patients who have a phonological loop of reduced capacity will not be able to exploit this buffer storage, and so will experience impaired comprehension.

Recent data by Martin and Feher (1990), however, has challenged this interpretation. They attempted to diagnose working memory involvement in sentence comprehension by identifying the sentence types in which STM patients gained most benefit from data-unlimited presentations (in which the printed forms of sentences remained available for as long as the patients wished) over brief fixed-period presentations. Their argument was that working memory load is reduced in the latter condition, so that memory-demanding sentences should show greatest benefit in this case. The patients performed relatively poorly over all sentence types, but only improved with unlimited viewing conditions for the Token Test-type sentences that contain large numbers of content words (e.g. "Touch the small yellow circle and the large green square"). With sentences containing highly complex syntactic structures, such as centre-embedded subject and object relative clauses, no improvement in performance was found when the sentences remained available. Martin and Feher argued that these results do not support a "forward-looking" role for the phonological loop in syntactically complex sentences. Instead, they proposed that it contributes to the comprehension of sentences containing many content words, by providing a verbatim backup representation with which to assign the arbitrary descriptors of the shapes used in the Token Test to the nouns.

This view that phonological working memory contributes to sentence processing after syntactic analysis has taken place, but before the sentence structure has been fully interpreted, represents a theoretical stance that is becoming increasingly favoured by cognitive neuropsychologists. According to this approach, phonological memory involvement is located in second-pass language processing. Waters, Caplan, and Hildebrandt (1991; see also, Caplan & Hildebrandt, 1988) claim that the comprehension problems of STM patients are due to an impaired ability to compare the semantic interpretations derived pragmatically from the major lexical items within a sentence with the interpretations achieved from full syntactic analysis. They suggest that in order to resolve the conflicting readings of the sentence, the listener (or reader) checks with the representation of the original form of the sentence held in the phonological loop. Neuropsychological support for this position is provided by the STM patient BO (Waters et al., 1991). Across a range of sentence processing tasks, BO's deficits were largely restricted to sentences containing three proper nouns (e.g. "John said that Bill kicked Eddie"). It was argued that this finding indicates that a phonological memory representation of the sentence is consulted postsyntactically in order to assign nouns to their thematic roles in the propositional list.

The view that STM provides a back-up store that may be used to avoid overload from particularly demanding sentences is the dominant one in the Vallar and Shallice volume, although there is little agreement as to what constitutes a "demanding" sentence. However, much more dramatic impairment in comprehension does occur in at least one case, arguing in favour of a more central role for STM in comprehension (Baddeley & Wilson, 1987). On balance, the current data do not allow us to distinguish in a clear-cut manner between the first-pass and second-pass theories of phonological loop involvement in language comprehension. It may be more productive at the present time to emphasis the common rather than the distinctive elements shared by the two positions: Both agree that the phonological loop contributes significantly to the comprehension of long and syntactically complex sentences.

Other researchers, however, have challenged the notion that phonological working memory is important in language comprehension *at all*. Campbell and Butterworth (1985; see also Butterworth, Campbell, & Howard, 1986), reported the case of RE, a psychology undergraduate student who had very poor phonological memory skills. Her auditory digit span was about four items, and she showed no recency effect in serial recall. Furthermore, her immediate memory performance was uninfluenced by either word length or phonological similarity. These characteristics suggest that RE had a moderately severe developmental impairment of the phonological store.

Despite RE's reduced span, Butterworth et al. suggest that her language comprehension is unimpaired. RE showed good performance in the Token Test. In fact, under conditions of articulatory suppression, RE performed *better* in one part of the test than controls, who were significantly disrupted by the concurrent task. In a sentence–picture matching test, which employs a wide range of syntactic forms (Bishop's 1982 TROG test), RE produced errorless performance, which corresponds to a minimum comprehension age of 13 years. RE also performed normally on a sentence–picture verification test, which included both semantically reversible sentences and embedded clauses. In a test involving judgements of syntactic legality of long sentences, RE performed well except when functors were transposed (e.g. "The electricity supply failed because of two wires that have should been touching each other but weren't").

Butterworth et al. (1986) claimed that RE "… shows no evidence of any deficit of sentence parsing or comprehension, even when long and syntactically complex sentences are involved" (p.729). On this basis, they argue that the phonological loop component of working memory must *not* be critically involved in the comprehension of either spoken or written language.

These findings challenge the current views about the contribution of the phonological loop to language comprehension, as they appear to show a dissociation between phonological memory skills and abilities to understand language. The strong claims made by Butterworth et al. (1986) concerning RE have not, however, been accepted by all researchers, and this case has generated a good deal of debate (Vallar & Baddeley, 1987, 1989; Howard & Butterworth, 1989). Vallar and Baddeley have questioned whether it is valid to use data from a developmentally disordered individual to infer the nature of normal skilled language processing. Patients with acquired disorders of phonological working memory presumably had normal comprehension abilities prior to the brain trauma. Studying the language comprehension abilities of patients with impaired phonological working memory is therefore likely to provide useful information concerning the functions that the cognitive system fulfils in normal language understanding.

With developmental disorders, however, the case for generalisation is less convincing. It seems very likely that RE has developed highly atypical strategies for language comprehension as a consequence of her lack of temporary memory capacity. Indeed, her atypicality is demonstrated by that she was more resistant to the effects of irrelevant articulation on sentence comprehension than controls. From this result, it is clear that RE is understanding language in a highly unusual manner. So, although the case is a provocative and interesting one, it certainly leaves open the possibility that in normal skilled language users, the phonological loop does contribute to the comprehension of long and syntactically complex linguistic structures.

A weakness of the neuropsychological evidence is that it relies upon association—between STM impairments and deficits in language processing tasks—rather than controlled experimental procedures. One particular concern is that the associated deficits do not reflect the causal role played by phonological working memory in language understanding at all, but rather the likelihood that the brain areas controlling both types of activity are adjacent; thus damage to one functional area will frequently be accompanied by damage to the other. However, at present the consistency of findings from neuro-psychological and experimental studies is of a sufficient degree to argue against this possibility, and to suggest that there probably is a genuine contribution of the phonological loop to language under-standing. Nonetheless, it is clear that most language processing appears to work without significantly taxing even the limited phono-logical memory capacities of most STM patients. Only when sentences are presented that are long and syntactically complex, and in which the correct interpretation cannot be derived pragmatically from the main lexical elements, do phonological memory factors appear to be significant.

Developmental Studies

The contribution of the phonological loop to language understanding in skilled language users appears to be restricted to the most difficult kinds of linguistic constructions that we encounter. It is, however, possible that phonological working memory is rather more important in children's understanding of language. Language processing is obviously more difficult and less automatised in early childhood, when the child is struggling to master the many different forms that spoken language can take. During this period of language acquisition, phono-logical working memory may therefore fulfil a more critical role in off-line comprehension processes than in adulthood when language processing has become highly practised and near-automatic.

In this section we consider research which has focused on links between individual differences in working memory skills and com-prehension abilities during childhood. The work of a team of researchers from the Haskins Laboratories interested primarily in the phonological memory deficits in children of low reading ability (see Chapter 6) has been particularly influential. This group has proposed that the link between poor phonological processing skills and low reading ability may be mediated by a direct influence of memory ability on higher-level language processes, such as comprehension (e.g. Shankweiler & Crain, 1986; Smith, Macaruso, Shankweiler, & Crain, 1989). They argue that if reading skills build directly upon existing language structures, than any deficits in spoken language abilities will directly influence the development of language understanding.

In order to test the hypothesis that phonological memory skills influence the development of language comprehension, Smith, Mann, and Shankweiler (1986) studied eight-year-old children of high and low reading abilities. The poor readers performed at a significantly lower level in an immediate serial recall test than the good readers, confirming that the two reading ability groups were indeed distinguished by their phonological memory skills.

Comprehension was tested by a task that involves the subject manipulating objects in response to instructions such as "Touch the green circle" spoken by the experimenter. The poor readers were impaired on the section of the test which uses sentences containing two tokens, each modified by an adjective (e.g. "Touch the black circle and then the red square"). This result corresponds with neuro-psychological evidence reviewed earlier in the chapter, which has shown that STM patients also have problems with Token Test sentences containing many content words (Vallar & Shallice, 1990). It should be noted, however, that we have recently failed to find a correspondingly comprehension deficit in this part of the Token Test in eight-year-old children with poor phonological memory skills (Willis & Gathercole, in prep. a). It is therefore unclear whether it was the phonological memory problems of the poor readers in the Smith et al. (1986) study that underpinned their highly selective comprehension deficits.

Also, the good and poor readers in the Smith et al. study did not differ in the final section of the Token Test, in which the sentences are of even greater syntactic complexity (e.g. "If there is a black circle pick up the red square"). This absence of a group difference for these structures appears to reflect a point of divergence between the developmental and neuropsychological evidence, as STM patients are typically most impaired on Token Test sentences containing long and complex syntactic constructions (Caramazza et al., 1981b; Saffran & Marin, 1975).

Other work in this area has also yielded rather inconsistent support for the phonological loop hypothesis. Mann, Shankweiler, and Smith (1984) tested groups of nine-year-old children on their capacity to repeat and act out (using toy animals) sentences containing embedded clauses in which word order was critical for meaning (e.g. "The dog that chased the sheep stood on the turtle"). The good and poor readers differed both in their accuracy of repeating the sentences (72% and 53%, respectively), and in their ability to act out the meaning of the sentences. Encouraged by these findings, Mann et al. suggested that the poor readers' "phonetic representation of the words of a long sentence is often insufficient to support full recovery of syntactic structure" (p. 642), in line with theories developed on the basis of work with skilled language users and neuropsychological patients. However, it clearly remains a possibility that the comprehension deficits of the poor readers detected in this task were a consequence of their poor literacy attainment rather than their inadequate phonological memory skills.

A further study by Shankweiler, Smith, and Mann (1984) failed to identify any differences in good and poor readers' abilities to comprehend sentences containing embedded clauses that were designed to maximise phonological memory requirements. In this study, the children's task was to choose which picture corresponded to a spoken sentence. Shankweiler et al. suggested that this sentence–picture verification procedure may not have been as sensitive to group differences as the acting-out task used in their earlier study. Recent work from our laboratory, however, suggests that sentence–picture matching is indeed an appropriate task for testing phonological memory involvement in sentence comprehension (Willis & Gathercole, in prep. b). However, our findings indicate that the syntactic structures that place significant burdens on phonological memory appear to vary considerably according to the age and linguistic maturity of the subjects.

In summary, there has been relatively little systematic research on phonological working memory involvement in young children's language understanding, and the results that are available lack consistency and also methodological rigour. In principle, though, it seems plausible that phonological memory has an even *greater* role to play in children's language comprehension than in adults' language understanding, simply because when children are learning to master decoding of complex syntactic structures, processing is by necessity likely to take place off-line rather than on-line. Using experimental tasks and linguistic materials developed in the study of comprehension in adults with neuropsychological deficits, we hope that it will prove possible to provide a systematic analysis of phonological memory involvement in children's understanding of language in future research.

THE CENTRAL EXECUTIVE AND COMPREHENSION

The comprehension of language in normal adults appears to depend critically on the verbal component of working memory—the phonological loop—only when difficult sentence structures that occur relatively infrequently in natural language are used. There is, however, considerable evidence that the central executive component of working memory makes a more general contribution to the processing of language for meaning. In this section we consider some of the principal findings that have linked the central executive with processes involved in language understanding in adults and in children, and evaluate the theoretical positions that have been advanced to account for these findings.

Studies of Skilled Comprehenders

The work and ideas of Daneman and Carpenter have been very influential in developing the notion that the understanding of ordinary connected language, whether in the form of spoken words or printed text, places demands on general-purpose cognitive resources furnished by the working memory system. Daneman and Carpenter (1980) used the term "working memory" to refer to these resources. In terms of the specific working memory model, however, it is clear that this entity corresponds more closely to the central executive component than to the more specialised phonological processing resources of the phonological loop.

Three principles have guided this research programme. The first principle is that the comprehension of language involves both *processing* and *storage*. Processing is needed to recognise the lexical items represented by the surface forms of language, access their syntactic and semantic specifications, and interpret the meaning of sentences. According to most models of language understanding, the intermediate representations resulting from these processes need to be stored, as they provide input to further levels of language processing activities. The second principle assumes that a common pool of limited-capacity resources serves both kinds of activity, so that a tradeoff between processing and storage is necessary whenever a language processing task exceeds the limited resources available to the comprehender. The final principle is that there are important individual differences in functional working memory capacity, and that these are due either to variation in the total capacity of resources available, or to the efficiency with which cognitive processes are executed. These individual differences will influence the points at which tradeoffs between processing and storage demands will be necessary for a particular individual.

These principles have recently been extended and elaborated as the basis for a computational model of reading (Just & Carpenter, 1992). Before discussing this model in detail, we consider some of the basic evidence consistent with the three principles outlined above. Most of the research has focused on individual differences in working memory capacities. Daneman and Carpenter (1980) developed the reading span test, which they interpret as providing a measure of an individual's working memory capacity. The reading span measure differs from conventional memory span measures, such as digit span that assess storage only, as it taps an individual's abilities to process as well as to store linguistic material. The subject is given a series of sentences to read, and at the end of each sentence is required to recall in sequence the last word from each of the preceding sentences. Span is calculated as the maximum number of sentences on which the subject can perform this task perfectly. Two other variants of the span paradigm were also used by Daneman and Carpenter (1980)—oral reading span (subjects have to read aloud each sentence as it is presented) and listening span (as with reading span, but subjects hear each sentence spoken by the experimenter rather than reading it).

In one experiment, each of these three span measures was correlated with a range of comprehension measures based on factual questions and knowledge of pronoun reference within a series of short passages. The measures were obtained for both heard and written passages. Verbal Scholastic Aptitude Test (SAT) scores were also available for each subject.

The correlations between the span measures, comprehension measures, and SAT scores are shown in Table 8.2. Each of the span measures correlated to a highly significant extent with all reading comprehension and listening comprehension measures, as well as with Verbal SAT scores. These strong positive links between span measures and scores in language comprehension tests have since been replicated in a number of other studies (e.g. Baddeley, Logie, Nimmo-Smith, & Brereton, 1985; Dixon, LeFevre, & Twilley, 1988). These findings led Daneman and Carpenter (1980) to suggest that individuals' capacities for processing and storing linguistic information (as indexed by the span measures) directly determine the accuracy and efficiency with which they process language for meaning. More specifically, they speculated that the basis for the working memory differences between individuals lies in the speed and efficiency with which cognitive operations are executed, rather than in variation in the total resources available.

TABLE 8.2
Correlations between Spans and Comprehension

Span Tests	Fact Questions	Pronoun Reference Questions	Verbal SAT
	Reading Comprehension Measures		
Oral reading span	0.81**	0.84**	0.55**
Silent reading span	0.74**	0.86**	0.49**
Listening span	0.67**	0.72**	0.53**
	Listening Comprehension Measures		
Oral reading span	0.42*	0.78**	
Silent reading span	0.43*	0.71**	
Listening span	0.47*	0.85**	

*$p < 0.05$ **$p < 0.01$
From Daneman and Carpenter (1980).

Further work has identified close links between the reading span measure and individual differences in processing difficult syntactic structures. King and Just (1991) compared the reading times and reading comprehension of subjects with low and high reading spans on various kinds of syntactically complex sentences. Differences in comprehension accuracy between reading span groups were greatest for the sentences containing the most complex embedded clauses (object-relative clauses), such as *The reporter the sentence attacked admitted the error.* Low span subjects were particularly slow in processing the critical part of the sentence at which the syntactic structure had to be interpreted. These findings lend support to the view that the sentence structures that place greatest demands on processing are the ones in which readers with low working memory resources show greatest deficits.

The consequences of poor functional working memory capacities for language processing were also explored by Daneman and Carpenter (1983). They hypothesised that working memory capacity may be critical to the ease with which a reader (or indeed, a listener) can integrate new material with preceding passages of a text. Consider, for example, the following text: ... *he went and looked among his baseball equipment. He found a bat that was very large and brown and was flying back and forth in the gloomy room.* Because of the preceding context, readers usually interpret *bat* as a baseball bat, but the subsequent information about the locomotion of the object forces the reader to interpret it as an animal. To achieve this reinterpretation successfully, Daneman and Carpenter claimed that the reader must recover active representations of the original surface form of the word *bat*. Readers with low working memory capacity, they argued, would be less likely to maintain active representations of earlier material, as a consequence of the heavy demands placed by incoming sentences on their relatively inefficient processing operations. In other words, these readers were hypothesised to have maintained the efficiency of sentence processing at a cost of failing to maintain recent working memory or long-term memory representations. Successful recovery from these "garden path" passages should therefore be less frequent for these low- than high- working memory capacity subjects.

The results were consistent with this prediction. Readers with small reading spans were especially poor at recovering from such textual ambiguities within text when a sentence boundary intervened between the ambiguous word and its disambiguating context.

MacDonald, Just, and Carpenter (1992) have recently extended this work. They introduce a model of sentence parsing, the Capacity Constrained Parsing Model, in which the comprehender's representations of alternative syntactic representations of ambiguous words is directly influenced by the available working memory capacity. According to this model, low-capacity readers will have less activation to support the alternative representations and as a consequence, unpreferred interpretations will not be maintained. They should therefore experience most difficulties in interpreting text when a low-preference interpretation is supported by subsequent information (e.g. *The horse raced past the barn fell*).

The results from the three experiments reported by MacDonald et al. are most counterintuitive although, they claim, consistent with their sentence parsing model. Subjects' reading times for each of the words in the sentences were measured. The high reading span subjects had consistently longer reading times than the low span subjects, and this cost was greatest when the sentences contained ambiguous words. So, the individuals with supposedly *greatest* working memory capacities for written language were actually *slower* at processing syntactically ambiguous sentences.

Why should this be? MacDonald et al. propose that the slower processing of the high than the low span group is a direct cost of maintaining alternative syntactic representations of the ambiguous words: The activation necessary to satisfy these extra storage requirements reduces the resources that can be allocated to on-line processing of the text. Some of the findings in this study do, however, appear to stand in direct contradiction with the model outlined by the authors. In particular, the model predicts that low span readers will find it difficult to adjust to unpreferred contexts for ambiguous words, as there should be no representation available of the correct syntactic interpretation to support the reinterpretation. In fact, though, the high span readers were found to be more impaired in this condition than the low span readers. Thus, although MacDonald et al.'s theoretical interpretation of these unexpected findings seems plausible, it could perhaps be more fairly characterised as a *post hoc* interpretation derived from a relatively unconstrained model than as a testable prediction generated from that model.

Just and Carpenter (1992) build upon the theoretical development of the earlier work, and present a computational model of comprehension—the Capacity Constrained READER. The model combines a production system and a connectionist system, and is based on the assumption that both processing ("computation") and storage ("information maintenance") are fuelled by a common resource—*activation*. Old elements (such as the representations of earlier passages within a text) are maintained by activation, and if the activation of an element exceeds a threshold, the item is said to be represented within working memory. If the total amount of activation available for a particular comprehension task exceeds the available activation resources, however, the activation used to maintain old elements is scaled back. Individual differences in working memory capacity are modelled by varying the total amount of activation that the system has available to support processing and storage.

The CCREADER model successfully models a range of findings relating working memory to sentence processing. For example, in the model the available activation determines whether one or two syntactic interpretations will be represented for syntactically ambiguous regions such as those employed in the Daneman and Carpenter (1983) paper discussed earlier. Thus in the low capacity simulation, the unpreferred interpretation is not supported due to lack of available activation, and the preferred interpretation is maintained. Interestingly, though, no simulation data are presented for the MacDonald et al. (1992) findings that low span subjects are faster at reading ambiguous sentences. The model also simulates the processing efforts involved in reading syntactically complex sentences such as subject-relative and object-relative clauses for both high and low span readers (King & Just, 1991).

It should be clear from this overview that there is now considerable evidence supporting the involvement of a limited-capacity resource system in comprehension, and it seems at least plausible to assume that this system is part of the central executive component of the working memory model. The strong theoretical claims that have been made by Daneman, Carpenter, and colleagues have not gone unchallenged, though. One problem is that the span measures of working memory involve subjects in a reading comprehension task; reading spans may therefore be closely related to measures of reading comprehension simply because they involve very similar processes. However, correlations of similar magnitude to the Daneman and Carpenter (1980) experiment have since been found across different surface forms of the span and comprehension tests, including conditions in which mental arithmetic is substituted for sentence reading, suggesting that the high correlations are not simply due to the part–whole relationship between the measures.

A further concern is that positive relationships found between the working memory span measures and performance in reading tasks could simply be a consequence of the common influence of a third unidentified variable, such as general intelligence, on both types of activity. This may not be a crucial objection, however, as the functional capacity of the central executive may correspond fairly directly with intelligence (Kyllonen & Chrystal, 1990).

In summary, the evidence linking general working memory capacity with language comprehension is interesting, but far from conclusive. One of the weaknesses at present is the dependence on correlational data linking individual differences in capacity measures with their comprehension performance; inevitably, this evidence cannot provide strong tests of causal interpretations, such as those advanced by Daneman, Carpenter, and colleagues. One solution is to investigate the consequences on language comprehension of experimental techniques that reduce central executive resources, by analogy with the articulatory suppression procedure developed in the context of the phonological loop, which has proved to be an exceptionally useful empirical tool. Waters et al. (1987) recently adopted this approach, and found that a task designed to burden the central executive (maintaining a random sequence of six digits) did indeed impair subjects' comprehension of syntactically complex sentences. Certainly, the prospects for furthering our understanding of the central executive contribution to language comprehension seem brightest if researchers can successfully combine a more experimental approach with the correlational data and theoretical development already achieved.

Children's Comprehension

There has as yet been little work focusing directly on central executive involvement in the development of language comprehension abilities during childhood, although there are some interesting recent papers in this area. In fact, there are good grounds for expecting that central executive function may be *even more* critical in the early stages of learning to comprehend language than in later years as a skilled adult comprehender, as the child may well not have automatised procedures for processing many language structures and, as a consequence, may need to rely heavily on the general purpose resources furnished by the central executive component of working memory. It seems quite plausible that the developmental course of the relationship between the central executive and language understanding is therefore one of increasing independence as the child becomes more skilled at language processing.

Oakhill and her colleagues have carried out an interesting series of experiments on the role of working memory in comprehension in children (summarised in Oakhill, Yuill, & Parkin, 1988). Oakhill was particularly interested in a subgroup of children who appeared to have good reading skills as measured by their capacity for reading aloud, but poor comprehension skills. She began with a more detailed analysis of comprehension, demonstrating that the two groups were equivalent in answering literal questions about passages they had just read, but differed in their capacity to make correct inferences from the passages (Oakhill, 1984), suggesting that the poor comprehenders might be undertaking less constructive and inferential processing during reading. Other studies (Oakhill, 1982; Oakhill, Yuill, & Parkin, 1986) provided further evidence on this point. Subjects read a passage, and then judged a series of sentences, deciding whether or not those sentences had been within the original passage. In addition to repeated sentences there were new sentences, some of which comprised a correct inference from the passage, while others were inferentially false. The two groups of subjects were equally good at identifying the repeated sentences, and made a similar number of false alarms, suggesting that they did not differ in general memory ability. However, the nature of the errors was very different, with the good comprehenders tending to accept correct inferences, while the poor comprehenders were equally likely to accept inferences that did not follow from the passage. Again the amount of inferential processing that goes on in reading appears to be different between the two groups.

From a working memory viewpoint, the limitation could be either in the operation of the phonological loop, or the central executive. Phonological loop capacity was measured by requiring subjects to remember sequences of pictures of objects having long or short names. The presence of a word-length effect would indicate subvocal rehearsal, while the overall level of performance would indicate the capacity of the phonological loop. There was no difference between the groups in either of these measures, suggesting that they were equivalent in phonological loop capacity.

The central executive hypothesis was tested using a variant on the Daneman and Carpenter working memory span measure described earlier. However, as mentioned before, this paradigm is potentially open to the objection that one is using a language processing measure in order to predict language comprehension. To avoid this problem, Yuill, Oakhill, and Parkin (1989) used digit material. The task was to read aloud a visually presented list consisting of a number of separable groups of three digits, and then to recall the final digit of each group in the correct sequence. For example, the correct response to the list *069-801-027* would be *9-1-7*. Lists containing two, three and four digit triples were given to each child, and mean accuracy scored for the trials at each of these three lengths.

This working memory task was given to two groups of seven-year-old children matched for word recognition ability, but of either high or low reading comprehension skills for their age. Note that these two groups are probably quite different from the groups of good and poor readers typically tested by researchers interested in reading development, who are typically *most* differentiated in measures of word recognition, and *least* differentiated in comprehension ability (see Chapter 5). Yuill et al.'s (1989) less skilled comprehenders performed at a significantly lower level in the digit memory test than the good comprehenders. Across all children participating in the study, there was a correlation between performance in the memory test and comprehension of 0.51. These results indicate that the same relationship between central executive function and comprehension abilities in normal adult language users extends back into childhood, too. More specifically, the findings are consistent with the view that the poorer comprehension abilities of the less skilled group in the Yuill et al. study are a direct consequence of their reduced working memory capacity.

In a final experiment Oakhill et al. (1988, Experiment 5) simultaneously vary memory load and inference within a comprehension study. Their good and poor comprehenders are required to read a series of passages, some of which comprise apparently anomalous information, which is subsequently resolved. Comprehension is tested by asking the child after the passage why a person should have acted in a particular way. For example, in one story a mother is pleased when her son refuses to share his sweets with his sister. It subsequently transpires that this is because his sister was on a strict diet. The resolving information can be presented either immediately after the apparent anomaly, or only after several intervening sentences. When questioned about the reason for the mother's action, both good and poor comprehenders answer the question correctly when the resolution comes immediately after the anomaly. When there are several sentences intervening however, the good comprehenders perform substantially better than the poor. Oakhill et al. suggest that the two groups differ in their capacity to read and remember the material simultaneously, a difference they attribute to differential capacity of the central executive component of working memory.

OVERVIEW

Findings from experimental, neuropsychological, and developmental sources converge on the view that language comprehension processes draw upon both the phonological loop and central executive components of working memory. The relationships between the working memory systems and language understanding are, however, far from straightforward. In skilled adult language users, the phonological loop appears to make a significant contribution to comprehending connected language when the linguistic constructions within the message are particularly complex, suggesting the possibility that it may only be necessary for off-line language processing. With children, unfortunately, there has as yet been little systematic investigation of phonological loop involvement in the development of language-understanding skills.

Links between the central executive and language understanding are rather more speculative, largely due to a reliance upon correlational evidence and the absence of a widely accepted measure of central executive function. Nonetheless, findings from a number of studies have provided the basis for considerable theoretical development in recent years. In both adults and children, measures of performance in tasks that require both linguistic processing and storage have consistently been found to be closely related to individual differences in the comprehension of demanding passages of text or speech. One influential theoretical interpretation of this relationship is that individuals vary in the working memory resources that they have available to support language processing and storage. These ideas have recently been made explicit in a computational model of understanding that has proved successful in simulating a range of working memory–comprehension relationships in adults. It seems likely that further progress will be achieved when experimental techniques are developed that allow researchers to manipulate directly central executive involvement in language understanding.

CHAPTER NINE

Theoretical and Practical Issues

The preceding chapters have examined the evidence relating working memory to language processing. Specific theories concerning the detailed nature of working memory involvement in different language skills based on evidence from relevant experimental, neuro-psychological, and developmental studies are to be found in individual chapters. In this final chapter, we take the opportunity to speculate about more general theoretical and practical issues arising from this examination of the links between working memory and language processing.

THEORETICAL PERSPECTIVES

As a platform for this discussion, the contributions of the two components of the working memory system that appear to make significant contributions to language processing—the phonological loop and the central executive—are summarised in Table 9.1. It is immediately apparent from this summary that there has been considerably less research in most of the language domains concerning the involvement of the central executive than the phonological loop, probably because experimental methods for identifying contributions of the loop system are more well-established. As yet, however, no explicit model of the central executive exists and there are no standard methods for establishing central executive

TABLE 9.1

Contribution of the Phonological Loop and Central Executive Components
of Working Memory to Different Language Processing Activities

Language Activity	Phonological Loop	Central Executive
Comprehension	Used to maintain a phonological record that can be consulted during off-line language processing	Involved in processing syntactic and semantic information and storing products of processing
Vocabulary acquisition	Critical for the long-term learning of phonological forms of new words	Involved in interpreting the semantic characteristics of new words?
Learning to read	Contributes to the development of a phonological recoding strategy	Unknown
Reading familiar words	None, except when complex judgements about phonological structure required	Unknown
Speech production	None	Involved in planning the conceptual content of speech?

involvement. The apparently closer links between language skills and the loop than the central executive therefore probably reflect the greater empirical tractability of the former component rather than a genuine lack of significant involvement of the latter.

None of the language processing activities that have been explored in the course of this book shows either complete dependence or independence from working memory. The domain of language processing in which working memory contributions have been most extensively investigated is sentence comprehension. The meaning of simple and unambiguous messages proceeds on-line and without recourse to the phonological loop. However, the loop does appear to provide a backup representation for incoming connected language that can be consulted on those occasions when language comprehension proceeds off-line, for example when the messages to be understood are long and syntactically complex. The central executive is also closely linked to the comprehension of written and spoken language. It has been suggested that this component of working memory provides the resources necessary to support both the processing and storage operations involved in extracting meaning from sentences.

The phonological loop also plays a major role in the acquisition of new vocabulary. It provides a temporary phonological representation of novel words that is used as the basis for constructing a more stable long-term representation of the new phonological form. The contribution of the central executive to learning new words has yet to be systematically explored, but first indications are that it may be critically involved in interpreting the semantic characteristics of unfamiliar concepts.

Contributions of working memory to reading appear to be most significant during childhood when the child is learning to develop reading strategies. In particular, the acquisition of a strategy of phonologically recoding unfamiliar letter strings is closely associated with phonological loop function. For both children and adults, however, recognition of familiar words does not appear to place notable demands upon working memory capacity. Comprehending printed text at the supra-word level, though, may require phonological loop support when the printed material is high in either syntactic or semantic complexity.

The weakest link of all lies between working memory and speech production. Despite the intuitive appeal of the notion that working memory is used for planning speech output, there is little indication of any contribution of the phonological loop to the skilled production of speech. There is, however, some indication that the central executive may be involved in constructing the conceptual content of spontaneous speech.

Given that working memory does appear to fulfil a range of important functions in language processing, it is interesting to consider whether the primary function of the system is to provide a language support system. Some theorists have argued this case. Caplan (1991) recently made this claim, proposing that verbal short-term memory is an integral part of the modular language system. More specifically, Crain et al. (1990) suggested that a primary function of central executive components of working memory is to direct the processing of linguistic material through a hierarchy of specialised submodules (corresponding approximately to phonology, syntax, and semantics).

Our preference is to view the language processing activities involved in speech production, vocabulary acquisition, reading, and comprehension as being largely dissociable from one another, and possessing different degrees of interdependence with the general purpose resources provided by the working memory system. The resources provided by the limited-capacity but flexible nature of the central executive, and the more specialised buffer facility of the phonological loop, do, however, seem to be ideally suited to meet a wide range of language processing requirements. It therefore seems reasonable to suppose that these aspects of working memory may have evolved at least partly to supply a flexible language support system. Note, though, that the contribution of these components of working memory extends well beyond the domain of cognitive activities typically associated with the language module. Recent work has identified central executive involvement in tasks as diverse as driving a car, planning actions, and conscious awareness (see Chapter 1). In addition, the phonological loop has been implicated in mental arithmetic (Hitch, 1980), an activity that is not generally considered to be served solely by the modular language system. The important point here is that although the phonological loop and central executive components of working memory may play an integral role in basic language processing activities, their contributions are by no means restricted to this domain. As such, they function (or at least, *appear* to do so) as independent cognitive components, which are not tied to any particular modular system. Viewing them as subsystems of the language module does not, in our view, fail to capture well this flexibility of function.

PRACTICAL APPLICATIONS

An important issue that has not as yet been directly touched upon concerns whether advances in understanding the nature of links between working memory and language processing can be put to practical use. The case for doing so, or at least trying to do so, is particularly compelling from a developmental perspective. Phonological memory skills appear to be directly associated with children's abilities to learn new words, to learn to read, and to understand language. And consistent with this conclusion, children with disordered language development across all of these language skills show phonological memory deficits that are even greater in magnitude than their impoverished language abilities (Gathercole & Baddeley, 1990b). So, the extent of the phonological memory impairments in such children and the broad constellation of accompanying language deficits indicate that phonological memory may indeed play a critical role in the development of a whole host of important language processing skills.

The implications of this close correspondence between phonological memory skills and the development of language ability are straightforward. A child whose ability to retain temporarily phonological material is inadequate will be at risk of experiencing either generalised problems in language development, or of having difficulties in acquiring more specific language skills, such as learning to read. Promoting phonological memory abilities in young children with below average memory skills should therefore yield benefits across a range of language abilities, and may potentially offer immunity from serious disorders of language development. This approach could be used either remedially, to improve the language abilities of children with developmental language problems that have already been identified, or preventatively, in younger children with no apparent language problems, but detectable phonological memory deficits.

The idea of training phonological memory in children as a way of boosting their language processing abilities has not so far received much attention, and as yet little is known about the nature of suitable training techniques. Traditional methods of promoting verbal short-term memory skills have involved recruiting resources from other components of the memory system, and using them to support or circumvent phonological memory mechanisms. In the use of imagery mnemonics, for example, immediate memory for verbal material is supplemented by using both long-term memory and the visuo-spatial sketchpad (Baddeley & Lieberman, 1980). Another successful technique for apparently expanding short-term memory span has involved chunking large units, and linking them with personally meaningful information stored in long-term memory (Ericsson, Chase, & Falloon, 1980). Although these techniques are undoubtedly effective in enhancing the functional capacity of the short-term memory system, they do so by alleviating loads on the limited-capacity phonological part of the working memory system, rather than by enhancing its operation directly. In the present case, our interest is with the latter possibility, namely of promoting phonological memory skills.

Mann (1984) considered several ways of developing phonological processing skills. Techniques considered to be of potential use for children at risk in reading problems included practice at naming letters and objects, at remembering spoken sentences, and at listening to stories and nursery rhymes. The final suggestion seems to be a particularly good one, as nursery rhymes and poetry naturally emphasise phonological structure without explicitly requiring the child to understand meta-linguistic concepts about the organisation of language. And, indeed, positive links between nursery rhyme learning and language abilities have already been established. Results from a recent longitudinal study have shown that children's knowledge of nursery rhymes at age three is an effective predictor of reading achievement up to three years later (Bryant, Bradley, Maclean, & Crossland, 1989; Maclean, Bryant, & Bradley, 1987). A project currently underway in our laboratory is concerned with exploring the nature of the relationship between phonological memory skills and nursery rhyme learning in preschool children, with the aim of assessing whether preschool phonological memory skills function as either contributor to or beneficiary of rhyme learning in children. The finding that phonological memory skills are enhanced by learning rhymes would provide us with a positive indication that phonological memory training and remediation programmes should include experience with rhyme and verse.

A further way of promoting phonological memory skills may be to provide practice in the repetition of unfamiliar phonological forms. In our studies of phonological memory and language skills in children, we have found that nonword repetition performance is a very effective predictor of general language ability. Providing children with plenty of opportunity to perceive and reproduce wordlike nonwords may promote their abstraction of the combinatorial basis of the phonetic code (Lindblom, 1989), which may in itself enhance their abilities to represent messages phonologically in working memory. Practice in the production of unfamiliar sound sequences may also indirectly promote the perception of those forms. According to the motor theory of speech perception (Liberman, Cooper, Shankweiler, & Studdert-Kennedy, 1967; Liberman & Mattingley, 1985), the phonetic structure of speech is recovered by reference to the articulatory gestures necessary to produce that utterance. In the course of enhancing children's skills in producing a wide variety of phonological forms, therefore, benefits may also be yielded in their perception and memory representation of speech forms.

Rather more attention has been given to the practical applications of research showing close associations between young children's phonological awareness and their early reading achievement (see Chapters 5 and 6). A number of structured educational techniques have been designed to promote skills in representing and manipulating the spoken structure of language (e.g. Lindamood & Lindamood, 1975). But although such techniques seem likely to boost later reading achievement, the precise cognitive benefits of the methods have yet to be identified. In particular, programmes designed to facilitate phonological awareness may also enhance other cognitive abilities such as phonological memory skills. This possibility seems to us to be entirely plausible: A procedure that emphasises phonological structure may well promote the child's skills in temporarily maintaining the phonological form to be manipulated in addition to the manipulation procedures. Testing this hypothesis, that phonological memory may be a beneficiary of meta-linguistic training programmes, is relatively straightforward. Measures of a range of cognitive skills including phonological memory as well as tests of phonological awareness should be taken at the beginning and end of the training programmes. By doing this, the precise modification in the armoury of cognitive skills that results from the training schedules can be assessed and competing explanations for positive results of such training studies can be ruled out.

One more general implication of the research linking phonological skills with reading success during the early school years concerns the importance of teaching children phonological strategies for learning to read. Methods of reading instruction that choose to emphasise the meaning of text at the expense of teaching phonics and specific word recognition skills may handicap many children learning to read, by failing to promote the phonological coding skills that appear to be critical to early reading success. Perhaps surprisingly, not all children appear to learn spontaneously to exploit the lawful relationship between letters and sounds if they are not taught to do so. Liberman, Shankweiler, and Liberman (1989) estimate that up to 25% of children will not use an alphabetic strategy for reading unless taught to do so. Similarly, Johnston and Thompson's (1989) comparison of the reading strategies of Scottish children (explicitly taught phonics) and New Zealand children (taught to read via the "whole word" method) suggests that a phonological recoding strategy may not emerge spontaneously. Comparative studies of this type are rare, as most school systems use a range of approaches for teaching reading, but are potentially extremely valuable for testing the strongly held competing claims for different philosophies of reading instruction.

The training programmes and practical issues discussed so far have been concerned with the facilitation of early reading achievement. Phonological working memory skills, however, are linked with the development of a range of other language abilities, including vocabulary acquisition and language comprehension. Techniques for training phonological memory may therefore possibly yield generalised benefits in language development, and may potentially be useful for remediation of children with developmental disorders of language. The intervention programmes for children with impaired language development that are in wide clinical use do not, however, focus on these relatively low-level cognitive skills, which may plausibly lie at the centre of the general language problems. The programmes aim instead to teach specific language production skills, through a variety of different techniques such as imitation and modelling (see Leonard, 1982, for a critical review). The techniques appear effective to varying degrees in improving or extending use of a particular set of grammatical forms, but clearly focus on symptoms of the language impairment rather than directing treatment at the underlying deficits. As an alternative to these symptom-directed programmes, we suggest that a valuable approach would be to assess the long-term linguistic consequences of phonological memory training in young children (preferably of preschool ages) with poor language development.

EPILOGUE

Working memory, as conceptualised by Baddeley and Hitch in 1974, plays an active role in processing and storing information in the course of a variety of complex cognitive activities and skills. At the conclusion of the present assessment of data and theory, it appears that this concept has been successful in its application to the important domain of language processing. Working memory is closely linked with vocabulary acquisition, language comprehension, and reading. And changes in working memory function that occur either naturally during childhood or accidentally through acquired brain damage do explain many normal developmental changes and abnormal disturbances in language processing.

There are, however, two important qualifications to the conclusions drawn here about the links between short-term memory and language processing. Firstly, we certainly do not wish to claim that the working memory perspective on any particular aspect of language processing does or indeed could ever provide a complete account of that specialised domain of linguistic activity. There is much more to word learning, speaking, reading, and comprehension than working memory alone, and each of these areas of language processing is represented by areas of extensive research activity and theoretical development that have gone unmentioned in this book. The reason for this selectivity is that our aim has been to examine the interface between working memory and language, rather than language processing in its own right. Secondly, it would be misleading to indicate that the nature of working memory involvement in language is now established beyond debate. This is an empirical area in its infancy that is characterised by healthy debate concerning both research methods and theory, as a cursory glance at any of the individual chapters reveals. In writing this book, we have aimed to provide an interim report on ongoing research and to draw some preliminary theoretical conclusions about the nature of working memory involvement in language.

References

Aguiar, L. & Brady, S. (1991). Vocabulary acquisition and reading ability. *Reading & Writing, 4,* 115–127.

Anderson, J. R. (1983). *The architecture of cognition.* Cambridge, MA: Harvard University Press.

Anderson, R. C. & Freebody, P. (1981). Vocabulary knowledge. In J. T. Guthrie (Ed.), *Comprehension and teaching: Research reviews.* Newark, DE: International Reading Association.

Aram, D. M. & Nation, J. E. (1975). Patterns of language behavior in children with developmental language disorders. *Journal of Speech & Hearing Research, 18,* 229–241.

Arthur, T., Hitch, G. J., & Halliday, M. S. (in press). The role of the articulatory loop in children's reading. *British Journal of Psychology.*

Aslin, R. N., Pisoni, D. B., & Jusczyk, P. W. (1983). Auditory development and speech perception in infancy. In M. M. Haith & J. J. Campos (Eds.), *Infancy and the biology of development, Vol. II of Carmichael's Manual of Child Psychology* (4th edn). New York: Wiley.

Baddeley, A. D. (1966a). The capacity for generating information by randomisation. *Quarterly Journal of Experimental Psychology, 18,* 119–129.

Baddeley, A. D. (1966b). Short-term memory for word sequences as a function of acoustic, semantic, and formal similarity. *Quarterly Journal of Experimental Psychology, 18,* 362–365.

Baddeley, A. D. (1978). Working memory and reading. In P. A. Kolers, M. E. Wrolstad, & H. Bouma (Eds.), *Processing of visible language,* Vol. 1, pp. 355–370. New York: Plenum Press.

Baddeley, A. D. (1986). *Working memory.* Oxford: Oxford University Press.

Baddeley, A. D. (in press). Working memory and conscious awareness. In A.F. Collins, S.E. Gathercole, M.A. Conway, & P.E. Morris (Eds.), *Theories of memory*. Hove, UK: Lawrence Erlbaum Associates Ltd.

Baddeley, A. D., & Dale, H. C. A. (1966). The effects of semantic similarity on retroactive interference in long- and short-term memory. *Journal of Verbal Learning and Verbal Behavior, 5,* 417–420.

Baddeley, A. D., Eldridge, M., & Lewis, V. (1981). The role of subvocalisation in reading. *Quarterly Journal of Experimental Psychology, 33A,* 439–454.

Baddeley, A. D., Grant, S., Wight, E., & Thomson, N. (1975). Imagery and visual working memory. In P. M. A. Rabbitt & S. Dornic (Eds.), *Attention and performance, V,* pp. 205–217. London: Academic Press. New York: Academic Press.

Baddeley, A. D. & Hitch, G. J. (1974). Working memory. In G. Bower (Ed.), *The psychology of learning and motivation,* (Vol. 8, pp. 47–90). New York: Academic Press.

Baddeley, A. & Lewis, V. (1981). Inner active processes in reading: The inner voice, the inner ear, and the inner eye. In A.M. Lesgold & C.A. Perfetti (Eds.), *Interactive processes in reading* (pp. 107–129). Hillsdale, NJ: Lawrence Erlbaum Associates Inc.

Baddeley, A. D., Lewis, V., Eldridge, M., & Thomson, N. (1984a). Attention and retrieval from long-term memory. *Journal of Experimental Psychology: General, 113,* 518–530.

Baddeley, A. D., Lewis, V. J., & Vallar, G. (1984b). Exploring the articulatory loop. *Quarterly Journal of Experimental Psychology, 36,* 233–252.

Baddeley, A. D. & Lieberman, K. (1980). Spatial working memory. In R. Nickerson (Ed.), *Attention and performance, VIII* (pp. 521–539). Hillsdale, NJ: Lawrence Erlbaum Associates Inc.

Baddeley, A. D., Logie, R., Bressi, S., Della Salla, S., & Spinnler, H. (1986). Dementia and working memory. *Quarterly Journal of Experimental Psychology, 38A,* 603–618.

Baddeley, A. D., Logie, R., Nimmo-Smith, I., & Brereton, N. (1985). Components of fluid reading. *Journal of Memory and Language, 24,* 119–131.

Baddeley, A. D., Logie, R. H., & Ellis, N. C. (1988a). Characteristics of developmental dyslexia. *Cognition, 29,* 197–228.

Baddeley, A. D., Papagno, C., & Vallar, G. (1988b). When long-term learning depends on short-term storage. *Journal of Memory and Language, 27,* 586–596.

Baddeley, A. D., Thomson, N., & Buchanan, M. (1975). Word length and the structure of short-term memory. *Journal of Verbal Learning and Verbal Behavior, 14,* 575–589.

Baddeley, A. D., Vallar, G., & Wilson, B. (1987). Sentence comprehension and phonological memory: Some neuropsychological evidence. In M. Coltheart (Ed.), *Attention and performance, XII* (pp. 509–529). Hove, UK: Lawrence Erlbaum Associates Ltd.

Baddeley, A. D. & Wilson, B. (1985). Phonological coding and short-term memory in patients without speech. *Journal of Memory and Language, 24,* 490–502.

Barrett, M. (1989). Early language development. In A. Slater & G. Bremner (Eds.), *Infant development*. Hove, UK: Lawrence Erlbaum Associates Ltd.

Barron, R. W. & Baron, J. (1977). How children get meaning from words. *Child Development, 48,* 587–594.

Beauvois, M.-F., & Dérouesné, J. (1979). Phonological alexia: Three dissociations. *Journal of Neurology, Neurosurgery and Psychiatry, 42,* 1115–1124.

Beech, J. R. & Harding, L. M. (1984). Phonemic processing and the poor reader from a developmental lag viewpoint. *Reading Research Quarterly, 19,* 357–366.

Benton, A. (1978). The cognitive functioning of children with developmental aphasia. In M. Wyke (Ed.), *Developmental dysphasia.* New York: Academic Press.

Berndt, R. & Caramazza, A. (1980). A redefinition of the syndrome of Broca's aphasia. *Applied Psycholinguistics, 1,* 225–278.

Berry, M. F. & Eisenson, J. (1956). *Speech disorders: Principles and practices of speech therapy.* London: Peter Owen.

Bertelson, P., Morais, J. Alegria, J., & Content, A. (1985). Phonetic analysis capacity and learning to read. *Nature, 313,* 73–4.

Berwick, R. C., & Weinberg, A. (1985). Deterministic parsing and linguistic explanation. *Language and Cognitive Processes, 1,* 109–134.

Besner, D. (1987). Phonology, lexical access in reading, and articulatory suppression: A critical review. *Quarterly Journal of Experimental Psychology, 39A,* 467–478.

Besner, D. & Davelaar, E. (1982). Basic processes in reading: Two phonological codes. *Canadian Journal of Psychology, 36,* 701–711.

Besner, D., & Davelaar, E. (1983). Seudohomofoan effects in visual word recognition: Evidence for phonological processing. *Canadian Journal of Psychology, 37,* 300–305.

Besner, D., Davies, J., & Daniels, S. (1981). Reading for meaning: The effects of concurrent articulation. *Quarterly Journal of Experimental Psychology, 33A,* 415–437.

Bird, J. (1989). *The auditory perception, phonemic awareness and literacy skills of phonologically disordered children.* Unpublished PhD thesis, Department of Psychology, University of Manchester.

Bishop, D. (1982). *Test for the reception of grammar (TROG).*

Bishop, D. V. M. & Robson, J. (1989). Unimpaired short-term memory and rhyme judgment in congenitally speechless individuals: Implications for the notion of "Articulatory Coding". *Quarterly Journal of Experimental Psychology, 41A,* 123–140.

Bishop, D. V. M. & Rosenbloom, L. (1987). Childhood language disorders: Classification and overview. In W. Yule & M. Rutter (Eds.), *Language development and disorders.* Oxford: Blackwell.

Bloom, L. (1973). *One word at a time.* The Hague: Mouton.

Bock, J. K. (1982). Towards a cognitive psychology of syntax: Information processing contributions to sentence formulation. *Psychological Review, 89,* 1–49.

Boder, E. (1973). Developmental dyslexia: A diagnostic approach based on three atypical reading-spelling patterns. *Developmental Medicine and Child Neurology, 15,* 663–687.

Bower, G. H. (1970). Analysis of a mnemonic device. *American Scientist, 58,* 496–510.

Bradley, L. & Bryant, P. E. (1978). Difficulties in auditory organization as a possible cause of reading backwardness. *Nature, 271,* 746–747.

Bradley, L. & Bryant, P. E. (1983). Categorizing sounds and learning to read—a causal connection. *Nature, 301,* 419–420.

Brady, S. (1991). The role of working memory in reading disability. In S.A. Brady & D.P. Shankweiler (Eds.), *Phonological processes in literacy*. Hillsdale, NJ: Lawrence Erlbaum Associates Inc.

Brady, S., Mann, V., & Schmidt, R. (1987). Errors in short-term memory for good and poor readers. *Memory & Cognition, 15*, 444–453.

Brady, S., Shankweiler, D., & Mann, V. (1983). Speech perception and memory coding in relation to reading ability. *Journal of Experimental Child Psychology, 35*, 345–367.

Brandimonte, M. A., Hitch, G. J., & Bishop, D. V. M. (1992). Influence of short-term memory codes on visual image processing: Evidence from image transformation tasks. *Journal of Experimental Psychology: Learning, Memory and Cognition, 18*, 157–165.

Brooks, L. R. (1967). The suppression of visualisation by reading. *Quarterly Journal of Experimental Psychology, 19*, 289–299.

Brown, R. A. (1973). *A first language: The early stages*. Cambridge, MA: Harvard University Press.

Bryant, P. E. (1986). Phonological skills and learning to read and write. In B. R. Foorman & A. W. Siegel (Eds.), *Acquisition of reading skills: Cultural constraints and cognitive universals*. Hillsdale, NJ: Lawrence Erlbaum Associates Inc.

Bryant, P. E. & Bradley, L. (1980). Why children sometimes write words they do not read. In U. Frith (Ed.), *Cognitive processes in spelling* (pp. 355–370). London: Academic Press.

Bryant, P. E. & Bradley, L. (1985). *Children's reading problems*. Oxford: Blackwell.

Bryant, P. E., Bradley, L., Maclean, M., & Crossland, J. (1989). Nursery rhymes, phonological skills and reading. *Journal of Child Language, 16*, 407–428.

Bryant, P. E. & Impey, L. (1986). The similarities between normal readers and acquired dyslexics. *Cognition, 24*, 121–137.

Bryant, P. E., Maclean, M., Bradley, L., & Crossland, J. (1990). Rhyme and alliteration, phoneme detection, and learning to read. *Developmental Psychology, 26*, 429–438.

Burani, C., Vallar, G., & Bottini, G. (1991). Articulatory coding and phonological judgements on written words and pictures: The role of the phonological output buffer. *European Journal of Cognitive Psychology, 3*, 379–398.

Butterworth, B., Campbell, R., & Howard, D. (1986). The uses of short-term memory: A case study. *Quarterly Journal of Experimental Psychology, 38*, 705–737.

Byrne, B. & Fielding-Barnsley, R. (1989). Phonemic awareness and letter knowledge in the child's acquisition of the alphabetic principle. *Journal of Educational Psychology, 81*, 313–321.

Campbell, R. & Butterworth, B. (1985). Phonological dyslexia and dysgraphia in highly literate subjects: A developmental case with associated deficits of phonemic processing and awareness. *Quarterly Journal of Experimental Psychology, 37A*, 435–476.

Campbell, R., Rosen, S., Solis-Macias, V., & White, T. (1991). Stress in silent reading: Effects of concurrent articulation on the detection of syllabic stress patterns in written words in English speakers. *Language and Cognitive Processes, 6*, 29–47.

Campbell, R., & Wright, H. (1990). Deafness and immediate memory for pictures: Dissociations between "inner speech" and "inner ear". *Journal of Experimental Child Psychology, 50,* 259–286.

Caplan, D. (1991). Potential pitfalls in neuropsychological studies: The case of short-term memory. *Behavioral and Brain Sciences, 14,* 443–444.

Caplan, D. & Hildebrandt, N. (1988). *Disorders of syntactic comprehension.* Cambridge, MA: MIT Press.

Caplan, D. & Waters, G. S. (1990). Short-term memory and language comprehension: A critical review of the psychological literature. In G. Vallar & T. Shallice (Eds.), *Neuropsychological impairments of short-term memory* (pp. 337–389). Cambridge: Cambridge University Press.

Caramazza, A., Basili, A. G., Koller, J. J., & Berndt, R. S. (1981a). An investigation of repetition and language processing in a case of conduction aphasia. *Brain and Language, 14,* 235–271.

Caramazza, A. & Berndt, R.S. (1985). A multicomponent view of agrammatic Broca's aphasia. In M.-L. Kean (Ed.), *Agrammatism.* New York: Academic Press.

Caramazza, A., Berndt, R. S., Basili, A. G., & Koller, J. J. (1981b). Syntactic processing deficits in aphasia. *Cortex, 17,* 333–348.

Carey, S. (1978). The child as word learner. In M. Halle, J. Bresnan, & G. Miller (Eds.), *Linguistic theory and psychological reality.* Cambridge, MA: MIT Press.

Carey, S. & Bartlett, E. (1978). Acquiring a single new word. *Papers and Reports on Child Language Development, 15,* 17–29.

Carr, T. H. & Levy, B. A. (1990). *Reading and its development: Component skills approaches.* New York: Academic Press.

Carr, T. H. & Pollatsek, A. (1985). Recognising printed words: A look at current models. In D. Besner, T. G. Waller, & G. E. Mackinnon (Eds.), *Reading research: Advances in theory and practice* (Vol. 5, pp. 1–82). San Diego, CA: Academic Press.

Case, R., Kurland, D. M., & Goldberg, J. (1982). Operational efficiency and the growth of short-term memory span. *Journal of Experimental Child Psychology, 33,* 386–404.

Cermak, L. S. & Moreines, J. (1976). Verbal retention deficits in aphasic and amnesic patients. *Brain and Language, 3,* 16–27.

Cermak, L. S. & Tarlow, S. (1978). Aphasic and amnesic patients' verbal vs. nonverbal retentive abilities. *Cortex, 14,* 32–40.

Chomsky, N. (1957). *Syntactic structures.* The Hague: Mouton.

Clark, H. H., & Clarke, E. V. (1977). *Psychology and language.* New York: Harcourt Brace Jovanovich.

Colle, H. A. & Welsh, A. (1976). Acoustic masking in primary memory. *Journal of Verbal Learning and Verbal Behavior, 15,* 17–32.

Coltheart, M., Masterson, J., Byng, S., Prior, M., & Riddoch, J. (1983). Surface dyslexia. *Quarterly Journal of Experimental Psychology, 35A,* 469–495.

Conrad, R. (1972). Speech and reading. In J. F. Kavanagh & I. G. Mattingley (Eds.), *Language by ear and by eye* (pp. 205–240). Cambridge, MA: MIT Press.

Conrad, R. & Hull, A. J. (1964). Information, acoustic confusion, and memory span. *British Journal of Psychology, 55,* 429–432.

Content, A., Kolinsky, R., Morais, J., & Bertelson, P. (1986). Phonetic segmentation in pre-readers: Effect of corrective information. *Journal of Experimental Child Psychology, 42,* 49–72.

Cowan, N., Day, L., Saults, J. S., Keller, T. A., Johnson, T., & Flores, L. (1992). The role of verbal output time in the effects of word length on immediate memory. *Journal of Memory and Language, 31*, 1–17.

Cowan, N., Saults, J. S., Winterowd, C., & Sherk, M. (1991). Enhancement of 4-year old children's memory span for phonologically similar and dissimilar word lists. *Journal of Experimental Child Psychology, 51*, 30–52.

Crain, S., Shankweiler, D., Macaruso, P., & Bar-Shalom, E. (1990). Working memory and comprehension of spoken sentences: Investigations of children with reading disorder. In G. Vallar & T. Shallice (Eds.), *Neuropsychological impairments of short-term memory.* (pp. 477–508). Cambridge: Cambridge University Press.

Crano, W. D. & Mellon, P. M. (1978). Causal influence of teachers' expectations on children's academic performance: A cross-lagged panel analysis. *Journal of Educational Psychology, 70*, 39–49.

Cromer, R. F. (1983). Hierarchical planning disability in the drawings and construction of a special group of severely aphasic children. *Brain and Cognition, 2*, 144–164.

Cromer, R. F. (1987). Language acquisition, language disorder and cognitive development. In W. Yule & M. Rutter (Eds.), *Language development and disorders.* Oxford: Blackwell.

Cromer, R. F. (1991). *Language and thought in normal and handicapped children.* Oxford: Blackwell.

Crystal, D. (1982). *Profiling linguistic disability.* London: Edward Arnold.

Crystal, D., Fletcher, P., & Garman, M. (1976). *The grammatical analysis of language disability: A procedure for assessment and remediation.* London: Edward Arnold.

Cunningham, A. E. & Stanovich, K. E. (1991). Tracking the unique effects of print exposure in children: Associations with vocabulary, general knowledge and spelling. *Journal of Educational Psychology, 83*, 264–274.

Cutler, A. & Isard, S. D. (1980). The production of prosody. In B. Butterworth (Ed.), *Language production, Vol. I: Speech and talk.* London: Academic Press.

Daneman, M. & Carpenter, P. A. (1980). Individual differences in working memory and reading. *Journal of Verbal Learning and Verbal Behavior, 19*, 450–466.

Daneman, M. & Carpenter, P. A. (1983). Individual differences in integrating information within and between sentences. *Journal of Experimental Psychology: Learning, Memory and Cognition, 9*, 561–584.

Daneman, M. & Green, I. (1986). Individual differences in comprehending and producing words in context. *Journal of Memory and Language, 25*, 1–18.

Daneman, M. & Stainton, M. (1991). Phonological recoding in silent reading. *Journal of Experimental Psychology: Learning, Memory and Cognition, 17*, 618–632.

Denckla, M. & Rudel, R. (1976). Rapid automatised naming: Dyslexia differentiated from the other learning disabilities. *Neuropsychologia, 14*, 471–479.

De Renzi, E. & Nichelli, P. (1975). Verbal and nonverbal short-term memory impairment following hemispheric damage. *Cortex, 11*, 341–354.

Dickinson, D. K. (1984). On words gained from a single exposure. *Applied Psycholinguistics, 5*, 359–373.

Dixon, P., LeFevre, J.-A., & Twilley, L. C. (1988). Word knowledge and working memory as predictors of reading skill. *Journal of Educational Psychology, 80*, 465–472.

Doctor, E. A. & Coltheart, M. (1980). Children's use of phonological encoding when reading for meaning. *Memory and Cognition, 8,* 195–209.

Dollaghan, C. (1987). Fast mapping in normal and language-impaired children. *Journal of Speech and Hearing Disorders, 52,* 218–222.

Duncan, J. (in press). Selection of input and goal in the control of behaviour. In A. D. Baddeley & L. Weiskrantz (Eds.), *Attention: Selection, awareness and control.* Oxford: Oxford University Press.

Duncan, J., Williams, P., Nimmo-Smith, I., & Brown, I. D. (1991). In D. Meyer & S. Kornblum (Eds.), *Attention and performance, XIV.* Hillsdale, NJ: Lawrence Erlbaum Associates Inc.

Dunn, L. M. & Dunn, L. M. (1982). *British Picture Vocabulary Scale.* Windsor: NFER-Nelson Publishing Company Ltd.

Ehri, L. (1985). Sources of difficulty in learning to spell and read. In M. L. Wolraich & D. Routh (Eds.), *Advances in developmental and behavioral paediatrics.* Greenwich, CT: Jai Press Inc.

Elley, W. B. (1989). Vocabulary acquisition from listening to stories. *Reading Research Quarterly, 24,* 174–187.

Elliott, C. D. (1983). *British Abilities Scales.* Windsor: NFER-Nelson Publishing Company Ltd.

Elliott, L. L., Hammer, M. A., & Scholl, M. E. (1989). Fine-grained auditory discrimination in normal children and children with language-learning problems. *Journal of Speech and Hearing Research, 32,* 112–119.

Ellis, A. (1979). Speech production and short-term memory. In J. Morton & J. C. Marshall (Eds.), *Psycholinguistics series, Vol. 2: Structures and processes,* (pp. 157–187). London: Paul Elek/Cambridge, MA: MIT Press.

Ellis, A. (1980). Errors in speech and short-term memory: The effects of phonemic similarity and syllable position. *Journal of Verbal Learning and Verbal Behavior, 19,* 624–634.

Ellis, A. (1985). The cognitive neuropsychology of developmental (and acquired) dyslexia: A critical survey. *Cognitive Neuropsychology, 2,* 169–205.

Ellis, A. W. & Young, A. W. (1988). *Human cognitive neuropsychology.* Hove, UK: Lawrence Erlbaum Associates Ltd.

Ellis, N. (1989). Reading development, dyslexia and phonological skills. *Irish Journal of Psychology, 10,* 551–567.

Ellis, N. & Cataldo, S. (in press). The role of spelling in learning to read. *Language and Education.*

Ellis, N. C. & Hennelly, R. A. (1980). A bilingual word-length effect: Implications for intelligence testing and the relative ease of mental calculation in Welsh and English. *British Journal of Psychology, 71,* 43–52.

Ellis, N. & Large, B. (1988). The early stages of reading: A longitudinal study. *Applied Cognitive Psychology, 2,* 47–76.

Ericsson, K.A., Chase, W.G., & Falloon, S. (1980). Acquisition of a memory skill. *Science, 208,* 1181–1182.

Estes, W. K. (1973). Phonemic coding and rehearsal in short-term memory. *Journal of Verbal Learning and Verbal Behavior, 12,* 360–372.

Farah, M. J. (1988). Is visual imagery really visual? Overlooked evidence from neuropsychology. *Psychological Review, 95,* 307–317.

Farah, M. J., Hammond, K. L., Levine, D. N., & Calvanio, R. (1988). Visual and spatial mental imagery: Dissociable systems of representation. *Cognitive*

Psychology, 20, 439–462.

Ferreiro, E. (1978). What is written in a written sentence? A developmental answer. *Journal of Education, 160,* 25–39.

Fodor, J. A. (1983). *The modularity of mind,* Cambridge, MA: MIT Press.

Fowler, A. E. (1991). How early phonological development might set the stage for phoneme awareness. In S. Brady & D. Shankweiler (Eds.), *Phonological processes in literacy.* Hillsdale, NJ: Lawrence Erlbaum Associates Inc.

Fox, B. & Routh, D. K. (1975). Analysing spoken language into words, syllables and phonemes: A developmental study. *Journal of Psycholinguistic Research, 4,* 331–342.

France, N. (1981). *Primary Reading Test (revised edition).* Windsor: NFER-Nelson Publishing Company Ltd.

Friedrich, F. J., Martin, R., & Kemper, S. J. (1985). Consequences of a phonological coding deficit on sentence processing. *Cognitive Neuropsychology, 2,* 385–412.

Frith, U. (1985). Beneath the surface of developmental dyslexia. In K. E. Patterson, J. C. Marshall, & M. Coltheart (Eds.), *Surface dyslexia.* Hove, UK: Lawrence Erlbaum Associates Ltd.

Fromkin, V. (1973). *Speech errors as linguistic evidence.* The Hague: Mouton .

Funnell, E. (1983). Phonological processes in reading: New evidence from acquired dyslexia. *British Journal of Psychology, 74,* 159–180.

Funnell, E. & Davison, M. (1989). Lexical capture: A developmental disorder of reading and spelling. *Quarterly Journal of Experimental Psychology, 41A,* 471–488.

Garrett, M. F. (1975). The analysis of sentence production. In G. Bower (Ed.), *Psychology of learning and motivation* (Vol. 9). New York: Academic Press.

Garrett, M. F. (1980). Levels of processing in sentence production. In B. L. Butterworth (Ed.), *Language production* (Vol. 1). London: Academic Press.

Gathercole, S. E. & Adams, A. M. (in press). Phonological working memory in very young children. *Developmental Psychology.*

Gathercole, S. E. & Baddeley, A. D. (1989a). Evaluation of the role of phonological STM in the development of vocabulary in children: A longitudinal study. *Journal of Memory and Language, 28,* 200–213.

Gathercole, S. E. & Baddeley, A. D. (1989b). The role of phonological memory in normal and disordered language development. In C. von Euler, I. Lundberg, & G. Lennestrand (Eds.), *Brain and reading* (pp. 245–255). Macmillan Press.

Gathercole, S. E. & Baddeley, A. D. (1990a). Phonological memory deficits in language disordered children: Is there a causal connection? *Journal of Memory and Language, 29,* 336–360.

Gathercole, S. E. & Baddeley, A. D. (1990b). The role of phonological memory in vocabulary acquisition: A study of young children learning arbitrary names of toys. *British Journal of Psychology, 81,* 439–454.

Gathercole, S. E. & Baddeley, A. D. (in press). Phonological working memory: A critical building block for reading development and vocabulary acquisition? *European Journal of the Psychology of Education.*

Gathercole, S. E. & Hitch, G. J. (in press). Developmental changes in short-term memory: A revised working memory perspective. In A.F. Collins, S.E. Gathercole, M.A. Conway, & P.E. Morris (Eds.), *Theories of memory.* Hove, UK: Lawrence Erlbaum Associates Ltd.

Gathercole, S. E., Willis, C. S., & Baddeley, A. D. (1991a). Differentiating phonological memory and awareness of rhyme: Reading and vocabulary development in children. *British Journal of Psychology, 82,* 387–406.

Gathercole, S. E., Willis, C., Emslie, H., & Baddeley, A. (1991b). The influences of number of syllables and word-likeness on children's repetition of nonwords. *Applied Psycholinguistics, 12,* 349–367.

Gathercole, S. E., Willis, C., Emslie, H., & Baddeley, A. (1992). Phonological memory and vocabulary development during the early school years: A longitudinal study. *Developmental Psychology, 28,* 887–898.

Gopnik, M. & Crago, M. B. (1991). Familial aggregation of a developmental language disorder. *Cognition, 39,* 1–50.

Goswami, U. (1986). Children's use of analogy in learning to read: A developmental study. *Journal of Experimental Child Psychology, 42,* 73–83.

Goswami, U. & Bryant, P. (1990). *Phonological skills and learning to read.* Hove, UK: Lawrence Erlbaum Associates Ltd.

Graham, N. C. (1980). Memory constraints in language deficiency. In F. Margaret Jones (Ed.), *Language disability in children.* Baltimore: University Park Press.

Hall, J. W., Wilson, K. P., Humphreys, M. S., Tinzmann, M. B., & Bowyer, P. M. (1983). Phonemic similarity effects in good vs. poor readers. *Memory and Cognition, 11,* 520–527.

Halliday, M. S., Hitch, G. J., Lennon, B., & Pettifer, C. (1990). Verbal short-term memory in children: The role of the articulatory loop. *European Journal of Cognitive Psychology, 2,* 23–38.

Hanley, J. R., Young, A. W., & Pearson, N. A. (1991). Impairment of the visuospatial sketchpad. *Quarterly Journal of Experimental Psychology, 43A,* 101–126.

Harris, M., Barrett, M., Jones, D., & Brookes, S. (1988). Linguistic input and early word meaning. *Journal of Child Language, 15,* 77–94.

Hayes, D. P. (1988). Speaking and writing: Distinct patterns of word choice. *Journal of Memory and Language, 27,* 572–585.

Haynes, C. (1982). *Vocabulary acquisition problems in language disordered children.* Unpublished M.Sc. thesis, Guys Hospital Medical School, University of London.

Henry, L. A. (1991). The effects of word length and phonemic similarity in young children's short-term memory. *Quarterly Journal of Experimental Psychology, 43A,* 35–52.

Herman, P. A. & Dole, J. (1988). Theory and practice in vocabulary learning and instruction. *The Elementary School Journal, 89,* 43–54.

Hitch, G. J. (1980). Developing the concept of working memory. In G. Claxton (Ed.), *Cognitive psychology: New directions* (pp.156–196). London: Routledge & Kegan Paul.

Hitch, G. J. & Halliday, M. S. (1983). Working memory in children. *Philosophical Transactions of the Royal Society, Series B, 302,* 324–340.

Hitch, G. J., Halliday, M. S., Dodd, A., & Littler, J. E. (1989a). Development of rehearsal in short-term memory: Differences between pictorial and spoken stimuli. *British Journal of Developmental Psychology, 7,* 347–362.

Hitch, G. J., Halliday, M. S., & Littler, J. E. (1989b). Item identification time and rehearsal rate as predictors of memory span in children. *Quarterly Journal of Experimental Psychology, 41A,* 321–328.

Hitch, G. J., Halliday, M. S., Schaafstal, A. M., & Heffernan, T. M. (1991). Speech, "inner speech", and the development of short-term memory: Effects of picture-labeling on recall. *Journal of Experimental Child Psychology, 51,* 220–234.

Hitch, G. J., Halliday, M. S., Schaafstal, A. M., & Schraagen, J. M. C. (1988). Visual working memory in young children. *Memory and Cognition, 16,* 120–132.

Howard, D. & Butterworth, B. (1989). Short-term memory and sentence comprehension: A reply to Vallar and Baddeley, 1987. *Cognitive Neuropsychology, 6,* 455–463.

Howard, D. & Franklin, S. (1990). Memory without rehearsal. In G. Vallar & T. Shallice (Eds.), *Neuropsychological impairments of STM* (pp. 287–319). Cambridge: Cambridge University Press.

Hulme, C. (1987). The effects of acoustic similarity on memory in children: A comparison between visual and auditory presentation. *Applied Cognitive Psychology, 1,* 45–52.

Hulme, C., Maughan, S., & Brown, G. D. A. (1991). Memory for familiar and unfamiliar words: Evidence for a long-term memory contribution to short-term memory span. *Journal of Memory and Language, 30,* 685–701.

Hulme, C., Thomson, N., Muir, C., & Lawrence, A. (1984). Speech rate and the development of short-term memory span. *Journal of Experimental Child Psychology, 38,* 241–253.

Hulme, C. & Tordoff, V. (1989). Working memory development: The effects of speech rate, word length, and acoustic similarity on serial recall. *Journal of Experimental Child Psychology, 47,* 72–87.

Jenkins, J. R., Matlock, B., & Slocum, T. A. (1989). Two approaches to vocabulary instruction: The teaching of individual word meanings and practice in deriving word meaning from context. *Reading Research Quarterly, 24,* 215–234.

Johnston, R. S. (1982). Phonological coding in dyslexic readers. *British Journal of Psychology, 73,* 455–460.

Johnston, R. S., Johnson, C., & Gray, C. (1987). The emergence of the word-length effect in young children: The effects of overt and covert rehearsal. *British Journal of Developmental Psychology, 5,* 243–248.

Johnston, R. S. & McDermott, E. A. (1986). Suppression effects in rhyme judgement tasks. *Quarterly Journal of Experimental Psychology, 38A,* 111–124.

Johnston, R. S., Rugg, M. D., & Scott, T. (1987). Phonological similarity effects, memory span and developmental reading disorders: The nature of the relationship. *British Journal of Psychology, 78,* 205–211.

Johnston, R. S. & Thompson, G. B. (1989). Is dependence on phonological information in children's reading a product of instructional approach? *Journal of Experimental Child Psychology, 48,* 131–145.

Jorm, A. (1983). Specific reading retardation and working memory: A review. *British Journal of Psychology, 74,* 311–342.

Jorm, A. F. & Share, D. L. (1983). Phonological recoding and reading acquisition. *Applied Psycholinguistics, 4,* 103–147.

Just, M. A. & Carpenter, P. A. (1992). A capacity theory of comprehension: Individual differences in working memory. *Psychological Review, 99,* 122–149.

Kamhi, A. G., Catts, H. W., & Mauer, D. (1990). Explaining speech production deficits in poor readers. *Journal of Learning Disabilities, 10,* 632–636.

Kay, J. & Marcel, T. (1981). One process not two in reading aloud: Lexical analogies do the work of nonlexical rules. *Quarterly Journal of Experimental Psychology, 33A,* 397–413.

Kelter, S., Cohen, R., Engel, D., List, G., & Strohner, H. (1977). Verbal coding and visual memory in aphasics. *Neuropsychologia, 15,* 51–60.

Kimura, Y. & Bryant, P. (1983). Reading and writing in English and Japanese: A cross-cultural study of young children. *British Journal of Developmental Psychology, 1,* 143–154.

King, J. & Just, M. A. (1991). Individual differences in syntactic processing: The role of working memory. *Journal of Memory and Language, 30,* 580–602.

Kintsch, W. & Van Dijk, T. A. (1978). Toward a model of text comprehension and production. *Psychological Review, 85,* 363–394.

Kirchner, D. & Klatzky, R. L. (1985). Verbal rehearsal and memory in language-disordered children. *Journal of Speech and Hearing Research, 28,* 556–565.

Klapp, S. T. (1974). Syllable-dependent pronunciation latencies in number naming: A replication. *Journal of Experimental Psychology, 102,* 1138–1140.

Klapp, S. T. (1976). Short-term memory as a response preparation state. *Memory and Cognition, 4,* 721–729.

Klapp, S. T., Greim, D. M., & Marshburn, E. A. (1981). Articulation and the articulatory loop: Two names for the same mechanism or two distinct components of short-term memory? In J. Long & A. Baddeley (Eds.), *Attention and performance IX* (pp. 459–472). Hillsdale, NJ: Lawrence Erlbaum Associates Inc.

Klee, T. & Fitzgerald, M. D. (1985). The relation between grammatical development and mean length of utterance in morphemes. *Journal of Child Language, 12,* 251–269.

Kyllonen, P. C., & Chrystal, R. E. (1990). Reasoning ability is (little more than) working memory capacity. *Intelligence, 14,* 389–433.

Lenneberg, E. H. (1973). The neurology of language. *Daedalus, 102,* 115–133.

Leonard, L. B. (1982). Phonological deficits in children with developmental language impairment. *Brain and Language, 16,* 73–86.

Levy, B. A. (1971). The role of articulation in auditory and visual short-term memory. *Journal of Verbal Learning and Verbal Behavior, 10,* 123–132.

Liberman, A. M. (1970). The grammars of speech and language. *Cognitive Psychology, 1,* 301–323.

Liberman, A.M., Cooper, F.S., Shankweiler, D.P., & Studdert-Kennedy, M. (1967). Perception of the speech code. *Psychological Review, 74,* 431–461.

Liberman, A. M. & Mattingley, I. G. (1985). The motor theory of speech perception revisited. *Cognition, 21,* 1–36.

Liberman, I. Y. (1989). Phonology and beginning reading revisited. In C. von Euler (Ed.), *Wenner-Gren international symposium series: Brain and reading* (pp. 207–220). Basingstoke: Macmillan.

Liberman, I. Y., Shankweiler, D., & Liberman, A. M. (1989). The alphabetic principle and learning to read. In D. Shankweiler & I. Y. Liberman (Eds.), *Phonology and reading disability: Solving the reading puzzle.* IARLD Research Monograph Series. Ann Arbor: University of Michigan Press.

Liberman, I. Y., Mann, V. A., Shankweiler, D., & Werfelman, M. (1982). Children's memory for recurring linguistic and nonlinguistic material in relation to reading ability. *Cortex, 18,* 367–375.

Liberman, I. Y., Shankweiler, D., Fischer, F. W., & Carter, B. (1974). Explicit syllable and phoneme segmentation in the young child. *Journal of Experimental Child Psychology, 18,* 201–212.

Lindamood, C.H. & Lindamood, P.C. (1969). *The A.D.D. Program: Auditory discrimination in depth.* Boston: Teaching Resources Corporation.

Lindblom, B. (1989). Some remarks on the origin of the phonetic code. In C. von Euler, I. Lundberg, & G. Lennestrand (Eds.), *Brain and reading* (pp. 27–44). Macmillan Press.

Linebarger, M. C., Schwartz, M. F., & Saffran, E. M. (1983). Sensitivity to grammatical structure in so-called grammatical aphasics. *Cognition, 13,* 361–392.

Locke, J. L. & Scott, K. K. (1979). Phonetically mediated recall in the phonetically disordered child. *Journal of Communication Disorders, 12,* 125–131.

Logie, R. H. (1986). Visuo-spatial processes in working memory. *Quarterly Journal of Experimental Psychology, 38A,* 229–247.

Logie, R. H., Cubelli, R., Della Salla, S., Alberoni, M., & Nichelli, P. (in press). In J. Crawford & D. Parker (Eds.), *Developments in clinical and experimental neuropsychology.* New York: Plenum Press.

Logie, R. H., Zucco, G. M., & Baddeley, A. D. (1990). Interference with visual short-term memory. *Acta Psychologica, 75,* 55–74.

Lundberg, I. (1988). Lack of phonological awareness: A critical factor in dyslexia. In C. von Euler, I. Lundberg, & G. Lennestrand (Eds.), *Brain and reading.* Basingstoke: Macmillan.

Lundberg, I., Frost, J., & Petersen, O.-P. (1988). Effects of an extensive program for stimulating phonological awareness in preschool children. *Reading Research Quarterly, 23,* 263–284.

Lundberg, I., Olofsson, A., & Wall, S. (1980). Reading and spelling skills in the first school years predicted from phonemic awareness skills in kindergarten. *Scandinavian Journal of Psychology, 21,* 159–173.

McCutcheon, D. & Perfetti, C. A. (1982). The visual tongue-twister effect: Phonological activation in silent reading. *Journal of Verbal Learning and Verbal Behavior, 21,* 672–687.

MacDonald, M. C., Just, M. A., & Carpenter, P. A. (1992). Working memory constraints on the processing of sentence ambiguity. *Cognitive Psychology, 24,* 56–98.

Maclean, M., Bryant, P., & Bradley, L. (1987). Rhymes, nursery rhymes, and reading in early childhood. *Merrill-Palmer Quarterly, 33,* 255–281.

Mackay, D. G. (1970). Spoonerisms and the structure of errors in the serial order of speech. *Neuropsychologia, 8,* 323–350.

Mann, V. A. (1984). Longitudinal prediction and prevention of early reading difficulty. *Annals of Dyslexia, 34,* 117–136.

Mann, V. A. & Liberman, I. Y. (1984). Phonological awareness and verbal short-term memory. *Journal of Learning Disabilities, 17,* 592–599.

Mann, V. A., Liberman, I. Y., & Shankweiler, D. (1980). Children's memory for sentences and word strings in relation to reading ability. *Memory and Cognition, 8,* 329–335.

Mann, V. A., Shankweiler, D., & Smith, S. T. (1984). The association between comprehension of spoken sentences and early reading ability: The role of phonetic representation. *Journal of Child Language, 11,* 627–643.

Marsh, G., Friedman, M., Welch, V., & Desberg, P. (1981). A cognitive- developmental theory of reading acquisition. In G. E. Mackinnon & T. G. Waller (Eds.), *Reading research: Advances in theory and practice.* New York: Academic Press.

Marshall, J. C. & Newcombe, F. (1973). Patterns of paralexia: A psycholinguistic approach. *Journal of Psycholinguistic Research, 2,* 175–199.

Marslen-Wilson, W. D. (1987). Function and process in spoken word recognition. *Cognition, 25,* 71–102.

Marslen-Wilson, W. D. & Tyler, L. K. (1980). The temporal structure of spoken language understanding. *Cognition, 8,* 1–71.

Martin, R. C. (1987). Articulatory and phonological deficits in short-term memory and their relation to syntactic processing. *Brain and Language, 32,* 159–192.

Martin, R. C. (1990). Neuropsychological evidence on the role of short-term memory in sentence processing. In G. Vallar & T. Shallice (Eds.), *Neuropsychological impairments of short-term memory* (pp. 390–427). Cambridge: Cambridge University Press.

Martin, R. C., & Feher, E. (1990). The consequences of reduced memory span for the comprehension of semantic versus syntactic information. *Brain and Language, 38,* 1–20.

Martin, R. C., Wogalter, M. S., & Forlano, J. G. (1988). Reading comprehension in the presence of unattended speech and music. *Journal of Memory and Language, 27,* 382–398.

Meyer, D. E. & Gordon, P. C. (1984). Dependencies between rapid speech perception and production: Evidence for a shared sensorimotor voicing mechanism. In H. Bouma & D. G. Bouwhuis (Eds.), *Attention and performance X*, (pp. 365–377). Hove, UK: Lawrence Erlbaum Associates Ltd.

Miller, J. F. & Chapman, R. S. (1981). The relation between and and mean length of utterance in morphemes. *Journal of Speech and Hearing Research, 24,* 156–161.

Mitterer, J. O. (1982). There are at least two kinds of poor readers: Whole-word poor readers and recoding poor readers. *Canadian Journal of Psychology, 36,* 445–461.

Monsell, S. (1984). Components of working memory underlying verbal skills: A "distributed capacities" view. In H. Bouma & D. G. Bouwhuis (Eds.), *Attention and performance X: Control of language processes.* Hove, UK: Lawrence Erlbaum Associates Ltd.

Morais, J., Alegria, J., & Content, A. (1987). The relationships between segmental analysis and alphabetic literacy: An interactive view. *Cahiers de Psychologie Cognitive, 7,* 462–464.

Morais, J., Cary, L., Alegria, J., & Bertelson, P. (1979). Does awareness of speech as a sequence of phones arise spontaneously? *Cognition, 7,* 323–331.

Morais, J., Content, A., Bertelson, P., Cary, L., & Kolinsky, R. (1988). Is there a critical period for the acquisition of segmental analysis? *Cognitive Neuropsychology, 5,* 347–352.

Morton. J. (1970). A functional model for memory. In D. A. Norman (Ed.), *Models of human memory.* New York: Academic Press.

Morton, J. & Patterson, K. (1980). A new attempt at an interpretation, or, an attempt at a new interpretation. In M. Coltheart, K. Patterson, & J. C. Marshall (Eds.), *Deep dyslexia.* London: Routledge & Kegan Paul.

Murray, D. J. (1967). The role of speech responses in short-term memory. *Canadian Journal of Psychology, 21,* 263–276.

Nagy, W. E. & Anderson, R. C. (1984). How many words are there in printed school English? *Reading Research Quarterly, 19,* 304–330.

Nagy, W. E. & Herman, P. A. (1987). Breadth and depth of vocabulary knowledge: Implications for acquisition and instruction. In M. G. McKeown & M. E. Curtis (Eds.), *The nature of vocabulary acquisition* (pp. 19–35). Hillsdale, NJ: Lawrence Erlbaum Associates Inc.

Naveh-Benjamin, M. & Ayres, T. J. (1986). Digit span, reading rate, and linguistic relativity. *Quarterly Journal of Experimental Psychology, 38A,* 739–751.

Neale, M. (1989). *Neale Analysis of Reading Abilities (revised British edition).* Windsor: NFER-Nelson Publishing Company Ltd.

Nelson, L. K. & Bauer, H. R. (1991). Speech and language production at age 2: Evidence for tradeoffs between linguistic and phonetic processing. *Journal of Speech and Hearing Research, 34,* 879–892.

Nelson, K. (1973). Structure and strategy in learning to talk. *Monographs of the Society for Research in Child Development, 38,* (1–2, Serial No. 149).

Nicolson, R. (1981).The relationship between memory span and processing speed. In M. Friedman, J. P. Das, & N. O'Connor (Eds.), *Intelligence and learning.* New York: Plenum Press.

Nittrouer, S., Studdert-Kennedy, M., & McGowan, R. S. (1989). The emergence of phonetic segments: Evidence from the spectral structure of fricative-vowel syllables spoken by children and adults. *Journal of Speech and Hearing Research, 30,* 319–329.

Nooteboom, S. G. & Cohen, A. (1975). Anticipation in speech production and its implications for perception. In A. Cohen & S. G. Nooteboom (Eds.), *Structure and process in speech perception.* Berlin: Springer Verlag.

Norman, D. A. & Shallice, T. (1980). *Attention to action: Willed and automatic control of behavior.* University of California, San Diego, CHIP Report 99.

Oakhill, J. V. (1982). Constructive processes in skilled and less skilled comprehenders' memory for sentences. *British Journal of Psychology, 73,* 13–20.

Oakhill, J. V. (1984). Inferential and memory skills in children's comprehension of stories. *British Journal of Educational Psychology, 54,* 31–39.

Oakhill, J.V. & Garnham, A. (1988). *Becoming a skilled reader.* Oxford: Blackwell.

Oakhill, J. V., Yuill, N., & Parkin, A. J. (1986). On the nature of the difference between skilled and less-skilled comprehenders. *Journal of Research in Reading, 9,* 80–91.

Oakhill, J. V., Yuill, N., & Parkin, A. J. (1988). Memory and inference in skilled and less skilled comprehenders. In M. M. Gruneberg, P. E. Morris, & R. N. Sykes (Eds.), *Practical aspects of memory: Current research and issues* (Vol. 2, pp. 315–320). Chichester: Wiley.

Olofsson, A., & Lundberg, I. (1985). Evaluation of long-term effects of phonemic awareness training in kindergarten. *Scandinavian Journal of Psychology, 26,* 21–34.

Olson, R. K., Davidson, B. J., Kliegl, R., & Davies, S. E. (1984). Development of phonetic memory in disabled and normal readers. *Journal of Experimental Child Psychology, 37,* 187–206.

Olson, R. K., Wise, B., Conners, F. A., & Rack, J, P. (1990). Organisation, heritability, and remediation of component word recognition and language skills in disabled readers. In T. H. Carr & B. A. Levy (Eds.), *Reading and its development: Component skills approaches.* New York: Academic Press.

Ostergaard, A. L. & Meudell, P. R. (1984). Immediate memory span, recognition memory for subspan series of words, and serial position effects in recognition memory for supraspan series of verbal and nonverbal items in Broca's and Wernicke's aphasia. *Brain and Language, 22,* 1–13.

Paivio, A. (1971). *Imagery and Verbal Processes.* New York: Holt, Rinehart and Winston.

Papagno, C. & Vallar, G. (1992). Phonological short-term memory and the learning of novel words: The effects of phonological similarity and item length. *Quarterly Journal of Experimental Psychology, 44A,* 47–67.

Papagno, C., Valentine, T., & Baddeley, A. (1991). Phonological short-term memory and foreign-language vocabulary learning. *Journal of Memory and Language, 30,* 331–347.

Parkin, A. J. (1982). Phonological recoding in lexical decision: Effects of spelling-to-sound regularity depends upon how regularity is defined. *Memory and Cognition, 10,* 43–53.

Parkin, A. J. (1988). Review of "Working Memory". *Quarterly Journal of Experimental Psychology, 40A,* 187–189.

Pascual-Leone, J.A. (1970). A mathematical model for the transition rule in Piaget's developmental stages. *Acta Psychologica, 32,* 301–345.

Patterson, K. E. (1982). The relation between reading and phonological recoding: Further neuropsychological observations. In A. W. Ellis (Ed.), *Normality and pathology in cognitive functions.* London: Academic Press.

Patterson, K. & Coltheart, V. (1987). Phonological processes in reading: A tutorial review. In M. Coltheart (Ed.), *Attention and performance, XII: The psychology of reading* (pp. 421–447). Hove, UK: Lawrence Erlbaum Associates Ltd.

Perfetti, C. A. & Zhang, S. (1991). Phonological processes in reading Chinese characters. *Journal of Experimental Psychology: Learning, Memory and Cognition, 17,* 633–643.

Peterson, L. R. & Johnson, S. T. (1971). Some effects of minimising articulation on short-term retention. *Journal of Verbal Learning and Verbal Behavior, 10,* 346–354.

Phillips, W. A. & Christie, D. F. M. (1977). Interference with visualisation. *Quarterly Journal of Experimental Psychology, 29,* 637–650.

Power, M. J. (1985). Sentence production and working memory. *Quarterly Journal of Experimental Psychology, 37A,* 367–386.

Rapala, M. M. & Brady, S. (1990). Reading ability and short-term memory: The role of phonological processing. *Reading and Writing, 2,* 1–25.

Raven, J. C. (1984). *Raven's progressive coloured matrices.* London: H. K. Lewis & Co. Ltd.

Read, C., Zhang, Y., Nie, H., & Ding, B. (1986). The ability to manipulate speech sounds depends on knowing alphabetic spelling. *Cognition, 24,* 31–44.

Rice, M. L. (1990). Preschoolers QIL: Quick incidental learning of new words. In G. Conti-Ramsden & C. E. Snow (Eds.), *Children's language* (Vol. 7). Hillsdale, NJ: Lawrence Erlbaum Associates Inc.

Rice, M. L. & Woodsmall, L. (1988). Lessons from television: Children's word learning when viewing. *Child Development, 59,* 420–429.

Riege, W. H., Metter, E. J., & Hanson, W. R. (1980). Verbal and nonverbal recognition memory in aphasic and nonaphasic stroke patients. *Brain and Language, 10,* 60–70.

Rodgers, B. (1983). The identification and prevalence of specific reading retardation. *British Journal of Educational Psychology, 53,* 369–373.

Rubenstein, H., Lewis, S. S., & Rubenstein, M. A. (1971). Evidence for phonemic recoding in visual word recognition. *Journal of Verbal Learning and Verbal Behavior, 10,* 645–657.

Rutter, M. & Yule, W. (1975). The concept of specific reading retardation. *Journal of Child Psychology and Psychiatry, 16,* 181–197.

Saffran, E. M. (1982). Neuropsychological approaches to the study of language. *British Journal of Psychology, 73,* 317–338.

Saffran, E. M. & Marin, O. S. M. (1975). Immediate memory for word lists and sentences in a patient with deficient auditory short-term memory. *Brain and Language, 2,* 420–433.

Saffran, E. M. & Martin, N. (1990). Short-term memory impairment and sentence processing: A case study. In G. Vallar & T. Shallice (Eds.), *Neuropsychological impairments of short-term memory* (pp. 428–447). Cambridge: Cambridge University Press.

Salamé, P. & Baddeley, A. D. (1982). Disruption of memory by unattended speech: Implications for the structure of working memory. *Journal of Verbal Learning and Verbal Behavior, 21,* 150–164.

Salamé, P. & Baddeley, A. D. (1986). Phonological factors in STM: Similarity and the unattended speech effect. *Bulletin of the Psychonomic Society, 24,* 263–265.

Scarborough, H. S., Rescorla, L., Fowler, A. E., & Sudhalter, V. (1991). The relation of utterance length to grammatical complexity in normal and language-disordered groups. *Applied Psycholinguistics, 12,* 23–46.

Scarborough, H., Wyckoff, J., & Davidson, R. (1986). A reconsideration of the relation between age and mean utterance length. *Journal of Speech and Hearing Research, 29,* 394–399.

Schneider, W. & Shiffrin, R. M. (1977). Controlled and automatic human information processing: Detection, search and attention. *Psychological Review, 81,* 1–66.

Seidenberg, M. S., Bruck, M., Fornarolo, G., & Backman, J. (1986). Who is dyslexic? Reply to Wolf. *Applied Psycholinguistics, 7,* 77–83.

Seidenberg, M. S., Waters, G. S., Barnes, M. A., & Tanenhaus, M. K. (1984). When does irregular spelling or pronunciation influence word recognition? *Journal of Verbal Learning and Verbal Behavior, 23,* 383–404.

Selkirk, E. O. (1980). The role of prosodic categories in English word stress. *Linguistic Enquiry, 11,* 563–605.

Service, L. (1992). Phonology, working memory, and foreign-language learning. *Quarterly Journal of Experimental Psychology, 45A,* 21–50.

Seymour, P. H. K. & Elder, L. (1986). Beginning reading without phonology. *Cognitive Neuropsychology, 3,* 1–36.

Seymour, P. H. K. & MacGregor, C. J. (1984). Developmental dyslexia: A cognitive experimental analysis of phonological, morphemic and visual impairments. *Cognitive Neuropsychology, 1,* 43–82.

Shallice, T. (1982). Specific impairments of planning. *Philosophical Transactions of the Royal Society London, Series B, 298,* 199–209.

Shallice, T. (1988). *From neuropsychology to mental structure.* Cambridge: Cambridge University Press.

Shallice, T. & Burgess, P. (1991). Deficits in strategy application following frontal lobe damage in man. *Brain, 114,* 727–741.

Shallice, T. & Burgess, P. (in press). Supervisory control of action and thought selection. In A. D. Baddeley & L. Weiskrantz (Eds.), *Attention: Selection, awareness and control.* Oxford: Oxford University Press.

Shallice, T. & Butterworth, B. (1977). Short-term memory impairment and spontaneous speech. *Neuropsychologia, 15,* 729–735.

Shallice, T. & McCarthy, R. (1985). Phonological reading: From patterns of impairment to possible procedures. In K. E. Patterson, M. Coltheart & J. C. Marshall (Eds.), *Surface dyslexia.* Hove, UK: Lawrence Erlbaum Associates Ltd.

Shallice, T., & Warrington, E. K. (1970). Independent functioning of verbal memory stores: A neuropsychological study. *Quarterly Journal of Experimental Psychology, 22,* 261–273.

Shallice, T., & Warrington, E. K. (1977). Auditory-verbal short-term memory impairment and conduction aphasia. *Brain and Language, 4,* 479–491.

Shallice, T., & Warrington, E. K. (1980). Single and multiple component central dyslexia syndromes. In M. Coltheart, K. Patterson, & J. C. Marshall (Eds.), *Deep dyslexia,* London: Routledge & Kegan Paul.

Shankweiler, D. & Crain, S. (1986). Language mechanisms and reading disorder: A modular approach. *Cognition, 24,* 139–168.

Shankweiler, D., Liberman, I.Y., Mark, L.S., Fowler, C.A., & Fischer, F.W. (1979). The speech code and learning to read. *Journal of Experimental Psychology: Human Learning and Memory, 5,* 531–545.

Shankweiler, D., Smith, S. T., & Mann, V. A. (1984). Repetition and comprehension of spoken sentences by reading-disabled children. *Brain and Language, 23,* 241–257.

Share, D. L., Jorm, A. F., Maclean, R., & Matthews, R. (1984). Sources of individual differences in reading acquisition. *Journal of Educational Psychology, 76,* 1309–1324.

Siegel, L. S. (1988). Evidence that IQ scores are irrelevant to the definition and analysis of reading disability. *Canadian Journal of Psychology, 42,* 201–215.

Siegel, L. S. & Linder, B. A. (1984). Short-term memory processes in children with reading and arithmetic learning disabilities. *Developmental Psychology, 2,* 200–207.

Smith, S. T., Macaruso, P., Shankweiler, D., & Crain, S. (1989). Syntactic comprehension in young poor readers. *Applied Psycholinguistics, 10,* 429–454.

Smith, S. T., Mann, V. A., & Shankweiler, D. (1986). Spoken sentence comprehension by good and poor readers: A study with the Token test. *Cortex, 22,* 627–632.

Snowling, M. J. (1980). The development of grapheme-phoneme correspondences in normal and dyslexic readers. *Journal of Experimental Child Psychology, 29,* 294–305.

Snowling, M. J. (1981). Phonemic deficits in developmental dyslexia. *Psychological Research, 43,* 219–234.

Snowling, M., Chiat, S., & Hulme, C. (1991). Words, nonwords and phonological processes: Some comments on Gathercole, Willis, Emslie, & Baddeley. *Applied Psycholinguistics, 12,* 369–373.

Snowling, M., Goulandris, N., Bowlby, M., & Howell, P. (1986). Segmentation and speech perception in relation to reading skill: A developmental analysis. *Journal of Experimental Child Psychology, 41,* 489–507.

Stahl, S. A., Jacobson, M. G., Davis, C. E., & Davis, R. L. (1989). Prior knowledge and difficult vocabulary in the comprehension of unfamiliar text. *Reading Research Quarterly, 24,* 27–43.

Stanovich, K.E. (1980). Toward an interactive-compensatory model of individual differences in the development of reading fluency. *Reading Research Quarterly, 16,* 32–71.

Stanovich, K. E., Cunningham, A. E., & Cramer, B. B. (1984a). Assessing phonological awareness in kindergarten children: Issues of task comparability. *Journal of Experimental Child Psychology, 38,* 175–190.

Stanovich, K. E., Cunningham, A. E., & Feeman, D. J. (1984b). Intelligence, cognitive skills, and early reading progress. *Reading Research Quarterly, 14,* 278–303.

Stanovich, K. E., Nathan, R. G., & Vala-Rossi, M. (1986). Developmental changes in the cognitive correlates of reading ability and the developmental lag hypothesis. *Reading Research Quarterly, 11,* 267–283.

Stanovich, K. E., Nathan, R. G., & Zolman, J. E. (1988). The developmental lag hypothesis in reading: Longitudinal and matched reading-level comparisons. *Child Development, 59,* 71–86.

Stark, R. & Tallal, P. (1981). Selection of children with specific language deficits. *Journal of Speech and Hearing Disorders, 46,* 114–122.

Sternberg, R. (1987). Most vocabulary is learned from context. In M. McKeown & M. Curtis (Eds.), *The nature of vocabulary acquisition* (pp. 89–106). Hillsdale, NJ: Lawrence Erlbaum Associates Inc.

Sternberg, S., Monsell, S., Knoll, R. L., & Wright, C. E. (1978). The latency and duration of rapid movement sequences: Comparisons of speech and typewriting. In G. E. Stelmach (Ed.), *Information processing in motor control and learning.* New York: Academic Press.

Stuart, M. & Coltheart, M. (1988). Does reading develop in a sequence of stages? *Cognition, 30,* 139–181

Tallal, P. & Piercy, M. (1975). Developmental aphasia: The perception of brief vowels and extended stop consonants. *Neuropsychologia, 13,* 69–74.

Tallal, P., Stark, R. E., & Mellitts, E. D. (1985). Identification of language-impaired children on the basis of rapid perception and production skills. *Brain and Language, 25,* 314–322.

Taylor, H. G., Lean, D., & Schwartz, S. (1989). Pseudoword repetition ability in learning-disabled children. *Applied Psycholinguistics, 10,* 203–219.

Taylor, M. & Gelman. S. A. (1988). Adjectives and nouns: Children's strategies for learning new words. *Child Development, 59,* 411–419.

Teasdale, J. D., Proctor, L., & Baddeley, A. D. (in prep.). Working memory and stimulus-independent thought.

Temple, C. M. (1987). The nature of normality, the deviance of dyslexia and the recognition of rhyme: A reply to Bryant and Impey, 1986. *Cognition, 27,* 103–108.

Temple, C. (1988). Red is read but eye is blue: A case study of developmental dyslexia and follow-up report. *Brain and Language, 34,* 13–37.

Temple, C. & Marshall, J. C. (1983). A case study of developmental phonological dyslexia. *British Journal of Psychology, 74,* 517–533.

Thorndyke, R. (1973). *Reading comprehension education in fifteen countries.* New York: Wiley.

Thorstad, G. (1991). The effect of orthography on the acquisition of literacy skills. *British Journal of Psychology, 82,* 527–537.

Torgesen, J. K. (1978). Performance of reading-disabled children on serial memory tests: A selective review of recent research. *Reading Research Quarterly, 1,* 57–87.

Treiman, R. & Hirsch-Pasek, K. (1985). Are there qualitative differences in reading behavior between dyslexics and normal readers? *Memory and Cognition, 13,* 357–364.

Tunmer, W. E., Herriman, M. L., & Nesdale, A. R. (1988). Metalinguistic abilities and beginning reading. *Reading Research Quarterly, 23,* 134–158.

Tunmer, W. E. & Nesdale, A. R. (1985). Phonemic segmentation skill and beginning reading. *Journal of Educational Psychology, 77,* 417–427.

Vallar, G. & Baddeley, A. D. (1982). Short-term forgetting and the articulatory loop. *Quarterly Journal of Experimental Psychology, 34,* 53–60.

Vallar, G. & Baddeley, A. D. (1984a). Fractionation of working memory: Neuropsychological evidence for a short-term store. *Journal of Verbal Learning and Verbal Behavior, 23,* 151–161.

Vallar, G. & Baddeley, A. D. (1984b). Phonological short-term store, phonological processing, and sentence comprehension: A neuropsychological case study. *Cognitive Neuropsychology, 1,* 121–141.

Vallar, G. & Baddeley, A. D. (1987). Phonological short-term store and sentence processing. *Cognitive Neuropsychology, 4,* 417–438.

Vallar, G. & Baddeley, A.D. (1989). Developmental disorders of verbal short-term memory and their relation to sentence comprehension: A reply to Howard and Butterworth. *Cognitive Neuropsychology, 6,* 465–473.

Vallar, G., Basso, A., & Bottini, G. (1990). Phonological processing and sentence comprehension: A neuropsychological case study. In G. Vallar & T. Shallice (Eds.), *Neuropsychological impairments of short-term memory.* Cambridge: Cambridge University Press.

Vallar, G. & Cappa, S. F. (1987). Articulation and verbal short-term memory: Evidence from anarthria. *Cognitive Psychology, 4,* 55–78.

Vallar, G. & Papagno, C. (in press). Preserved vocabulary acquisition in Down's syndrome: The role of phonological short-term memory. *Cortex.*

Vallar, G. & Shallice, T. (1990). *Neuropsychological impairments of short-term memory.* Cambridge: Cambridge University Press.

Van Dijk, T. A. & Kintsch, W. (1983). *Strategies of discourse comprehension.* New York: Academic Press.

Vellutino, F. R. (1979). *Dyslexia: Theory and research,* Cambridge, MA: MIT Press.

Vellutino, F. R. & Scanlon, D. M. (1987). Linguistic coding and reading ability. In S. Rosenberg (Ed.), *Advances in psycholinguistics* (pp. 1–69). New York: Cambridge University Press.

Veneziano, E., Sinclair, H., & Berthoud, I. (1990). From one word to two words: Repetition patterns on the way to structured speech. *Journal of Child Language, 17,* 633–650.

Wagner, K. R. (1985). How much do children say in a day? *Journal of Child Language, 12*, 475–487.

Wagner, R. K. & Torgesen, J. K. (1987). The nature of phonological processing and its causal role in the acquisition of reading skills. *Psychological Bulletin, 101*, 192–212.

Waters, G. S., Caplan, D., & Hildebrandt, N. (1987). Working memory and written sentence comprehension. In M. Coltheart (Ed.), *Attention and performance XII* (pp.531–555). Hove, UK: Lawrence Erlbaum Associates Ltd.

Waters, G. S., Caplan, D., & Hildebrandt, N. (1991). On the structure of verbal short-term memory and its functional role in sentence comprehension: Evidence from neuropsychology. *Cognitive Neuropsychology, 8*, 81–126.

Waters, G. S., Komoda, M. K., & Arbuckle, T. Y. (1985). The effects of concurrent tasks on reading: Implications for phonological recoding. *Journal of Memory and Language, 24*, 27–45.

Waters, G. S., Rochon, E., & Caplan, D. (1992). The role of high-level planning in rehearsal: Evidence from patients with apraxia of speech. *Journal of Memory and Language, 31*, 54–73.

Wechsler, D. (1974). *Manual for the Wechsler intelligence scale for children–revised.* New York: Psychological Corporation.

Wells, G. (1985). *Language development in the preschool years.* Cambridge: Cambridge University Press.

White, T. G., Power, M. A., & White, S. (1989). Morphological analysis: Implications for teaching and understanding vocabulary growth. *Reading Research Quarterly, 24*, 283–304.

Wiig, E. & Semel, E. M. (1976). *Language disabilities in children and adolescents.* Columbus, OH: Charles E. Merrill.

Wijnen, F. (1990). The development of sentence planning. *Journal of Child Language, 17*, 651–675.

Wilding, J. & White, W. (1985). Impairment of rhyme judgments by silent and overt articulatory suppression. *Quarterly Journal of Experimental Psychology, 37A*, 95–107.

Willis, C. S. & Gathercole, S. E. (a, in prep.). Children's spoken sentence comprehension and working memory: A study using the Token test.

Willis, C. S. & Gathercole, S. E. (b, in prep.). The relation between phonological memory skills and spoken language comprehension in 5- and 8-year-old children.

Wilson, J. T. L., Scott, J. H., & Power, K. G. (1987). Developmental differences in the span of visual memory for pattern. *British Journal of Developmental Psychology, 5*, 249–255.

Wolfus, B., Moscovitch, M., & Kinsbourne, M. (1980). Subgroups of developmental language impairment. *Brain and Language, 10*, 152–171.

Yuill, N., Oakhill, J., & Parkin, A. (1989). Working memory, comprehension ability and the resolution of text anomaly. *British Journal of Psychology, 80*, 351–361.

Author Index

Subject Index